Rigidity

Faithfulness or Heterodoxy?

Pedro Gabriel

En Route Books and Media, LLC
St. Louis, MO

⊕ENROUTE
Make the time

En Route Books and Media, LLC
5705 Rhodes Avenue
St. Louis, MO 63109

Cover credit: Pedro Gabriel

Copyright © 2024 Pedro Gabriel

ISBN-13: 979-8-88870-206-2
Library of Congress Control Number: 2024942291

No part of this book may be reproduced, stored in a retrieval system, or transmitted in any form, or by any means, electronic, mechanical, photocopying, or otherwise, without the prior written permission of the author. For information contact: pedrogabrielbooks@gmail.com

Dedication

I dedicate this book to Our Lady Untier of Knots, to whom my dear Pope Francis is particularly devout. May the Blessed Virgin untie the knots of rigidity in our heartstrings, for she was always a model of motherly tenderness and mercy, always open to God's will even when it was surprising and strange, humbly keeping all things in her heart.

I also dedicate this book to the Apostle St. Paul, to St. Augustine of Hippo, to St. Alphonsus Liguori, and to St. Francis de Sales, for their spiritual insights which helped me so much while writing these pages. I pray for their intercession, so that this publication may be successful.

May God, through the intercession of these saints, show me the path to truth and help me assist the Church in this time of need. May I never fall into error, but rather help bring clarity where there is confusion, a merciful spirit where there is rigidity, and unity where there is disunity. May I, useless servant, always be an instrument of His will, and never of my own. Amen.

Table of Contents

Acknowledgments v
List of Abbreviations vii
Foreword by Rocco Buttiglione xi
Introduction 1

Chapter 1: Laxism and the Golden Mean 17
    Aristotle and the virtue 23
    Aquinas and the theological virtues 30
    Discernment and epikeia 34

Chapter 2: Scrupulosity and Slavery to the Law 41
    The spiritual danger of scruples 44
    The freedom of God's children 48
    Obedience: the antidote to scrupulous rigidity 54

Chapter 3: Pharisaism and the Double Life 63
    The Pharisees in Pope Francis's teaching 68
    The outward mask 73
    Spirit vs. letter of the law 78
    Hardness of heart vs. fulfilling the law 90

Chapter 4: The Judaizers and Indietrism 101
    Being fixed during the journey 104
    Peter and "the God of surprises" 111
    Paul's geography of salvation 118
    Synodality and the Council of Jerusalem 124
    Paul corrects Peter's indietrism 130

Chapter 5: Donatism and Lack of Mercy 137
Mortal sins and communion 142
Submission to the urgencies of the times................................. 149
Purity, Mercy, and Unity 153
Leniency vindicated 162
History repeats itself 166
Suspicion and lack of love.. 171

Chapter 6: Pelagianism and Self-Sufficiency 179
Moral athletes and frail humans 185
The Possibility of Sinlessness 190
Redefining grace.. 197
The victorious law of love 203

Chapter 7: Medieval Heresies and Spiritual Worldliness 213
The Cathars.. 218
The Fraticelli 231
The Flagellants... 247

Chapter 8: Jansenism and Rigorism 257
The eve of Jansenism: Calvin and Baius.................................. 261
Facts that were not right 268
Rigorism, Laxism, and Probabilism.. 278
Eucharist: not a reward for virtue 287

Conclusion 301

Bibliography 307

Acknowledgments

I wish to thank my beautiful wife, Claire Navarro Domingues, for all her support during the writing of this book and all my previous books. I could not have achieved this without her by my side.

I thank Prof. Rocco Buttiglione for reviewing my book, for writing the foreword, and for offering support and kindness throughout the whole process.

I also thank Prof. Robert Fastiggi for his support and encouragement, as well as for his input and testimonial.

Finally, I thank Prof. Rodrigo Guerra López, Mike Lewis, and Andrew Likoudis for their beta-reading and their help in publicizing the book.

List of Abbreviations

Biblical Abbreviations:

1 Cor—First Epistle of the Apostle St. Paul to the Corinthians
2 Cor—Second Epistle of the Apostle St. Paul to the Corinthians
1 Sam—First Book of Prophet Samuel
Acts—Book of the Acts of the Apostles
Exod—Book of Exodus
Ezek—Book of Prophet Ezekiel
Gal—Epistle of the Apostle St. Paul to the Galatians
Gen—Book of Genesis
Jer—Book of Prophet Jeremiah
John—Gospel according to St. John
Lev—Book of Leviticus
Luke—Gospel according to St. Luke
Mark—Gospel according to St. Mark
Mt—Gospel according to St. Matthew
Rev—Book of Revelation
Rom—Epistle of the Apostle St. Paul to the Romans

(Note: All of the biblical quotes were taken from the Douay-Rheims, except in the cases where they were quoted as embedded in other documents, in which case the version of said document was followed.)

Non-biblical Abbreviations:

CCC—Catechism of the Catholic Church.
CFD—Congregation for the Doctrine of the Faith.

"Another thing that prevents moving forward in knowledge of Jesus, in belonging to Jesus, is rigidity: rigidity of heart... Which is not faithfulness: faithfulness is always a gift to God; rigidity is a security for myself."

—Francis,
Homily "Attitudes that prevent us from knowing Christ"

Foreword

This book on rigidity by Pedro Gabriel offers a criterion for moving the ongoing discussion in the Church between so-called "innovators" and so-called "traditionalists" to a greater level of depth. While reading this book, I was reminded of a dialogue many years ago with Nickolaus Lobkowicz, a great philosopher and freedom fighter. We were talking about the preconciliar Church with the steadfastness of its doctrine, the splendor of its liturgy, the certainty of its moral convictions. . . And yet all that greatness was exposed to a risk: that of presuming to be saved simply through the observance of a rule, that is, basically by one's own merits and moral perfection.

A few days ago, I was talking somewhat about the same things with Father Wojciech Giertych, OP, a theologian of the Pontifical Household. Father Giertych was telling me about the risk in educational practice of putting the cardinal virtues first and the theological virtues only after. The cardinal virtues are those of the good man and good citizen that the ancients already knew: prudence, justice, fortitude, and temperance. The theological virtues, on the other hand, are the virtues of the Christian: faith, hope, and charity. In English these virtues are called, very appropriately, divine virtues. Divine because they are not the result of human effort but a gift that comes from God and brings us into the very life of God. The risk Father Giertych foresaw was to think that man should and could by his moral effort conquer the cardinal virtues. God would then reward him by granting him the theological virtues.

St. Paul tells us the opposite: man is unable to keep the Law by the effort of his will alone. And even if he could, it would do him no good because he would inevitably fall into the gravest of all sins: that of pride, of the claim to save himself alone. Pope Francis, following in Paul's footsteps, warns us: grace is not a prize granted to the perfect. It is a support given to sinners that changes their hearts and enables them to become righteous.

Let us try to put it another way. Many have struggled to discover a difference between Jesus' moral doctrine and that of the Pharisees. The differences are not there and, if there are, they are really small, at least if we refer to the teaching of Gamaliel. The difference is the person of Christ and the proclamation of mercy, that is, grace.

Grace and mercy do not take away the Law but change the way we approach it: not the way of the servant full of fear but the way of the son full of trust and hope. This is exactly the attitude that Pedro Gabriel tries to explain and communicate.

Think of the parable of the talents. Servants who have trafficked their talents are rewarded. The one who kept his talents, on the other hand, is punished. The Gospel comments, "from the one who has will be given, from the one who does not have will be taken away even what he has." To understand the Master's strange behavior, we must ask a question: what would have happened if the first two had trafficked their talents and lost them? To traffic is not simply to conserve and increase with one's labor. To traffic is to sell and buy with the hope of gaining but also exposing oneself to the risk of losing everything. And if they had really lost everything what would the Master have done?

A great saint who once explained this parable to me simply said, "he would have forgiven them." Then the third servant's fault is that he did not trust in mercy. That is the idea he had of the Master. The first two servants look to the Master as a Father, or at least a Friend. The Third has a spirit of fear and distrust.

In the language of Pope Francis, we could say that the first two servants are animated by a missionary spirit. They obviously know that they must keep the Law of the Lord, but their first concern is not to commit themselves to the law alone. Their first concern is to traffic in the talents they have received; that is, to bring to others the gift of faith. This exposes them to unforeseen problems for which they must invent new, sometimes risky solutions.

Think of St. Paul going to preach Jesus to the pagans and finding that those pagans did not want to observe the ritual prescriptions of the Law of Israel. They were used to eating ham and sausage and did not see why this should be an obstacle to following Christ. In fact, it is not a hindrance, although it was not easy to make this clear to Jewish Christians attached to the practices of the Law.

Paul's problems were still small compared with those of St. Joseph de Anchieta. He needed to preach the Gospel to the Tupi Indians who were accustomed to putting to the coals, not sausages, but enemy captives. Here, the missionary was not able to make any concessions.

Think of the problems of poor Matteo Ricci who went on mission to China and discovered that the Chinese wanted to be baptized along with their ancestors. Here, the situation required extensive theological reflection that would last for hundreds of years.

Paul of Tarsus, Joseph de Anchieta, and Matteo Ricci did not have the obsessive preoccupation with one's individual impeccability. They were all men of great moral integrity, but their own moral integrity did not lie at the center of their thoughts; it did not cause them to shy away from the adventure of life. Rather, their moral integrity is God's gift to those who take their vocation, their life's mission, to heart.

The gift of faith, the memory of the encounter with Christ, is preserved by communicating it to others, by creating community and, in this movement, by taking on the difficulties and problems of those we meet, accompanying them on their journey of faith.

Rigidity is the attitude of those who hear the proclamation of the Gospel. . . but are afraid to break away from the sense of security that the Law gives them. Let's be clear: I am not saying that observance of the Law does not matter. I am saying that observance of the Law becomes truly possible only in following the freedom of Christ. Jesus was criticized for eating with publicans and prostitutes, going out to meet sinners. He did not stay in the circle of the good, the pure, and the perfect, but went to find sinners in the places of real life where they actually were. This is the model of the "outgoing Church."

Pedro Gabriel gives us a wonderful book on an "outgoing Church," a plea for the education of a Christian personality that is flexible but with a strong backbone. He discovers in the faith not an obstacle to the fullness of human life but a path—not only to eternal life but also to a life one hundred times more human here on earth.

- Rocco Buttiglione,
Member of the Pontifical Academy of Social Sciences
and of the Pontifical Academy of St. Thomas.

Introduction

"You're being so rigid!"—every Catholic taking his or her faith seriously has probably heard this line before. John Doe may be bailing on his friends' impromptu Sunday stroll, because he must attend Mass. Antony does not want to eat a tasty burger, because it is Lent Friday. Sixteen-year-old Michael does not want to play on Ouija boards with his friends. Jeremy is upset that a certain popular show is ridiculing his faith.

The dreadful sentence may arise in other settings, that the world may not recognize as directly related to faith, but morals—particularly sexual mores. Mary does not want to watch a certain movie, because it contains too much explicit content. Agnes tells her boyfriend she wants to wait until marriage before engaging in intercourse. Louis and Zelia tell a teacher how concerned they are with the sexual education being given to their children without their knowledge and consent. Gianna's gynecologist scolds her because her family, though healthy, is already too big in size, so she should take contraceptives. Tom is at a family gathering when a controversial topic—like say, abortion—comes up, and he expresses his opinion just like anyone else.

"You're being so rigid!" In all these situations and more, our fellow Catholics have heard it. Coming from their friends and family, those who they love the most, the people closest to them. Coming from non-Catholics or even from other Catholics, who do not practice their faith, but hold a more secularized, "live and let live" mindset. "You're being so rigid!" They heard it simply because they followed or expressed their faith, as it should be followed and expressed.

I must be very clear, in all these examples, this slur is being unjustly applied. The world is being excessively lax, allowing and tolerating things a Catholic cannot hold or do, as a matter of principle. From an excessively lax point of view, everything not validating or playing along with this leniency is considered "rigid," even if it would be considered mere decency or common sense in a less relaxed society.

However, there is a hidden danger here to our fellow Catholics, concealed like a bear-trap underneath the foliage on the ground. A lax world calls them "rigid" for being faithful, and Catholics rightfully reject the label. But Catholics may then start viewing "rigidity" as a dog whistle i.e., a code word for faithfulness.[1] They may begin, by a process of association, to equate "rigidity" with "faithfulness."[2] From that point onward, whenever someone criticizes rigidity, this is to be taken as a badge of honor.[3] Catholics have reacted strongly

---

[1] Pokorsky. "Rigidity Dog Whistle."

[2] Lambert, "What Does the Pope Mean By 'Rigid'?": "The problem is made clear from this very fact: Catholics see rigidity - faithfulness as a good thing! Of course we do! I recall as a young man a priest telling me that the Catholic Church was like a great anchor in the sea of chaos. . . It stands firm. It is the Rock. We are Faithful, steady. . . Rigid. The use of this term as a pejorative seems counter-intuitive to any Catholic because we are by definition rigid in our faith."

[3] "Being 'Rigid' Is a Badge of Honor, Your Holiness." *One Peter Five*. See also LiMandri, "Faithful Catholics are condemned for being too rigid. They should wear the label proudly."

and appropriately against a false accusation, but then proceeded to dwell in the reaction.

Things get more complicated when the Pope, the visible head of the Catholic Church, the guarantor of unity and orthodoxy, starts criticizing rigidity as a vice. Worse still: when he elevates this criticism to a hallmark of his pontificate. This is precisely what happened. So, what is a Catholic to do? In my experience, there are two different responses, flowing from two diametrically opposite premises.

The first response is: the Catholic will sit down for a moment and digest the Pope's words. He will meditate on them. And he will arrive at the conclusion that the Pope is indeed warning against a spiritual danger, as a good shepherd should do. The Catholic should then take an examination of conscience to gauge whether he is indeed engaging in rigidity or not. This becomes even more urgent if the Catholic discovers that Francis's words are touching a nerve. Obedient, humble, eager to progress in his or her spiritual journey, this Catholic will try to assimilate the pontiff's lessons into his being and praxis,[4] even if this may be accompanied with much struggling and many falls along the way.

---

[4] See, for example, Lewis. "Why does Pope Francis pick on 'rigid Christians'?": "Francis is clearly touching a nerve with this type of speech, based on the reaction he receives every time he does it. . . Once people begin to open themselves up to the person of Christ, and desire to build a relationship with him, that's when their hearts become open to difficult moral teachings. . . For those of us who have a tendency towards rigidity in our faith, let us take the Holy Father's words to heart, rather than mocking or criticizing the pope for calling us out. We should, as Francis reminds us, examine our hearts and consciences to discern where we have closed

The second response is invariably: "Why is Pope Francis picking on faithful Catholics?"[5] Here, we can see the inherent mental association between "rigidity" and "faithfulness." Pope Francis has not decried faithfulness, only rigidity. But the Catholic here asserts that Francis is slamming "faithful Catholics," defined as such by the very Catholic who feels the sting of the pontiff's words.[6] Since it is not proper for a pope to bash faithful Catholics, then something else must be afoot. "Rigidity" must be a concept created by Francis to simply stamp out resistance against him.[7] Or it must be a smokescreen from a liberal pope, a distraction to obfuscate the real

---

ourselves off to others and the movement of the Holy Spirit in our lives. Only then can we become the evangelizing Church that we are called to be."

[5] Chretien, "Pope Francis on the young": "Pope Francis frequently criticizes *faithful Catholics* using this type of rhetoric. He has blasted the 'excessive rigidity' of Catholics who believe in moral absolutes." See also "Pope Spits At Faithful Catholics Again," *Catholicism Pure & Simple*.

[6] Lawler. "Pope Francis has become a source of division": "If the Holy Father were rebuking me for my sins, I would have no reason to complain. But day after weary day the Pope upbraids me—and countless thousands of other faithful Catholics—for clinging to, and sometimes suffering for, the truths that the Church has always taught. We are rigid, he tells us."

[7] Lambert, "What Does the Pope Mean By 'Rigid'?": "This term [rigid] does not appear in Scripture or the Tradition of the Church, it is a Bergoglian innovation. It is something he uses as a hammer against those who he disagrees with." See also "Pope Spits At Faithful Catholics Again," *Catholicism Pure & Simple*: "Is all this 'rigid is bad' talk part of a strategy to get us to swallow Amoralis Lamentia?" (a play of words with Francis's magisterial document *Amoris Laetitia*, so that it would mean "amoral lamentation.")

Introduction

enemy: the world's laxity, so widespread in our days.[8] Or maybe the pope is just confused and does not know what he is doing. Regardless, one thing seems to be certain among those who respond like this: the Pope's warnings are to be ignored if one is to remain faithful.[9]

It seems to me obvious that these two responses are irreconcilable. So, if one is to make a solid decision, one must ask: which one of the two approaches is correct? Is there such a thing as "rigidity" in Catholic tradition? Is there such a thing as being "too faithful"?

Let me start by answering the latter question. No, there is no such thing as being "too faithful." God demands a radical faithfulness from us, more radical than what we can ever provide.

---

[8] Lambert, "What Does the Pope Mean By 'Rigid'?": "What do you say to that apart from 'Mental!' - It's just mental! Mental to engage in internal navel gazing and exacerbate divisions within the Church when we have so many challenges to the Gospel from the secular culture. Relativism & the cult of self-idolatry and self-worship is pushing in on Christianity from every angle and all the Catholic Church seems to do is accommodate and appease. The powerful medicine the Catholic Church has for these societal ills - which are causing real harm to our culture and our children right now - is locked in the cabinet while the pope rolls up his sleeves and deals with. . . RIGIDITY." See also "Pope Spits At Faithful Catholics Again," *Catholicism Pure & Simple*: "Have you ever noticed how many times he assails us, yet utters not one peep about those who play loosey-goosey with the teachings of Jesus Christ regarding faith and morals?"

[9] "Being 'Rigid' Is a Badge of Honor, Your Holiness." *One Peter Five*: "Francis expects as much; he wants his public insults to cause us to disavow rigidity, repenting. . . Instead, we will rejoice. . . Therefore, we desire to remain attached, even in a rigid way, to the traditions of the Church, which have been protected and handed down for the honor and glory of God throughout all generations."

Therefore, our faithfulness can never, by definition, be enough. But even if there is no such thing as being too faithful, this does not entail that there is no such thing as rigidity, because "rigidity" and "faithfulness" are two distinct concepts. The problem is: rigidity may indeed be confused with "being too faithful." Therein lies the thorn.

If I may be so bold, I would like to borrow a metaphor from the famous apologist C.S. Lewis. Granted, he used this analogy for another purpose, but I think I can adequately adapt it to better illustrate what I mean. Let us imagine we are hikers, leaving the bustle of the city to go on a mountain walk towards a small town in the countryside.

> At mid-day we come to the top of a cliff where we are, in space, very near [the town] because it is just below us. We could drop a stone into it. But as we are no cragsmen we can't get down. We must go a long way round; five miles maybe. At many points during that *détour* we shall, statically, be farther from the village than we were when we sat above the cliff. But only statically. In terms of progress, we shall be far "nearer" our baths and teas.[10]

The small town in the countryside is our goal, the end of our spiritual journey. It is very likely we will only reach it at the time of our final decision after we die. Still, it is our duty as Christians to position ourselves as closely as possible to that town, so that death

---

[10] Lewis. *The Four Loves*, 5.

will be merely the final step. The closer one is to the town, the closer one is to the finish line, the closer one is to complete faithfulness.

So, the Catholic has two ways of assessing how close he is to the finish line. In terms of *static distance* and in terms of *progress*. If we return to the analogy at hand, I think it is obvious that thinking in terms of progress is a much more profitable endeavor. Thinking in terms of static distance may be interesting when entertaining certain theoretical considerations, but no one organizes a hike with the purpose of arriving at the mathematically closest point possible without any detour. That would mean that one could not get closer to the town than the tip of the cliff—without falling to his death, at least. But it is indeed possible to arrive at the town if we see our path as progress. This is the principle behind Pope Francis's famous axiom: "time is greater than space."[11] Progress towards faithfulness is more important than the absolute distance. Someone sitting at the top of the cliff because that is the point of lesser static distance has frozen his spiritual journey at that point. He is, therefore, in a less favorable

---

[11] Francis, *Evangelii Gaudium*, 222-3: "Broadly speaking, 'time' has to do with fullness as an expression of the horizon which constantly opens before us, while each individual moment has to do with limitation as an expression of enclosure. People live poised between each individual moment and the greater, brighter horizon of the utopian future as the final cause which draws us to itself. Here we see a first principle for progress in building a people: *time is greater than space*. This principle enables us to work slowly but surely, without being obsessed with immediate results. It helps us patiently to endure difficult and adverse situations, or inevitable changes in our plans. It invites us to accept the tension between fullness and limitation, and to give a priority to time."

position than someone who is stubbornly moving towards the goal, even if the latter is still at the beginning of the journey.[12]

A critic may object that he is not static, that he is also progressing. Many of these Catholics draw their conclusions from their own experiences. They *did* struggle and progress. They abandoned—or are bravely in the process of abandoning—certain erroneous beliefs, sexual behaviors, or other addictions considered normal or even healthy by our lax society. Their "rigidity" derives from a thirst for truth, a thirst only sated when someone told them the fulness of the Catholic faith. Only then were they cured of the ensnaring and reassuring lies of the world. They obviously wish all humankind to experience the same liberation—and that is very generous of them.

But please note that the hiker sitting atop of the cliff *also* progressed. He did not teleport to that point. He abandoned the comforts of the city, with its parlors and its bars, with its motels and its Wi-fis, with its branded shops and its movie theaters, to undergo a journey through the craggy, rough, perilous mountain trails. Surely, arriving at the top of that cliff was a triumph one must not downplay.

Still, notice that C.S. Lewis places the hiker at the cliff by midday. The journey is only halfway through. The hiker conquered the mountain, but if he is to achieve his goal, he must now descend to

---

[12] Buttiglione, *Risposte Amichevoli*, 119: "If no one can escape one's cross, it is also true that no story begins with the cross. It is a path. In this journey, 'time is greater than space.' In what direction is the sinner moving? Towards the house of the Father, or away from it? The direction of the movement (marked by time) counts more than the absolute distance." (my translation from the original Italian).

the town. Having conquered the sins of the flesh—an ascending journey of struggle—he must now conquer the much more dangerous sins of the spirit—a descending journey of humility.[13]

I may even complete Lewis's metaphor with another formidable apologist's idea: G.K. Chesterton once said that he wished to write about someone journeying the whole world, only to arrive at the same place, the house he had left at the beginning of the book.[14] Maybe our hiker must descend from the mountain and return to the city from whence he came, not to indulge on the pleasures of city life once again, but to try to convince those who are swamped in its alienation to come with him to breathe the mountain's fresh air.

One may argue that it is safer to just stay at the mountaintop, without descending. After all, that is the closest point to the destination that you can achieve without meandering. If we conceive of faithfulness as a state of the soul, or as a kind of sacred place emanating its radiance towards us, then we may feel like the best choice is to just strive to be as close as possible from it without necessarily achieving it—which would be impossible. A bit like a cold person that tries to stay as close as possible to the fireplace without being inside the fireplace. On the other hand, our hiker may get lost if he proceeds further away from the cliff, through paths seeming, on the surface, to move farther away from the goal. Why risk that if you are

---

[13] Francis, "Press Conference on the return flight from Cyprus and Greece": "This is sin, but one of the more grave sins, because sins of the flesh are not the gravest sin: the gravest sins are those that have more of an 'angelic' character; pride, hatred… these are the most grave." This reasoning is actually very traditional, as decisively proven by Schneider. "Aquinas: Some Sins Worse Than Sexual Sins."

[14] Chesterton. *The Everlasting Man*, 9.

as close as possible to the target as you can get? Likewise, it can be argued that Francis's focus on rigidity is counterproductive. Even if he may have a point, is it not safer to err on the side of rigidity than laxity?

We will come back to this point in chapter 8. For now, I must say that I believe this thinking to be wrongheaded for three reasons. First of all, we are not meant to be "safe" on our journey. Another mountaintop, taken from the Bible, tells us as much. During the transfiguration episode atop Mount Tabor, Peter proclaims: "Master, it is good for us to be here; and let us make three tents."[15] Peter is so dazzled with the majesty of the miracle, he wants to set up tents and linger there. But the Bible quickly adds he knew not what he said.[16] The transfiguration soon ends, and they must descend from the mountain, where toil—and even the cross—await.

Following Christ is not meant to be a "safe" endeavor. Even those who advocate for rigidity as a virtue admit to this, though they usually argue it to eschew lax theologies. This laxism tries to soothe us into a reassuring worldview, telling us that we do not need to move beyond our comfort zone.[17] But Jesus asks us for a radical

---

[15] Paraphrased from Luke 9:33.

[16] Luke 9:33.

[17] "Being 'Rigid' Is a Badge of Honor, Your Holiness." *One Peter Five*: "Satan does not speak in terms that frighten us; he speaks words of encouragement. All God said isn't what he really meant! It's all really quite equivocal. Death is not a punishment for disobedience: 'Did he say you will die? Surely you will not die!' Use God's mercy for your comfort: 'Command these stones to become loaves of bread!' 'He will give his angels charge of you and on their hand they will bear you up, lest you strike your foot against a stone.'"

following: "If any man come to me, and hate not his father, and mother, and wife, and children, and brethren, and sisters, yea and his own life also, he cannot be my disciple. And whosoever doth not carry his cross and come after me, cannot be my disciple."[18] Following Christ is not about lingering in the safer position, but rather about a continuous journey, where we are asked to sacrifice everything for His sake: even our rigidity.

But why must we sacrifice our safe position for the sake of the journey? This brings us to the second point: while we are journeying, there are no safe positions. Whether we sit idly or proceed, the danger will come knocking on our door. The hiker atop our metaphorical cliff may think he is better in that spot, as mathematically close to the goal as possible. Who knows what dangers lurk ahead if he continues walking? Maybe he will be attacked by wolves or fall into a ditch from whence he will be unable to get off. If the hiker sits on top of the cliff, he will be able to see danger approaching from every direction. But this is an illusion, caused by the bright noon sun. Sooner or later, night will set in, and wolves will roam as much near the cliff as anywhere else. Or it may happen that the cliff is not as firm as the hiker thought. It may crack, plunging him into his doom. Or the hiker may become overconfident in his safe position and venture too near the cliff, tripping and falling into the darkness.

The only safe spot is home. No spot alongside the journey is a home: at most it is a camping site. Only an inn in the town, with its walls and roof, its teas and baths, is safe. We may be under the illusion that moving away from the safety of the cliff is leading into an

---

[18] Luke 14:26-27.

unsafe position. But by bringing us closer to our goal by means of progress—not static distance—the journey is actually bringing us into the safer position, the only one that really exists.

Finally, the third misgiving is to think that rigidity is the most prudent course of action to begin with. It is, as I said, easy to confuse faithfulness with rigidity. But historical precedent shows us that rigidity is as much prone to unfaithfulness as laxity. Throughout Church history, there have been as many rigorist heresies as there have been lax ones. The purpose of this book is precisely to bring these to light, so that the reader may understand how the prudential calculus involving rigorism is not as favorable to his or her soul as previously thought.

But one may object: these rigid heresies of the past have nothing to do with what Francis decries! Current day traditionalists or conservatives are not Pharisees or Donatists. They do not share the same tenets. There are substantive theological and ideological differences between the rigorisms of yore and the alleged rigorisms of today. After all, even those who criticize Pope Francis often concede that there *is* a danger to rigidity.[19]

---

[19] See, for example, Pokorsky. "Rigidity Dog Whistle": "But the average bishop fears clerical obduracy – a fear, *I gather, that is well-founded.* Hence, seminarians lived in dread of being charged with 'rigidity,' i.e., of holding fast to the Faith. . . I've committed many sins, and I know a rigid attachment to my predominant faults is among them. But I'm glad my confessions are protected by the Church's rigid 'Seal of Confession.' May this and many other rigid planks of the Barque of Peter support our faith now and forever." See also Williamson. "Moral Rigorism and the Jansenist Monster": "In the modern world, moral rigorism is not the scourge it once

This is a fair objection. Yet, there must be something common among these different kinds of rigidity, otherwise they would not share the same category. Even if we must not confuse them, maybe we can gain insight by learning from the lessons of the past.

Furthermore, if we acknowledge that there are indeed different kinds of rigidity, we are questioning the premise that rigidity and faithfulness are one and the same thing. If there is a difference between Donatist rigidity and the rigidity condemned by Pope Francis today, then there can also be a difference between the rigidity condemned by Pope Francis and the rigidity of faithfulness. By taking a nuanced look at the phenomenon of rigidity in Catholic history, we can accept that Pope Francis may be warning the faithful of a true spiritual danger, not scolding them for their faithfulness.

But what does Francis mean by "rigidity," after all? Those who do not accept his teachings have claimed that the term is ambiguous, and that it is impossible to know what the pope really means unless he clarifies its meaning.[20] Unfortunately, the term "ambiguity" has been reflexively used throughout Francis's pontificate as a stamp for

---

was. *Yes, we all must guard against it, for it is easy to fall into, especially for pious practicing Catholics. However...*"

[20] Lambert, "What Does the Pope Mean By 'Rigid'?": "Let's be honest, this term is typically Bergoglian. No one is even sure what, exactly, it means. I don't get why someone at the Vatican doesn't grab hold of him and tell him to either explain himself or just shut up... At best, the term is a vague metaphor which in and of itself, calls for clarification - how very Pope Francis!... Brian Holdsworth does an excellent job of pointing out why the Pope should STOP using this confusing, ambiguous term in this video."

every teaching of his not conforming to a certain mindset[21]—ironically the mindset that tends to defend rigidity. This use of the word "ambiguity," by effectively undermining Francis's magisterium, avoids the clarifications that it allegedly seeks.

Nevertheless, at the time of the writing of this book, a search for the keyword "rigidity" on the Vatican website yields a total of 144 results for Pope Francis. It is hard to argue that a word used so often remains ambiguous. In fact, it is more plausible to argue that such a widespread use of the word may actually be an attempt to provide the "clarification" so often requested. And in fact, when we start reading these papal speeches and writings with an open mind, we start to notice certain recurring ideas. These form patterns that help us elucidate what the Pope means by the word "rigidity."

I have taken these recurring patterns and tried to relate them to what they share with the rigorist heresies of the past. Once again, this is not to establish a perfect parallel between the rigidity decried by Pope Francis and those past heresies, but to highlight what we can learn from those past heresies and apply it today. By doing so, I hope, at least, to help the reader to understand the fundamental distinction between rigidity and faithfulness, so that he or she may not be afraid to follow Francis's magisterium.

I have, therefore, divided this book into the following chapters:

- ❖ Chapter 1: How to oppose both laxity and rigidity, by taking recourse to Thomistic-Aristotelian virtue ethics.

---

[21] See, for example, Hitchens. "An Ambiguous Exhortation."

- Chapter 2: The spiritual problem of scrupulosity, in contrast to the freedom afforded by the Gospel.
- Chapter 3: The doctors of the law at the time of Jesus according to Pope Francis's concerns about a "double life."
- Chapter 4: The Judaizer heresy and the error of remaining frozen in the past.
- Chapter 5: The Donatist controversy and the need for mercy.
- Chapter 6: Pelagianism and the question of self-sufficiency.
- Chapter 7: The medieval heresies of the Cathars, the *Fraticelli*, and the Flagellants, considering the temptation of spiritual worldliness.
- Chapter 8: The Jansenists and the error of Rigorism.

I hope the reader will find this reading productive, both from a spiritual point of view and from an apologetical perspective. Spiritual, that it might help the reader identify the spiritual danger of rigidity, even more pernicious because it tends to evade the soul's radar by disguising itself as faithfulness. Apologetical, so that more Catholics may get to know Pope Francis's spirituality and magisterium, dispelling erroneous and prejudiced ideas around his pontificate, so that his teachings may be more profitable to each individual in particular and for the Church in general. So, without further ado, let us begin.

Chapter 1

Laxism and the Golden Mean

And one needs to see oneself from two opposite extremes: rigorism and laxism. Neither of the two are beneficial, because in reality they do not take care of the penitent. Mercy instead truly listens with the heart of God and wants to accompany the soul along the path of reconciliation.

—Francis, Address to a Course Sponsored by the Apostolic Penitentiary

The first major controversy around Francis's pontificate burst out when he published the apostolic exhortation *Amoris Laetitia*. In this document, the pontiff instituted a new sacramental discipline. Before *Amoris Laetitia*, divorced and remarried couples could only take communion if they would live without sexual intercourse, "as brother and sister." But now, divorced and remarried people could commune if, during an examination of conscience, they would have found that they had not committed a mortal sin due to mitigating circumstances diminishing their subjective culpability.[1]

---

[1] For an in-depth explanation as to why this is *Amoris Laetitia*'s most cogent interpretation and why it is perfectly orthodox, see Gabriel. *The Orthodoxy of Amoris Laetitia*.

Francis's critics pointed out that such a loosening of the previous restrictions incurred the danger of laxity,[2] especially when received by a hedonistic, secularized society. Some of these critics, more moderate, would say that *Amoris Laetitia* was not expressly lax, but could be interpreted in a lax way.[3] Some would argue that this ambiguity was intentional, so the laxists could get their way, while maintaining a plausible deniability.[4] Others, more daring, went as

---

[2] See, for example, Leone. "The Church and the Asmodeus": "As noted above, the great novelty of *Amoris Laetitia* is the advocacy of adultery. In the light of this laxity one cannot but be alarmed at the Pope's analysis of the sexuality of contemporary youth in exclusively sociological and psychological terms, without so much a hint at morality. Impurity, alone or with another, is nowhere condemned. Indeed, as we observed above, it seems actively to be encouraged." See also Harrison, "*Amoris Laetitia* Laxity Trickles Down."

[3] See, for example, van den Aardweg et al. *Correctio filialis*: "Those statements in [Amoris Laetitia] that on the face of them contradict the faith could be due to simple error on Pope Francis's part, rather than to a voluntary rejection of the faith. When it comes to the document itself, however, there is no doubt that it constitutes a grave danger to Catholic faith and morals. It contains many statements whose vagueness or ambiguity permit interpretations that are contrary to faith or morals, or that suggest a claim that is contrary to faith and morals without actually stating it." See also Longley, "*Amoris Laetitia*: Pope Francis Has Created Confusion Where We Needed Clarity": "[*Amoris Laetitia*] is a mess. In those circumstances the only possible advice is to follow the instincts and intuitions of one's conscience as honestly as possible, consulting whomever one likes in the process. Let liberals interpret the document liberally and conservatives conservatively. But don't let anybody tell them they are wrong, because nobody knows that for sure."

[4] See, for example, Reno. "A Stubborn Givenness": "Francis doesn't actually say that divorced and remarried Catholics can receive

Chapter 1: Laxism and the Golden Mean

far as saying that Pope Francis was actively promoting adultery,[5] a most extreme laxity in Catholic teaching.

Is this an accurate reading of Pope Francis's manifest mind and will on the subject? It seems hard to argue this, since the pontiff has explicitly decried a laxist interpretation of his document. A few days after the publication of *Amoris Laetitia*, Francis gave an interview during the return flight from his visit to the Greek island of Lesbos. In this interview, Francis was asked by Frank Rocca, correspondent of the *Wall Street Journal*, if there were new, concrete possibilities for eucharistic access to the divorced and remarried that did not exist before the publication of the exhortation. Francis referred the journalists to the presentation made by Cardinal Christoph Schönborn during the press conference presenting *Amoris Laetitia* a few days earlier.[6]

---

communion. *Amoris Laetitia* explicitly affirms the church's teaching on marriage. But in long digressions into the complexities of moral and pastoral discernment, Francis provides plenty of justifications for others to say that, yes, in particular situations, divorced and married Catholics can receive communion. All the while, Francis insists that the Catholic teaching on marriage must be affirmed. The ambiguity seems intentional, designed to increase scope for pastoral discretion."

[5] See, for example, McCusker. "Key Doctrinal Errors and Ambiguities of *Amoris Laetitia*": "The implication of this, is that it might sometimes be appropriate to tolerate, or even, perhaps, as would be the logical consequence, to encourage, adultery." See also, once again, Leone. "The Church and the Asmodeus": "As noted above, the great novelty of *Amoris Laetitia* is the advocacy of adultery."

[6] Francis, "In-flight Press Conference from Lesbos to Rome."

In this presentation, Schönborn was literally asked whether *Amoris Laetitia* did not favor a certain laxism, a disregard for ecclesial teaching. The cardinal replied:

> The pope leaves no room for doubt about Church teaching and, to avoid any errant interpretation, he points out that "in no way must the Church desist from proposing the full ideal of marriage, God's plan in all its grandeur" (AL 307). But he affirms too, using strong words, that "it is petty simply to consider whether or not an individual's actions correspond to a general law or rule, because that is not enough to discern and ensure full fidelity to God in the concrete life of a human being." (AL 304). Let us not be petty![7]

Elsewhere in the same presentation, Schönborn once again sets laxism and rigorism as two equally erroneous extremes of the same spectrum:

> [*Amoris Laetitia*] is realist, and certainly does not give in to alarmism: there is no obsession with critical cases or complex situations. Francis writes about the things of our time, the risks, the challenges, the sufferings with a profound compassion for what is being lived out, *without falling into rigorism or laxism*... We have here the exposition of a morality that is inspired by the great Ignatian tradition (discernment of conscience) and the great Dominican one (the morality of

---

[7] Schönborn, "Conversation with Cardinal Schönborn."

virtues). *We have turned our backs on the moralities of obligation, whose extrinsicism generates both laxism and rigorism.* Instead, we reconnect to the great Catholic moral tradition.[8]

This is not to be taken lightly. Francis himself emphasized this idea, lest people overlook it. A couple of months later, Francis once again made reference to Schönborn's presentation, echoing the cardinal's crucial distinction:

> Both are not truth: *neither rigorism nor laxity are truth.* The Gospel chooses another way. . . For your tranquility, I must tell you that all that is written in the Exhortation —and I again take up the words of a great theologian who was the secretary of the Congregation for the Doctrine of the Faith, Cardinal Schönborn, who presented it —everything is Thomist, from beginning to end. It is the doctrine that is certain. But we often want the certain doctrine to have that mathematical certainty that does not exist, *neither with laxity, lenience, nor with rigidity.*[9]

This dichotomy appears in other occasions of his pontificate, not just related to *Amoris Laetitia*. Francis is very clear that his criticisms of rigidity are not to be construed as an endorsement of laxism. In one of his usual morning meditations, titled "Faith is not Sold," Francis explained that there is a temptation to downsize the faith, to

---

[8] Ibid.
[9] Francis. "Address at the Opening of the Pastoral Congress."

behave more or less "like everyone else," to "*not be too rigid.*"[10] Francis explained that we must resist this temptation, for this path ends in apostasy. Faith is not negotiable.[11] According to Francis, we must live a daily attitude of conversion, which requires "vigilance both over rigidity as well as excessive and comfortable tolerance."[12]

Another aspect where Francis often eschews laxism pertains to the sacrament of Reconciliation. Just like rigidity is sometimes confused with faithfulness, laxism is also sometimes confused with mercy (see chapter 5).[13] But neither the lenient confessor, nor the rigid one is truly merciful. The rigid confessor pontificates "No, the law says. . ." while the laxist advocates: "Go, don't worry, God forgives all. Go on, go!"[14] Both are, in effect, "washing their hands on the penitent": the former by simply "nailing the person to the law, understood in a cold and rigid way," the latter by "minimizing sin," by not taking "seriously the problems of that conscience."[15] In this respect, neither laxity nor rigorism foster holiness.[16] By merely repeating premanufactured mantras to the penitent, a "one-size fits all" approach, both the lenient and the rigid confessors are excusing themselves from the demanding task of accompanying the sinner. But being merciful means "carrying the burden of a brother and

---

[10] Francis. "Faith is not sold."
[11] Ibid.
[12] Francis. "Address to the Participants in the General Chapters."
[13] Francis. "Address to a Course Organized by the Apostolic Penitentiary."
[14] Ibid.
[15] Francis. "Address to the Parish Priests of the Diocese of Rome."
[16] Ibid.

sister and helping them walk."[17] "True mercy takes the person into one's care, listens to him attentively, approaches the situation with respect and truth, and accompanies him on the journey of reconciliation."[18] Therefore, priests are asked to be on guard against two opposing temptations: rigidity, leading to a sterile clericalism, and secularism, leading to worldliness.[19]

But is this teaching rooted in traditional Catholic theology? If one is to eschew laxism, as Pope Francis urges us to do, does this not mean that one must embrace rigidity? And if opposing laxism is faithfulness, does this not mean that rigidity is faithfulness? To answer these questions, we must dive into Thomistic-Aristotelian virtue ethics, the kind of ethics that informs much of contemporary Catholic thought.

Aristotle and the virtue

We are accustomed to thinking of virtue and vice as two polar opposites, standing against each other (see figure 1). According to this dualistic perspective, each individual is situated alongside a spectrum between two extremes: one of the extremes is virtue, the

---

[17] Francis. "Address to a Course Organized by the Apostolic Penitentiary."

[18] Francis. "Address to the Parish Priests of the Diocese of Rome." See also Francis. "Letter on the 160th Anniversary of the Curé of Ars": "Thank you for celebrating the Eucharist each day and for being merciful shepherds in the Sacrament of Reconciliation, *neither rigorous nor lax*, but deeply concerned for your people and accompanying them on their journey of conversion to the new life that the Lord bestows on us all."

[19] Francis. "Address to Pilgrims from Slovakia."

other is vice. The more one moves away from vice, the more one moves towards virtue and vice versa.

This dualistic model can be exacerbated by our hedonistic and lax society in a twofold way. On one hand, a Catholic observes how laxity is a vice and then seeks to counter it. On the other hand, this society does not acknowledge the existence of pure good or evil. In such a relativistic society, everything is morally ambiguous and "grey." Therefore, a Catholic may feel justified in opposing this "grey" relativism by positing the existence of "black" and "white" realities. Thus, the dualistic model is affirmed.

Figure 1. Dualistic model

| **Vice** | **Virtue** |
| (Laxity) | (Faithfulness / Rigidity) |

According to this dualistic model, if one considers laxity a vice, then that which is farther away from laxity must be a virtue. From this point onward, it is possible to formulate a sort of syllogism:

Premise 1: Rigidity is opposed to the vice of laxity.
Premise 2: The more one moves away from laxity, the more faithful one becomes.
Conclusion: Therefore, the more rigid one becomes, the more faithful one is.

Seems like a foolproof model, but it actually fails. It errs because it is too simplistic. Catholic moral theology is deeply imbued with Thomistic theology, which in turn relies heavily on Aristotelian philosophy. Aristotle, on his end, did not postulate a dualistic model, but a model based on the principle of "the golden mean."

According to this Aristotelian golden mean model, virtue is intermediate between a defect and an excess. The defect and the excess are what stand diametrically opposed to one another, while the mean is an intermediate state between the two extremes. Excess is a form of failure. The defect is also a form of failure. Only the intermediate state is a success.[20] So, for instance, courage is not merely the virtue that stands opposed to cowardice. Rather, courage is an intermediate state between cowardice (a defect of confidence) and rashness (an excess of confidence).[21] Rashness is not courage, because rashness is not a virtue. A courageous person is the one who has the right amount of confidence, without being cowardly or rash.

We may try to apply this golden mean model to rigidity. Before I proceed, two caveats. First: Aristotle does not list rigidity as one of its virtues or vices. But neither does he list faithfulness, for he was a pagan philosopher. Later, I will complement Aristotle's philosophy with St. Thomas Aquinas's theology. For now, let us see what we can learn from Aristotle that we can apply to the topic at hand, even if Aristotle himself did not do so.

Second: the golden mean applies to virtues, not actions. Virtues and vices are not actions, they are inclinations. Some actions—like, say adultery or murder—are always wrong. They, therefore, admit to no defects or excesses. Adultery is not a mean between an excess of adultery and a defect of adultery.[22] The Church has codified this

---

[20] Aristotle. "The Nicomachean Ethics," 27.
[21] Ibid., 28.
[22] Ibid.

in her doctrine of *intrinsece malum* i.e., "intrinsically evil acts": these are negative precepts of the universal moral law, in which certain acts (like adultery) are wrong according to their species (their "objects,") regardless of intentions and circumstances.[23]

Is this what we are dealing with when we are talking about laxity and rigidity? It does not seem that way. If it were so, rigidity would always be the virtuous course of action, because laxity would always be wrong. But even those who reject Pope Francis's teachings on rigidity often concede that rigidity is not always good.[24] Furthermore, the rest of this book will give several examples of rigorist heresies. Therefore, we are not dealing with an intrinsically evil act. Consequently, excesses and defects are possible, and the golden mean model is applicable.

Let us then apply the golden mean model. If faithfulness is a virtue, then it must be an intermediate state between a defect and an excess. The defect is obviously laxity. But the excess is rigidity. Faithfulness then, is different from rigidity. In fact, this model assumes that one must not be rigid to be faithful (see figure 2). The error of the dualistic Catholic was believing that he was succeeding by merely avoiding the failure of laxity. But there is not a single way to fail. Rather, there is a single way to succeed and many ways to fail.[25]

---

[23] John Paul II. *Veritatis Splendor*, 52, 79-80.

[24] See, for example, Pokorsky. "Rigidity Dog Whistle": "But the average bishop fears clerical obduracy – a fear, *I gather, that is well-founded.*" See also Williamson. "Moral Rigorism and the Jansenist Monster": "Pastors must warn against both moral rigorism and moral laxity"

[25] Aristotle. "The Nicomachean Ethics," 27.

Chapter 1: Laxism and the Golden Mean

Figure 2. "Golden mean" model

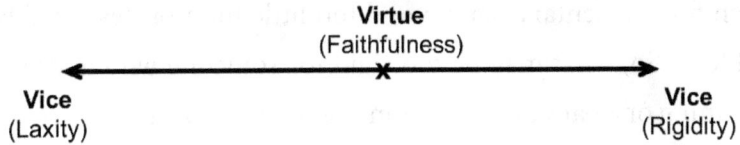

There are some nuances we must consider. The golden mean does not necessarily stand at the exact mathematical center between both extremes. As the reader can see in figure 2, the virtue lies slightly closer to one of the ends of the spectrum than the other. One of the extremes can be more erroneous.[26] This happens because one of the extremes is more alike the virtue than the other. So, for instance, rashness is more alike courage than cowardice, so cowardice is a greater vice than rashness.[27] In this sense, one can argue that rigidity stands closer to faithfulness than laxism does.[28]

But even granting this point, there are some other subtleties we need to acknowledge. If it is true that virtue is not equidistant from either extreme, it is also true that the distance between each extreme is not the same in each person. In a purely arithmetical perspective, one hundred pounds stands in the mean between zero and two hundred pounds. This happens always and everywhere. However,

---

[26] Ibid., 32.

[27] Ibid., 31.

[28] Williamson. "Moral Rigorism and the Jansenist Monster": "Simply put, Aristotle proposed virtue as the mean between two vices – but the virtue, he continued, does not fall directly between the two. Instead, it falls closer to one than the other... Pastors of souls especially are called to read the "signs of the times" and prepare their flocks for the particular errors of the day... In the modern world, moral rigorism is not the scourge it once was."

relatively to an individual, lifting one hundred pounds might be too much for a sedentary person and too little for a professional bodybuilder.[29] So, what may be too rigid for someone who is still at the beginning of a path of conversion might be too lax for someone who is already more advanced.

This poses a danger. If it is true that both extremes oppose each other, it is also true that both extremes oppose the virtuous intermediate state. Vices of defect are contrary to vices of excess, but both vices are contrary to virtue.[30] This produces an interesting effect. The people at each extreme lay claim to the middle place.[31] So, for the coward, the brave person is seen as rash. Conversely, for the rash person, the brave person is seen as a coward. Yet, the brave person is the one who is virtuous.[32]

If we apply this logic to our topic, we can infer that a lax person will see the faithful one as being too rigid (see the introduction to this book). But for the rigid person, the faithful one may be seen as too lax. This is what, in my experience, is happening when some Catholics claim that Pope Francis's teachings are lax. So, again, we must not merely consider the virtue in itself, but also relative to ourselves. According to Aristotle, the things to which we ourselves more naturally tend seem more contrary to the intermediate.[33] In other words, a lax person tends more naturally to laxity, so this person must guard himself more against laxity than rigidity. But if someone

---

[29] Aristotle. "The Nicomachean Ethics," 26-7.
[30] Ibid., 31.
[31] Ibid., 29.
[32] Ibid., 31.
[33] Ibid., 31-3.

tends more naturally to rigidity, then it is wise for this person to guard himself more against rigidity than against laxity. Thus, the importance of discernment, so continuously stressed by Pope Francis. We will return to the importance of discernment later in this chapter.

For now, let us say that figure 2 above is still too reductive to fully encompass the richness of Aristotle's ethics. It is not completely accurate to place virtue in a spectrum between two opposing vices, because that would mean that virtue lays in the same plane as the vices. In this model, we lost the spectrum between virtue and vice with which we started this chapter. For the model to account for the full complexity of reality, we must see it in three dimensions.

Figure 3. Aristotelian model

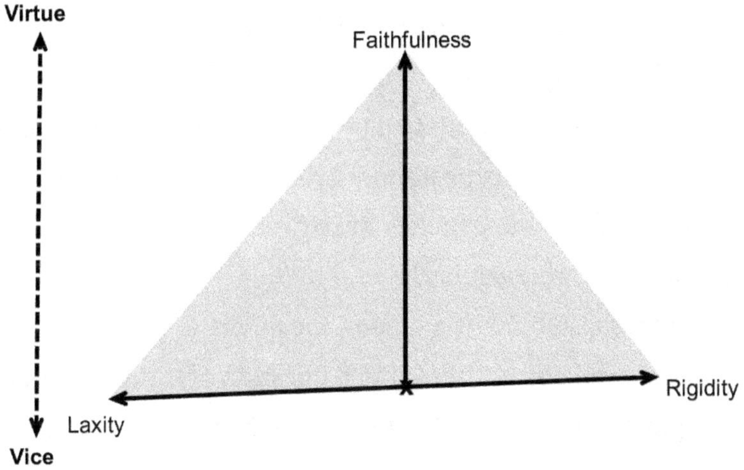

Here, each individual does not fall within a line, but along a certain point within that triangular grey area. Virtue is not merely a mean between two vices. Virtue is also an excellence.[34] It stands at a

---

[34] Ibid., 26.

higher plane than each vice. Virtue is doing the right thing to the right person, to the right extent, at the right time, with the right motive, and in the right way. Finding the golden mean is not an easy task.[35]

Faithfulness is not rigidity merely because rigidity opposes laxity. Rather, faithfulness stands at a higher plane than either rigidity or laxity, even if one grants that rigidity may be slightly more virtuous than laxity. A Catholic that seeks to live faithfully must, therefore, try to eschew rigidity, especially if such a Catholic feels more naturally drawn to rigidity than laxity.

Aquinas and the theological virtues

Let us now move to St. Thomas Aquinas. As is well known, Catholic theology and doctrine is highly indebted to Aquinas, who is held in singular honor by the Church.[36] Even in modern times, the Church recommends us to "go to Thomas."[37] One of the hallmarks of Aquinas's theology is its profound Aristotelianism. Thomas ransomed Aristotle from the clutches of paganism, thoroughly Christianizing the Greek philosopher.

Did Aquinas also borrow a golden mean virtue ethics from Aristotle? This is explicitly addressed in a question of the *Summa Theologiae*, Aquinas's master work. On the one hand, St. Thomas says that in things that can be ruled or measured, the good is what is in

---

[35] Ibid., 32.

[36] Leo XIII. *Aeterni Patris*, 17-24.

[37] See, for example, Vatican II. *Gravissimum educationis*, 10, and Francis. "Address to the International Thomistic Congress."

Chapter 1: Laxism and the Golden Mean

conformity with its rule. Likewise, evil is discordance with that same rule. From this, it would seem like Aquinas was a proponent of the dualistic model from figure 1. But he quickly adds that *discordance with the rule can happen either by exceeding the measure or by falling short of it.*[38]

St. Thomas acknowledges that virtue is, in a sense, always a maximum. Virtue is an extreme. On the other hand, as I said before, virtue is a mean between exceeding the rule and falling short of it.[39] How can this be? It depends on how we look at virtue. Just like in my one hundred pounds example earlier, we can consider virtue in relation to its absolute value, or in relation to the circumstances.[40]

If we consider virtue in relation to its absolute value, then virtue is a maximum. Virtue is when one does what is right, where it is right, when it is right, and for an end that is right.[41] There is no

---

[38] Aquinas. *Summa Theologiae*, I-II, q. 64, a. 1, co.

[39] Ibid., I-II, q. 64, a. 1, ad. 2.

[40] Ibid., I-II, q. 64, a. 1, ad. 1: "Moral virtue derives goodness from the rule of reason, while its matter consists in passions or operations. If therefore we compare moral virtue to reason, then, if we look at that which is has of reason, it holds the position of one extreme, viz. conformity; while excess and defect take the position of the other extreme, viz. deformity. But if we consider moral virtue in respect of its matter, then it holds the position of mean, in so far as it makes the passion conform to the rule of reason. Hence the Philosopher says (Ethic. ii, 6) that 'virtue, as to its essence, is a mean state,' in so far as the rule of virtue is imposed on its proper matter: 'but it is an extreme in reference to the 'best' and the 'excellent,'" viz. as to its conformity with reason."

[41] Ibid., I-II, q. 64, a. 1, ad. 2.

excess here. The more one conforms to this, the more virtuous one is. If virtue is viewed as an excellence,[42] then virtue is an extreme.

But if we consider virtue in relation to the circumstances, then virtue is a mean between two extremes. There is a deficiency when one fails to do what is right. But there is an excess when one tends to the maximum either when it is not right, or where it is not right, or for an undue end.[43]

In summary, and considering our earlier figures, it would seem like Aquinas proposes figure 2 when we are talking about virtue as a golden mean between two extremes, and figure 3 when we talk about virtue as an excellence.

In all of this, it seems like Aquinas agrees with Aristotle in everything we said previously. However, there is a catch. Whatever we said before relates to *moral* virtues. But as Catholics, we also promote the so-called *theological* virtues, which were alien to the pagan Aristotle. The theological virtues are the three listed by St. Paul in 1 Cor 13:13: *faith, hope, and charity.* These are, in fact, the most excellent of virtues. This is especially important because it would seem like faithfulness would, by definition, fall under the virtue of faith (hence its name.) So, in order to know whether faithfulness has a golden mean, we must ascertain whether the theological virtues also admit to a golden mean, just like the moral virtues.

The same *Summa Theologiae* question that addresses the golden mean in moral virtues also tackles whether the theological virtues have a golden mean. Here, the answer is different, for Aquinas says: "Wherever virtue observes the mean it is possible to sin by excess as

---

[42] Ibid., I-II, q. 64, a. 1, arg. 1.
[43] Ibid., I-II, q. 64, a. 1, ad. 2.

Chapter 1: Laxism and the Golden Mean

well as by deficiency. But *there is no sinning by excess against God, Who is the object of theological virtue.*"[44]

In other words, Aquinas posits what I have already said in the introduction to this book: there is no such thing as being too faithful. Whatever faithfulness we have, it will always be too short relative to what God deserves and mandates.

However, even here the answer is not as straightforward. Indeed, there is no excess as regards to theological virtues. But once again, it all depends on the perspective we take. If we measure a theological virtue in relation to God, then theological virtues do not accept a mean. It is not possible to love God too much or believe in God too much.[45] However, if instead we measure a theological virtue in relation to ourselves, "we should approach to Him by believing, hoping and loving, *according to the measure of our condition. Consequently, it is possible to find a mean and extremes in theological virtue, accidentally and in reference to us.*"[46]

Aquinas gives the example of hope. Relative to God, hope has no extreme, for it is not possible to hope in God too much. But relative to us, hope is the golden mean between the extremes of despair (defect) and presumption (excess),[47] the latter being when one has so

---

[44] Ibid., I-II, q. 64, a. 4, sc.

[45] See Aquinas. *Summa Theologiae*, I-II, q. 64, a. 4, co: "This measure surpasses all human power: so that never can we love God as much as He ought to be loved, nor believe and hope in Him as much as we should. Much less therefore can there be excess in such things. Accordingly the good of such virtues does not consist in a mean, but increases the more we approach to the summit."

[46] Ibid., I-II, q. 64, a. 4, co

[47] Ibid., I-II, q. 64, a. 4, ad. 3.

much hope in God's salvation, that one considers oneself saved, regardless of one's continuous sins.

Regarding the virtue of faith, St. Thomas also gives the examples of heresy—a sin against faith. Heresies usually do not appear in isolation, but often strike in opposite pairs. So, for instance, we have the heresy of Nestorianism, wherein it is believed that Jesus Christ was two persons (one human, one divine) with two natures (again, one human, one divine). On the other hand, the heresy of Monophysitism advocated that Jesus was one person with one nature. But orthodoxy holds a mean between those two extremes, believing that Jesus is one person with two natures.[48]

From a purely Thomistic-Aristotelian point of view, whether one considers faithfulness as falling under the theological virtue of faith or under a moral virtue, it is possible to consider a golden mean between two extremes, one being laxity (defect) and the other being rigidity (excess). This happens even if faithfulness, considered in itself, has no extreme, for it is not possible to ever be too faithful.

Discernment and epikeia

If a Catholic is to avoid both rigorism and laxism, what is a Catholic to do? How does one distinguish between faithfulness and mere rigidity? If we study Pope Francis's interventions, we will find several remedies for both laxity and rigidity. The first one is "perseverance," the true and healthy "rigidity." As Francis teaches, perseverance is defined as "being very strict." But not strict with oneself,

---

[48] Ibid., I-II, q. 64, a. 4, arg. 3 and ad. 3.

Chapter 1: Laxism and the Golden Mean

considering oneself not up to standard, neither with others, becoming rigid and inflexible. Rather, one must be strict, uncompromising, resolute, and persistent in "building upon what does not pass away. This then, is perseverance: it is building goodness every day. To persevere is to remain constant in goodness, especially when the reality around us urges us to do otherwise. . . Persevering, instead, is remaining in goodness."[49]

How does one remain in goodness? Francis gives us four words: "welcome, support, integrate, discern."[50] Of these, discernment seems to be the most recurring in Francis's thought. When something new presents itself in our lives, it is through discernment we may recognize whether this novelty is "an illusion created by the spirit of this world or the spirit of the devil," or the "new wine brought by God" (in which case, rigidly resisting it would be to "block the working of the Holy Spirit.")[51]

> Discernment is a choice of courage, contrary to *the more comfortable and reductive ways of rigorism and laxism, as I have repeated several times.* Educating in discernment means, indeed, fleeing from the temptation to seek refuge behind a rigid norm or behind the image of an idealized freedom.[52]

---

[49] Francis. "Angelus," November 13, 2022.
[50] Francis. "Address to the Parish Priests of the Diocese of Rome."
[51] Francis. *Gaudete et Exsultate*, 168.
[52] Francis. "Address to the Community of the Pontifical Seminary."

We have been exploring Thomistic-Aristotelianism until now. Can we find instances of this discernment in this philosophical and theological model? Here, I would like to appeal to the concept of *epikeia*, also called "equity." According to Aristotle, equity is a kind of justice, but a bizarre kind. Justice is giving to each one what is due to them, namely by correctly applying a universal law or principle. But equity mandates that, if a certain particular case is not covered by the universal rule, it is right to correct for this omission by not applying the rule. For Aristotle, being just is good, but being equitable is better.[53]

Now, one may argue: how can equity be a part of justice? Is it not the actual opposite: a break of the law and, consequently, the very denial of justice? Both Aristotle and Aquinas agree that such is not the case. *Epikeia* is not passing judgment either on the law or on the legislator. Both law and legislator are good. On the contrary, *epikeia* is passing judgment on the nature of that particular circumstance, which is not adequately covered by the law.[54] Therefore, the law and the legislator remain reliable, since *epikeia* corrects an omission: it judges according to what "the legislator himself would have said had he been present, and would have put into his law if he had known."[55]

The law takes the usual case, but acknowledges the possibility of error, since it cannot cover every particular circumstance. This is not because of an evilness of the law, but because of the nature of things.

---

[53] Aristotle. "The Nicomachean Ethics," 88-9.

[54] Ibid., 89. See also Aquinas. *Summa Theologiae*, II-II, q. 120, a. 1, ad. 2.

[55] Aristotle. "The Nicomachean Ethics," 89.

Chapter 1: Laxism and the Golden Mean

The complexity of reality is such that no law can account for every possible contingency. So says Aristotle:

> Hence, the equitable is just, and better than one kind of justice—not better than absolute justice but better than the error that arises from the absoluteness of the statement. And this is the nature of the equitable, a correction of law where it is defective owing to its universality... the rule adapts itself to the shape of the stone and *is not rigid*, and so too the decree is adapted to the facts.[56]

Aquinas agrees with Aristotle on this:

> Human actions, with which laws are concerned, are composed of contingent singulars and are innumerable in their diversity, it was not possible to lay down rules of law that would apply to every single case. Legislators in framing laws attend to what commonly happens: although if the law be applied to certain cases, it will frustrate the equality of justice and be injurious to the common good, which the law has in view.[57]

St. Thomas goes on to give a practical example of *epikeia*. The law requires deposits to be given back to the depositaries, because this is just in the vast majority of cases. But if a man had deposited a sword and asks it back when in a state of madness, it would not be

---

[56] Ibid.
[57] Aquinas. *Summa Theologiae*, II-II, q. 120, a. 1, co.

just to give the sword back. In fact, that would be as much madness as the one from the madman.[58]

From this discussion we can see that equity is indeed a part of justice. Therefore, it is a virtue. It is not virtuous to follow the letter of the law always and everywhere. What is virtuous is to follow the letter of the law *when it ought to be followed*. St. Thomas Aquinas explicitly says that following the letter of the law when it ought not to be followed is *sinful*. Someone who adheres to the letter of the law in order to defeat the intention of the lawgiver is also a transgressor of the law (see chapter 3).[59] Can we not say then that this is why rigidity is sinful and, ironically, a transgression of the very law it purports to defend?

Before I finish this chapter, I would like to point out that I am not equating discernment with equity here.[60] I am simply showcasing an instance in Thomistic-Aristotelian thought where discernment is obviously needed to overcome an inappropriate rigidity. As

---

[58] Ibid., II-II, q. 120, a. 1, co.

[59] Ibid., II-II, q. 120, a. 1, ad. 1

[60] Neither am I arguing that the sacramental discipline where *Amoris Laetitia* rests is based on *epikeia*. Even though I started this chapter by talking about *Amoris Laetitia*, I did so in the context of highlighting Pope Francis's opposition to both laxity and rigidity. Elsewhere, I argue that *Amoris Laetitia* does not rest in *epikeia*, but on applying to the divorced and remarried a general rule from which they were previously excluded. See Gabriel. *The Orthodoxy of Amoris Laetitia*, 102, 198—199. See also Buttiglione, *Risposte amichevoli*, 144-5: "Before, the divorced and remarried were sinners of a particular kind, almost excommunicated (even if not formally excommunicated, they could not partake of Communion unless they lived 'as brothers and sisters'). Now, they have become ordinary sinners."

we have seen above, virtue is doing the right thing to the right person, to the right extent, at the right time, with the right motive, and in the right way. *Epikeia* concerns itself only with laws that admit to exceptions, and to define *when* the law ought to be followed. Therefore, there are still many other considerations to discern if one is to follow the path of virtue. Still, from what was said above, it is undeniable that discernment has a role to play in Thomistic-Aristotelian ethics and, therefore, in Catholic tradition.

Chapter 2

Scrupulosity and Slavery to the Law

The law was not established in order to make us slaves, but to make us free, to make us children... those who are rigid suffer greatly when they are sincere, and they realize this, they suffer because they cannot have the freedom of the children of God.

—Francis, Morning Meditation
"Never Slaves of the law"

In 2016, Pope Francis stirred another major controversy in an interview by Fr. Antonio Spadaro. During this interview, Francis wondered why some young people would prefer to celebrate Mass according to the pre-Vatican II liturgy: "Why so much rigidity? Dig, dig, this rigidity always hides something, insecurity or even something else. Rigidity is defensive. True love is not rigid."[1]

Traditionalist commentators and their sympathetic allies were very critical of the Pope's remarks. They were once again puzzled at what Pope Francis meant with rigidity.[2] More importantly, they viewed the Holy Father's words as an unfair stereotype,[3] based on

---

[1] Wooden. "Texts of Argentina homilies."

[2] Olson. "Digging into Pope Francis' remarks": "And why the constant use of the term 'rigid'? What, exactly, does it refer to here? Is it the rubrics of the EF? The prayers? The culture in parishes that celebrate it? The attitude of those who celebrate it?"

[3] DeVille. "Rigidity in defense of the liturgy is no vice."

assumptions and name-calling. Pope Francis would be sounding more like a psychologist than like a pastor.[4]

Sed contra, I will show throughout this chapter how sometimes this is how a spiritual father acts and talks to those under his care. But regarding the accusation of broad brushing, I would like to point out that Francis's views on this matter are more nuanced than what he expressed in this interview. For the Holy Father, there are several types of rigidity. It is true that rigidity always "hides something" according to his thought. But not always the same thing. It may be insecurity, or it may be not. Hence, the need to "dig."

Around the same time, Pope Francis preached a morning meditation in his chapel at *Domus Sanctae Marthae*, suggestively titled: "Never slaves of the law." In this meditation, the pontiff reaffirms his stance that "behind rigidity there is something hidden in a person's life." However, he makes a distinction between two kinds of rigid people: 1) the hypocrites who live a "double life," and 2) those who are "sincere" and who "suffer," because they have "something like a disease." In both instances, the rigid person is a "slave of the law," lacking "the freedom of children."[5] I will address the former kind of rigid person in my next chapter. Here, I would like to focus on a specific subtype of the latter kind of rigid person: the scrupulous person.

For Pope Francis, there are two paths a person can take in his or her life: there are those who see God as a Father, so they hope in Him because they know He is forgiveness; and then there are those who take refuge in the slavery of rigidity, because they do not know God's

---

[4] Olson. "Digging into Pope Francis' remarks."
[5] Francis. "Never slaves to the law."

Chapter 2: Scrupulosity and Slavery to the Law

mercy.[6] Those who take the first path receive the treasures of God as a gift: in other words, they receive the Father's gifts in freedom. But those who take the second path do not know how to receive these things as a gift, but as justice. Therefore, they seek refuge in the rigidity of the commandments[7]: "to be justified, you need to do this, this, and this."[8] Inevitably, this trajectory leads them to think that there are too few commandments, and that they should engender more.[9]

To justify themselves and see themselves as good, rigid people replace God's spirit of freedom with rigidity.[10] But the Spirit of God is liberty. Justification is gratuitous, freely given. Those who take away the gratuitousness of salvation are also taking away the liberty of the Spirit of God[11]... and their own liberty as well.

This creates a very tragic reality: unlike the people who take the first path, the rigid person sees God as a master, rather than as a father. They make themselves cosmic orphans, with no father.[12] They, therefore, lose their ability for joy and praise.[13] However, if we look

---

[6] Francis. "A grandmother's lesson."
[7] Francis. "Two wonders."
[8] Francis. "Our relationship with God is gratuitous."
[9] Francis. "Two wonders."
[10] Francis. "A daily struggle."
[11] Francis. "Our relationship with God is gratuitous."
[12] Francis. "Flour and yeast."
[13] Francis. "A daily struggle." See also Francis. "Our relationship with God is gratuitous": "A religion of prescriptions, and thus they took away the Holy Spirit's freedom. And the people who followed them were rigid people, people who did not feel comfortable, they did not know the joy of the Gospel... The spirit of rigidity always brings turmoil. 'Did I do this all right? Did I not do that all right?' Scrupulosity. The Spirit of evangelical

at the lives of the saints, we see that they experienced joy, even in the midst of many tribulations.[14] Without joy, faith becomes a rigorous and oppressive exercise, and runs the risk of ailing with sadness. Francis quotes Evagrius Ponticus—a desert father—saying that sadness is "a worm that burrows into the heart," and corrodes life.[15]

The antidote for this ailment is freedom. Not the laxist freedom that we warned against in the last chapter, but Jesus's freedom, which contrasts with the lack of freedom of the doctors of the law. The latter were paralyzed by a rigorous interpretation of the law. But Jesus, while obeying the law, is not contented with a superficially "correct" observance of the law. Rather, Jesus obeys the law, by bringing the law into fulfilment (see chapter 3).[16]

With these foundations, I believe we are now able to delve into the phenomenon of scrupulosity, and how slavery to the law can destroy a soul.

The spiritual danger of scruples

Etymologically, "scruples" comes from the idea of a jagged stone stuck in one's footwear, preventing him or her from walking

---

freedom brings you joy because that is exactly what Jesus did by His resurrection: He brought joy!"

[14] It is telling that joy plays a pivotal role in Pope Francis's magisterium, as it is featured in the titles of many of his documents: *Amoris Laetitia* ("the joy of love"), *Evangelii Gaudium* ("the joy of the gospel"), *Gaudete et Exsultate* ("be glad and rejoice"), and *Veritatis Gaudium* ("the joy of truth").

[15] Francis. "Angelus," November 1, 2021.

[16] Francis. Homily at Enrique Olaya Herrera airport.

properly.[17] According to the *Catholic Encyclopedia*, scruples are "an unfounded apprehension and consequently unwarranted fear that something is a sin which, as a matter of fact, is not. It is not considered here so much as an isolated act, but rather as a habitual state of mind."[18] Several saints suffered from scruples throughout their life. However, they were saved and now enjoy the beatific vision *in spite of* those scruples, not *because* of them. Or rather, they were saved because they overcame their scruples, alongside many other trials in their saintly lives.

One such saint was Alphonsus Liguori. In his treatise on moral theology, St. Alphonsus distinguishes between several kinds of conscience. One of such kinds is the "scrupulous conscience," in which a person, without a reasonable basis, frequently lives in dread of sinning when there is in fact no sin.[19] Usually, a scrupulous conscience is plagued by one or more of three fears: 1) fear of bad thoughts that a person wrongly assumes to have assented to; 2) fear of having been too incomplete in past confessions, endangering the validity of the sacrament of reconciliation; and 3) fear of sinning in whatever thing they do.[20]

One may argue that, by forcing the scrupulous person to be so overly cautious towards sin, scrupulosity may be spiritually beneficial. After all, it is unlikely that someone so afraid of sin will ever commit a mortal sin, with full knowledge or full consent. However, it is not so. The *Catholic Encyclopedia* calls this misguided belief

---

[17] Liguori. *Conscience*, 171.
[18] Delany. "Scruple."
[19] Liguori. *Conscience*, 16-17.
[20] Ibid., 21-2.

about scrupulosity's supposed spiritual benefits a "grave error."[21] This is because scrupulous people will wear themselves out in search for a perfection that is unattainable on this side of eternity. Eventually, the scrupulous person will fall either into despair or, giving up from this futile attempt at perfection, indulge in his vices.[22] The end result of scrupulosity is either "this is impossible, God will doom me," or "this is impossible, might as well stop trying."

Once again, we can look at the phenomenon of scrupulosity through the lens of the Golden Mean, as we have seen in the last chapter. Scrupulosity is not virtue, because it stands in an extreme, not at the virtuous middle. St. Ignatius of Loyola, himself a saint who struggled with scrupulosity, wrote in his famous *Spiritual Exercises* that the Devil tempts the lax conscience to become even more lax, downplaying mortal sin the same way it underestimates venial sin. However, for the scrupulous conscience, the Devil will try to make it even more scrupulous. If Satan sees that he cannot make the person fall into any sin—be it mortal, venial, or even the mere appearance of sin—then he brings the person to judge as sinful something that is no sin at all.[23] The Enemy can then ensnare the soul in this downward spiral, driving the soul away from God and into the twin squalls of despair or indulgence.

Scrupulosity, of course, is not a heresy. It is not a denial, or even neglect for a revealed truth that one must believe with divine and Catholic faith.[24] Nor do I wish to burden a scrupulous reader with

---

[21] Delany. "Scruple."
[22] Ibid.
[23] Ignatius. *The Spiritual Exercises*, 210.
[24] CCC, 2089.

the idea that they are somehow heterodox. No. I must be very clear on that. However, I included scrupulosity in this book because we can learn from it and extrapolate our lessons to the doctrinal realm. Scruples can work a bit like heresy since, etymologically, the word heresy means "pick and choose." Just like the heretic, the scrupulous person "picks and chooses" from the Gospel, focusing on certain parts while disregarding others. Namely, as Pope Francis warns us, the scrupulous unwittingly ignore God's fatherhood, to understand Him merely as a master. Therefore, if they are to be loved by God, scrupulous people believe they must become perfect slaves. In other words, the scrupulous is a slave to the law, the same spiritual danger that Pope Francis warns against.

Since scruples are such a spiritual danger, how can one get rid of them? Before I proceed with an answer, there is an important caveat that must be addressed. Scrupulosity can be associated with obsessive-compulsive disorder: both consist in obsessions and compulsions. The scrupulous person is obsessed with sin and alleviates this anxiety by going to confession or performing acts of piety, turning them into compulsions. Catholics are particularly prone to this specific kind of religiously associated obsessive-compulsive disorder.[25] If a psychological component is present in one's scruples, the person must also address it through appropriate therapeutic means, guided by a proper professional. But for the purpose of this book, I am going to focus on scrupulosity as a religious phenomenon and explore its healing from a purely spiritual point of view.

---

[25] Buchholz *et al.* "Scrupulosity, Religious Affiliation and Symptom Presentation in Obsessive Compulsive Disorder."

To know how to heal scrupulosity, we must first ascertain what the healthy state is, so as to determine our end goal. Pope Francis already hinted at the solution, by distinguishing between two paths: the path of slavery to the law, and the path of the freedom of the children of God.

The freedom of God's children

Some Catholics may feel wary of the way the Holy Father wields the word "freedom" in opposition to the "rigidity" they view as faithfulness. After all, the word "freedom" has often been employed to oppose the Church and her teaching, since at least the French Revolution. The dreaded ideology of "liberalism" is derived from *liber*, the Latin word for "free." Freedom is conceived as a "condition of being free from any constraints, whether familial, societal, governmental or moral."[26] It is viewed as an end unto itself, almost as an idolatry.[27]

However, this is derived from a modern misuse of "freedom." Freedom is as much a part of Christian tradition as it is of the modern lexicon. Pope Francis's teachings are perfectly aligned with this Catholic tradition. The Holy Father's lessons are enshrined in the Catechism itself, in its section on theological virtues:

> The practice of the moral life animated by charity gives to the Christian *the spiritual freedom of the children of God*. He no longer stands before God as a slave, in servile fear, or as a

---

[26] Pocetto. "Freedom to Love," 1.
[27] Ibid.

mercenary looking for wages, but as a son responding to the love of him who "first loved us."[28]

The Catechism then goes on to quote the great fourth century Church Father St. Basil of Caesarea:

If we turn away from evil out of fear of punishment, we are in the position of slaves. If we pursue the enticement of wages, . . . we resemble mercenaries. Finally, if we obey for the sake of the good itself and out of love for him who commands . . . we are in the position of children.[29]

In fact, this concept goes even further back, being inerrantly inscribed in scripture itself. The first instance of the expression "freedom of the children of God" comes from St. Paul in his epistle to the Romans.[30] This "freedom of the children of God" is the kind of freedom Pope Francis is alluding to in his teachings. The Holy Father is not referring to the modern misconception about liberty. We can see that Francis makes this distinction very clearly when he discusses the life of St. Thérèse of Lisieux, another saint who struggled with scrupulosity throughout her life:

[Y]ou have touched upon a very serious problem, which is comfort in consecrated life: "we must do this…, let's be calm…, I keep all the commandments that I have to observe

---

[28] CCC, 1828.
[29] Ibid.
[30] Rom 8:21.

here, the rules..., I observe them..." But that is what St Thérèse of Jesus said about the strict, structured observance that takes away freedom. She was an independent woman, so free that she had to go to the Inquisition. *There is a freedom that comes from the Spirit and there is a freedom that comes from worldliness.* The Lord calls you —and he calls us all —to what Pierre called a "prophetic way" of freedom, namely, *the freedom that is linked to witness and fidelity.* A mother who is strict in raising her children —"it must be done, it must, it must, it must ..." and who does not allow the children to dream, to have dreams and who does not let the children grow, nullifies the creative future of the child. The children will be sterile...

And what St Thérèse called "*almas concertadas*" [the concerted soul] is a danger. It's a great danger. She was a cloistered nun, but she went through the streets throughout Spain, establishing foundations and convents. And she never lost the capacity for contemplation. Prophecy, the ability to dream is the contrary of rigidity. Those who are rigid cannot dream.[31]

This prophetic freedom that allows us to dream as a child is the "freedom of the children of God," referred to by Pope Francis, St. Basil, and the Catechism. What is the main difference between the two conceptions of freedom, the modern and the Catholic one? To put it simply, the former is a freedom *from* something, whereas the

---

[31] Francis. "Address to Young Consecrated Persons."

latter is a freedom *for* something.[32] Hence, Francis's emphasis on dreams. Dreams are what freedom is *for*.

We can even find a more practical example of this in one of the pontiff's namesakes: St. Francis de Sales. This seventeenth century saint was a masterful spiritual director. To this very day, his insights help priests with the spiritual direction of those under their care. One of the people St. Francis accompanied was Jane de Chantal, a widow and mother who, after her husband's passing, consecrated herself wholly to the Lord's service. She also struggled with scrupulosity.

In a letter sent to Jane in October 14, 1604, St. Francis de Sales also makes a distinction between two kinds of freedom, one of which he wishes his directee to attain: "I want you to have a spirit of liberty, not the kind that excludes obedience, for that is liberty of the flesh, but the kind that excludes constraint, scruples or over-eagerness."[33] Later in this letter, he would categorize the latter kind of liberty as the "liberty of the children who know that they are loved. . . a detachment of a Christian heart following God's known will."[34]

In other words, this liberty is about freedom of attachment to one's inclinations. St. Francis gives the example of someone who is interrupted during his meditation. Spiritual meditations are obviously good, but one may grow attached to them. This person will become irritated if he is interrupted. But a truly free person will not mind the interruption, because he will not mind whether he is

---

[32] Pocetto. "Freedom to Love," 2.
[33] Francis de Sales. *Selected letters*, 70.
[34] Ibid.

serving God by meditating or by bearing his neighbor.[35] St. Francis knew that people who are eager to deepen their spiritual lives may become attached to the consolations experienced in prayer, since these provide security and stability. Though it is not wrong to desire these consolations, the attachment to them may actually be a hindrance to following God's will.[36] On the other hand, keeping an open heart will allow the person to be more responsive to any fluctuation of the divine breath.[37] In other words, rigidity gets in the way of following God's will, and the antidote is the freedom of the children of God.

In typical Golden Mean fashion (see chapter 1), St. Francis de Sales tells Jane that she must avoid two opposite vices which beset liberty: lack of discipline and slavishness.[38] The former is laxity. As for slavishness, it is "a certain lack of liberty as a result of which the mind is overwhelmed with irritation or anger when it cannot carry out its plans, even though something better may offer."[39]

St. Francis also applies the same logic to the way Jane is raising her children. After all, if the metaphor "freedom of the children of God" is to hold water, then the signifier must accurately describe the signified. "Freedom of the children of God" only means anything if children are indeed free. Francis tells Jane that she should not "influence" the vocation of her children in advance, but only through

---

[35] Ibid., 71.

[36] Francis de Sales. *Selected letters*, 71. See also Pocetto. "Freedom to Love," 11.

[37] Pocetto. "Freedom to Love," 9.

[38] Francis de Sales. *Selected letters*, 71.

[39] Ibid., 72.

"gentle encouragement... graciously and without coercion," so that "generous motives may be implanted... little by little."[40] These children were to be free to dream, as Pope Francis intends.

The saintly spiritual director proceeds likewise when dealing with Jane's own scruples. He sets her anxious mind at ease. If she would happen to omit or forget anything she had been instructed to do (like a prayer), then she should not be concerned about it.[41] St. Francis de Sales knew that these instructions would only be salutary if Jane was not constrained to perform them. If she forgot to execute an act of piety, it would not be due to negligence, for she was an honest soul. Rather, it would have been probably due to her chores with her children and household,[42] which were also godly deeds. To hammer this point home, St. Francis writes in capital letters:

LOVE AND NOT FORCE SHOULD INSPIRE ALL YOU DO; LOVE OBEDIENCE MORE THAN YOU FEAR DISOBEDIENCE.[43]

This brings us to another important element when discussing scrupulosity: obedience.

---

[40] Ibid., 68.
[41] Ibid., 67.
[42] Pocetto. "Freedom to Love," 8.
[43] Francis de Sales. *Selected letters*, 67.

Obedience: the antidote to scrupulous rigidity

One of the characteristics of scrupulous people is "obstinacy." They are so attached to their own opinion, they will not listen to others, not even if they are their confessors or spiritual directors. They go so far as changing confessors often, and confessing already confessed sins over and over, in case the previous confession was invalid for some reason they imagined.[44] In other words, they are unwilling to heed the instructions of those who may recognize their ailment and recommend the appropriate treatment.

For this reason, St. Alphonsus Liguori dedicates a whole article of his moral theology treatise to "the importance of obedience" for the scrupulous mind. Alphonsus asks confessors to "be firm" with such people, trying to "persuade them" that they are "completely secure." On the contrary, the scrupulous person must be made aware that what places the salvation of the soul in jeopardy is disobedience.[45] "For St. Alphonsus, "the only remedy that can be applied to illnesses of this type is to submit completely to the judgment of one's superior or confessor."[46] He quotes several holy authors in support of this position.

This is especially important if we take into consideration how the soul can grow attached to certain practices, no matter how objectively good and pious they are. In another sermon, suggestively

---

[44] Delany. "Scruple."

[45] Liguori. *Conscience*, 20-21.

[46] Ibid., 17. See also Delany. "Scruple": "Their [the scruples'] chief remedy is, having reposed confidence in some confessor, to obey his decisions and commands entirely and absolutely."

titled "On obedience to your confessor," St. Alphonsus explains that the way to achieve sanctity may not be as straightforward as an undirected soul may think. For example, though it is usually holy to perform many works of penance, a sick man who does so by endangering his health or life is guilty of grievous sin. Although it is usually holy to pray or to attend Mass frequently, one sins if, by doing so, one neglects his or her own family. Sanctity is not necessarily attained through these works but rather, as we have seen in the last section, "by doing the will of God."[47]

How can one recognize the will of God? Not through a personal judgment of the soul. "There is nothing more dangerous than self-direction when it comes to a personal judgment,"[48] according to St. Alphonsus. Many believe that they are doing the will of God when, in fact, their passions are directing them to do their own will. The only way to be secure is to obey one's own confessor, for the soul that obeys the superior obeys Jesus Himself: "He who heareth you, heareth Me."[49] The confessor is to be obeyed, not as man, but as God.[50] If a person practices pious actions in disobedience to the confessor, this person is not doing the will of God. A person who takes delight in recreation in obedience to the confessor *is* doing the will of God. "Obedience is more pleasing to God than all the sacrifices of penitential works, or of alms-deeds, which we can offer to him."[51]

---

[47] Liguori. *The Sermons*, 182-183.
[48] Liguori. *Conscience*, 18-19.
[49] Luke 10:16. This biblical passage is quoted by St. Alphonsus in Liguori. *The Sermons*, 183. See also Liguori. *Conscience*, 20.
[50] Liguori. *The Sermons*, 185.
[51] Ibid., 183.

St. Alphonsus reminds us that the demons fell through disobedience. Obedience, therefore, places humans above devils. This is the reason why Satan tempts the scrupulous soul into disobedience, trying to make the soul walk the same errors he underwent. He tempts the soul under the pretext of doing good through actions that seem holy, but which are actually harmful.[52] The penitent then contends with their confessor, trying to make him adopt their own opinions.[53] But this is a snare. "Beware, lest, while you seek security, you rush into a pit."[54] The only security can be found in obedience, because the soul—so says St. Alphonsus—will not have to give account of what was done under obedience.[55]

But then, is there not a contradiction between what was said in this section of the chapter and in the previous section? Here, we see that the scrupulous person must be obedient. Previously, we have seen that the same person must seek the "freedom of the children of God." Are not obedience and freedom in opposition? How can this be?

Let us return to the case-study of Jane de Chantal's spiritual direction, Since Jane struggled with scruples, St. Francis asked her to be moderate in her fasting. Instead, she was to focus on mortifying her "choice."[56] For a modern mind, it would seem like cutting down on choice would stand opposed to freedom. However, Catholics

---

[52] Ibid., 185-6.
[53] Ibid., 187.
[54] Ibid., 186.
[55] Ibid., 184.
[56] Francis de Sales. *Selected letters*, 68. This mirrors St. Alphonsus's words about "self-will." See also Pocetto. "Freedom to Love," 9.

Chapter 2: Scrupulosity and Slavery to the Law

know that there is no contradiction between liberty and submitting to God. In a previous letter to Jane, St. Francis de Sales says:

> So there, dear sister. . . this is our bond, these are our chains which, the more they are tightened and press against us, the more they bring us joy and freedom. Their strength is gentleness; their violence, mildness; nothing is more pliable than that; nothing stronger.[57]

This makes sense. If scrupulosity is a kind of slavishness to the law, and if the spiritual director aims at curing the soul of this ailment, and if the soul is tempted to resist the spiritual direction through disobedience, then we can conclude that disobedience will only perpetuate this slavery, whereas liberty is only attainable through obedience.

Now, we can take what we have learned in this chapter about scrupulosity and apply it to the Magisterium and Pope Francis's teachings. Where else do we find the biblical quote: "He who heareth you, heareth Me"? In the encyclical *Humani Generis*, Venerable Pope Pius XII linked this scriptural passage to the "ordinary teaching authority of the pope"[58] i.e., to his non-infallible magisterial teachings. If Pope Francis *repeatedly* teaches us, even in his non-infallible magisterium, that Catholics must be on guard against spiritual dangers and sins associated with rigidity, should they not seek to obey him?

---

[57] As quoted in Pocetto. "Freedom to Love," 10.
[58] Pius XII. *Humani Generis*, 20.

Much has been written about "blind obedience" to the pope in recent years,[59] namely from people that eschew the pontiff's warnings against rigidity.[60] They will recycle the same quotes from saints[61] and appeal to the same precedents from the same saints (St. Paul, St. Catherine of Siena, St. Athanasius),[62] when in fact these do not show what they intend to show, because these are not applicable to the pontiff's magisterial teachings, only to his actions and policies.[63]

Certainly, St. Alphonsus also makes the caveat that the spiritual director / confessor is to be obeyed only insofar as he does not command one to sin.[64] But these critics of Pope Francis just seem to take for granted that the pontiff is commanding them to sin and proceed accordingly to disobey him. This raises the question: is this really the case? Or is it not possible that those who are disobedient are

---

[59] See, for example, Kwasniewski. "True Obedience."

[60] Kwasniewski. "Pope Francis's Hermeneutic of Anti-Continuity": "As I tried to wrap my mind around this address, I came to the conclusion that the key to understanding Francis is to see that he confuses the traditional concepts of spiritual oldness (sinfulness) and newness (renewal by the grace of Christ) with, respectively, tradition and change, and therefore with rigidity and flexibility, legalism and life in the Spirit."

[61] See once again, Gaspers. Kwasniewski. "True Obedience."

[62] See, for example, Schneider. "Catholics are not called to blind obedience."

[63] I deconstruct the precedents of St. Paul and St. Athanasius elsewhere. See Gabriel. *Heresy disguised as Tradition*, 102-105, 317. Regarding St. Catherine of Siena, see Alt, "Newman, St. Catherine, and St. Pius X."

[64] Liguori. *The* Sermons, 186: "Hence all the spiritual masters exhort us to obey our confessors in everything which is not manifestly sinful."

displaying signs of rigidity that parallel, in some way, what we have learned about scrupulosity so far?

If the pope is continuously warning against the spiritual dangers of rigidity, is it not likely that those affected by this ailment may be tempted into disobedience through private judgment and self-direction? Is it not possible that they may be excusing obedience a bit too hastily, and therefore, compromising the security that obedience affords the soul? Are they showing signs of mortifying their self-will and choices before proceeding into this dangerous realm? By perusing the writings of the saints—even those exceptional cases that for some reason, withstood the pope's actions and policies—we never see such a fierce apology for disobedience as we see in those who resist Pope Francis's magisterium.

One may object that one is disobeying in the name of something good. But, if we recall, the scrupulous disobeys also in the name of something good, like prayer or penitential acts. The problem is not the good thing in itself, but the attachment that leads to such rigidity that one compromises God's will to follow self-will.

Pope Francis teaches us that the Devil can disguise himself as an angel of light.[65] That is, in fact, the etymology of the name "Lucifer" ("light-bearer.") Someone who is under the influence of his temptation may feel like he is doing good, and that he has clarity over that good. The person is then "hooked" in this truth he "clearly saw" when he was tempted.[66] This creates a rigid attachment to this secondary good, which may then stand in the way of God's will:

---

[65] 2 Cor 11:14.

[66] Bergoglio. *Reflexiones en Esperanza*, 162-3.

[It is the case of someone who] himself believes that he's seeking the glory of God, the promotion of the Church. . . but he does so with a prearranged compromise, he does so after having chosen the path beforehand: "I will serve, but only in this way." Then, the generous self-giving which purports to be instrument, useless servant, drinking from the Lord's cup. . . turns itself into a negotiation. . .

[The self-sufficient man] puts his strength and his talents at the service of the Kingdom, heeds its calling, but on the condition that he will be allowed to choose the methods, the paths, the plans. A redemption according to his own measure. But there is ambition here, because one wants to impose his mark, demonstrate that God's decision is the same as one's own plan and power. This ambitious man does not know how to dialogue, he does not ask to be chosen, rather he is the one who chooses.[67]

Here, just like with scrupulosity, the antidote is obedience. The knots tied by the Virgin Eve's disobedience are untied by the Virgin Mary's obedience.[68] Lucifer's disobedience is combatted in the desert with Jesus Christ's full and detached obedience to the Father. As Pope Francis teaches, being a Christian is not just a way of living a spirituality that makes us good, which makes us better. It is not about following "that spiritual teacher" or "reading that book." It is

---

[67] Ibid., 148-9 (my translation from the original Spanish).

[68] Ibid., 145. For a more fleshed out essay on how to escape the temptation of the Angel of Light according to Bergoglian spirituality, see Gabriel. "Silence: the shield against the Suspicious Man."

not "an idea, a philosophy, or a power." Rather, it is being a "witness to obedience, like Jesus. . . If we are not on this path to grow in witness to obedience, we are not Christians." Obedience, it is true, is something more easily said than done. It requires grace.[69] Therefore, it is the opposite of the self-sufficiency demonstrated by those tempted by the Angel of Light (we are going to explore self-sufficiency in chapter 6).

This remedy of obedience worked well for Jane de Chantal, the widow under St. Francis de Sales's spiritual direction. Jane eventually founded the Order of the Visitandines and was canonized in 1767. St. Jane would often instruct the sisters of her order about this "freedom of spirit" she had learned with St. Francis. Certainly, given the "temper of our age," the Christian doctrine may become "more palatable and comprehensible if presented in terms of a spirit of freedom as Francis de Sales originally did."[70]

More importantly, those who promote these Christian teachings will be more credible if, having freed themselves from the slavery to the law, they find the *joy* that comes with the freedom of the children of God. Stocked with this joy, they can go out into the world and become the missionary, evangelizing Church Pope Francis dreams of.

---

[69] Francis. "Witnesses to obedience."
[70] Pocetto. "Freedom to Love," 12.

Chapter 3

Pharisaism and the Double Life

This is the difference between a sinner and a man who is corrupt. One who leads a double life is corrupt, whereas one who sins would like not to sin, but he is weak. . . A varnished putrefaction: this is the life of someone who is corrupt. And Jesus does not call them simply sinners. He calls them hypocrites.

—Francis, Morning Meditation
"Sinners yes, corrupt no."

As we have seen in the last chapter, Pope Francis makes a distinction between two kinds of "slavery to the law": 1) those who are "sincere" and who "suffer," because they have "something like a disease," and 2) the hypocrites who live a "double life."[1] In both situations, the person receives God's commandments as justice, not as a gift. Rigid people in the first group—the ones we discussed in the last chapter—see God not as a father, but as a master.[2] But those in the latter group end up as seeing *themselves* as the masters:

> They stole the inheritance, which belonged to another. A story of infidelity, of infidelity to their election, of infidelity to the promise, of infidelity to the covenant, which is a gift.

---

[1] Francis. "Never slaves to the law."
[2] Francis. "Flour and yeast."

> The election, the promise and the covenant are a gift from God. Disloyalty to God's gift. *Not understanding that it was a gift and taking it as though it were their possession. These people appropriated the gift. They took away the aspect as gift to turn it into their property...*
>
> This is the great sin. It is the sin of forgetting that God made a gift of Himself to us, that God gave us this as a gift and, forgetting this, *becoming owners.* And the promise is no longer a promise, the election is no longer election, and the covenant comes to be interpreted according to "my" opinion.[3]

These words immediately bring to our minds the parable of the wicked tenants as told in the Gospel according to St. Matthew. As Jesus recounts, there was a landlord (representing God) who planted a vineyard and left it to be tended by some husbandmen. When the harvest was ripe, the landlord sent his servants (the prophets) to collect the rent, but the tenants killed the servants instead of paying their dues. Finally, the landlord sent his own son (Jesus), but the wicked tenants murdered him to get the inheritance for themselves.[4] The tenants in this parable were meant to signify the Pharisees,[5] Jesus's greatest adversaries during His ministry.

---

[3] Francis. "Let us not forget the gratuitousness."

[4] Mt 24:33-43. Pope Francis's quote was, in fact, a commentary on this parable. See Francis. "Let us not forget the gratuitousness": "But what happens in this parable is that when the time came to reap the fruits, these people had forgotten that they were not the masters:"

[5] Mt 24:45. See also Su. "A Study in the Significance of Jesus," 148.

Chapter 3: Pharisaism and the Double Life

It would be very awkward to write a book on religious rigidity and not mention the Pharisees. But a chapter about Pharisaism needs to be written with much care and sensitivity. It is true that in Christian symbolism, the Pharisees have become an archetype for rigidity. For that same reason, the word "Pharisee" has become excessively loaded, often becoming a facile slur. It is not uncommon to see people accusing Catholics of being like Pharisees merely for following the traditional tenets of their faith.[6] This aggravates the confusion between rigidity and faithfulness. Consequently, Catholics may learn to reject the "Pharisee" label altogether, even when the Pope himself is using it to instruct them about rigidity.[7]

---

[6] See, for example, Wijngaards. *The Ordination of Women*, 8-9: "The pharisees rejected the carpenter from Nazareth. They refused to recognise him as their priest when they stood under his cross on Calvary. The idea that a woman could express the priesthood of Christ may seem equally upsetting." See also Kraus. "Queer Theology: Reclaiming Christianity," 107: "In John 8, the Pharisees bring a woman to Jesus and accuse her of adultery. Many would gladly condemn her and sentence her to be stoned to death, but Jesus refuses to condemn her. This lack of judgment by Jesus, when read with a queer perspective, can be understood as Jesus not seeing supposed sexual impropriety as important enough to warrant his disapproval... Queer theology can use this story to show how traditional Christian theology is like the Pharisees, viewing the queer community as sinners deserving of condemnation."

[7] See, for example, Douthat. "Jesus and the Pharisees": "There is a recurring theme in the papal rhetoric of the Francis era. To insist on the moral law too forcefully, the Pope and his allies often suggest, is to be like the Pharisees... And just as Jesus transcended Jewish legalism, Catholicism under Pope Francis must transcend its own legalities. The idea is powerful. But it is not an idea to be found anywhere in the traditional teachings of the Church; it is an idea, indeed, that the Church has rejected, out of fidelity to the Gospels." See also Stravinskas. "Good Pharisees, Bad

However, if the Pharisees became such an archetype of religious rigidity, it must be for a reason. Therefore, if we are to understand rigidity from a Catholic point of view, we must be able to peel away the negative connotations of the word "Pharisee" and try to undertake a dispassionate and objective study of Pharisaism: not to try to put other people down (even those who may disagree with us and the Pope,) but as a collective effort to learn and grow together.

Another point which demands caution is that modern-day Judaism has developed from first century Pharisaism. When the Temple of Jerusalem fell, religious practice shifted away from the rituals previously performed there and was refocused into the practices of daily purity belonging to the sphere of influence of the teachers of Mosaic law i.e., the Pharisees.[8] For that reason, there have been calls for Christians to stop using the word "Pharisee" as an insult, since this can lead to antisemitism.[9] These pleas have even been extended to some of Pope Francis's talks over this topic.[10]

On the other hand, the clashes between Jesus and the Pharisees are an integral part of the gospel and, therefore, of the Christian religion. So, how to solve this tension? The answer is: by placing these biblical episodes in their proper historical context. As we shall see in the remainder of this chapter, Jesus was not so much condemning

---

Catholics": "For eight years now, we have heard Pope Francis condemn the 'Pharisaism' or 'Pharisees' he thinks he has discovered in the Church; this is a genuine papal 'trigger,' which he uses against anyone who seems to hold the line on absolutes, you know, the 'rigid' ones."

[8] Su. "A Study in the Significance of Jesus," 49-50, 71. See also Cook. "A Gospel Portrait of the Pharisees," 221.

[9] See, for example, Huckabee. "Christians, Stop Using 'Pharisee.'"

[10] Staff. "Pope urged by Jews to take care over Pharisees talk."

the Pharisees for their beliefs, but for their actions. In other words, His criticisms were directed at the specific people performing those actions, not to any religions or ethnicities they may belong to. Jesus Himself was a Jew, and we cannot isolate that fact from what He said and did regarding the Pharisees. Jesus was not criticizing the Jews as an outsider, rather His invectives must be read as a Jewish prophetic critique seeking to restore a proper observance of the Torah.[11] In fact, some scholars think that these reproaches were not particularly original or harsh for that time period.[12] Far from being anti-Jewish, Jesus's criticisms were thoroughly Jewish. Therefore, an antisemitic reading of the gospels is anachronistic and wrongheaded.[13]

Instead of using "Pharisee" and "Pharisaism" as a slur against Judaism, we must be careful to see it as a label applicable to particular individuals of a historical context that is not replicable today.[14] We can then take what we learned from these historical episodes and extrapolate it to what we can change in ourselves as Christians, not to our fellow Jews. We know that Pope Francis is cognizant of this nuance.[15] Consequently, his comments on Pharisaism must be read accordingly.

---

[11] Duffield, "Difficult texts," 18. Su. "A Study in the Significance of Jesus," 102.

[12] Su. "A Study in the Significance of Jesus," 98.

[13] Duffield, "Difficult texts," 18.

[14] Staff. "Pope urged by Jews to take care over Pharisees talk": "According to Rabbi David Rosen, director of interfaith affairs at the American Jewish Committee (AJC)... People should put it in context, or at least use 'those Pharisees' or 'those Jews.'"

[15] Francis. "Address to the Pontifical Biblical Institute."

With these caveats in mind, we can now explore what the Pharisees of Jesus's time can teach us about rigidity. Namely, we can try to understand why Pope Francis likes to evoke the Pharisees of Jesus's time when he speaks about a certain expression that has become commonplace in his meditations and homilies: the "double life."

The Pharisees in Pope Francis's teaching

According to some scholars, the term "Pharisee" derives from the word "specifiers" (or, to be more precise: "those who are exact in the upholding of the law.") Most, however, affirm that the label arises from the Hebrew/Aramaic word "*Perisha*," meaning "the separated ones" or "separatists." The Pharisees arose during Israel's conquest by the Greeks, to distinguish them from the so-called Hellenists i.e., those who adopted pagan Greek customs. The Pharisees, therefore, were the ones who "separated" themselves from all pagan practices, so that they could live a pure Jewish faith.[16]

As time went on, the influence of the Pharisees steadily grew. By the time of Jesus, the Pharisees were seen as spiritual and religious leaders in Israelite society, holding sway even among high-ranking rulers.[17] Since the Pharisees believed that they were the ones upholding the exactness of the law, they sought as much control and authority in religious matters as possible.[18] They were not only considered the interpreters of the law, but its enforcers, with the power to

---

[16] Su. "A Study in the Significance of Jesus," 43.
[17] Ibid., 45-6.
[18] Ibid., 45.

determine who was and who was not a member in good standing of the Jewish community.[19] However, they abused this authority by exacting it in an excessive way among their countrymen.[20]

In this sense, "double life" can be understood as abusing religious authority as a way to grow in wealth and power. Pope Francis has taught that the chief priests and the scribes were angry at Jesus when He expelled the moneychangers from the Temple, because they were "connected" with these businessmen. This was a "holy bribe": the religious authorities "were attached to money and worshiped it as 'holy.'"[21] Also, the Pharisees put up a "hypocritical outward show" to present themselves with "worldly power rather than with the weakness that makes space for God." As Christians, we should be "free from dubious associations with power and from the fear of being misunderstood and attacked."[22]

Another way this "double life" can manifest itself is through "corruption." Jesus told His followers to observe everything the Pharisees said, but not what they did, "for they say, and do not."[23] Pope Francis says that the Pharisees were "corrupt, because rigidity of this sort can only go on in a double life." Mentioning some biblical episodes where women were condemned by corrupt judges, the Holy Father explains that those "who condemned these women later went to find them from behind, hidden, to have a good time."[24]

---

[19] Ibid., 54.
[20] Ibid., 46.
[21] Francis. "A daily struggle."
[22] Francis. Homily at Blessing of the Sacred Pallium.
[23] Mt 23:3.
[24] Francis. "Three women and three judges."

And even in our own times we have seen some apostolic organizations that seem to be quite well organized, who work well…, but all of them are rigid, everyone is exactly the same, and then we have learned about the corruption that was inside, even in the founders.[25]

Certainly, these papal denunciations of institutional corruption are most important and welcome in our present days. But is this all there is to it? What about the common folk, Catholics practicing their religion without any prospects of growing rich or powerful? Can they also learn something from the Pharisees' rigidity that can help them develop spiritually?

Let us recall Jesus's parable of the Merciful Father. When the father of that parable forgives the prodigal son, the elder son—who never left his father's house nor disobeyed him—resents both his father and his brother. Francis explains how the elder son's indignation stems from a fundamental error we have already explored throughout this book: "He bases his relationship with his Father solely on pure observance of commands, on a sense of duty." He does not see him as a father, but as a master. "Losing sight that he is a Father, and living a distant religion, made of prohibitions and duties," the elder son became estranged from his own family: "the consequence of this distance is rigidity towards our neighbor whom we no longer see as a brother or sister. In fact, in the parable, the elder son does not say 'my brother' to the Father. No, he says 'that son of

---

[25] Francis. "Our relationship with God is gratuitous."

Chapter 3: Pharisaism and the Double Life

yours,' as if to say: he is not my brother. In the end, he risks remaining outside of the house."[26]

Pope Francis's teachings are in continuity with what his predecessor Benedict XVI wrote about the same matter:

> [The elder son] sees only injustice. "And this betrays the fact that he too had secretly dreamed of a freedom without limits, that his obedience has made him inwardly bitter, and that he has no awareness of the grace of being at home, of the true freedom that he enjoys as a son. . . *Jesus is using these words of the father to speak to the heart of the murmuring Pharisees* and scribes who have grown indignant at his goodness to sinners. . .
>
> Their bitterness toward God's goodness reveals an inward bitterness regarding their own obedience, a bitterness that indicates the limitations of this obedience. In their heart of hearts, they would have gladly journeyed out into that great "freedom" as well. There is an unspoken envy of what others have been able to get away with. They have not gone through the pilgrimage that purified the younger brother and made him realize what it means to be free and what it means to be a son. They actually *carry their freedom as if it were slavery and they have not matured to real sonship.* They, too, are still in need of a path.[27]

Pope Francis further elaborates on this thought:

---

[26] Francis. "Angelus." March 27, 2022.
[27] Benedict XVI, *Jesus of Nazareth: from the Baptism*, 210-211.

> We think of those great things that Jesus said to those strict people of his time. . . Those are the rigid ones. And observance must not be rigid. If observance is rigid, it is not observance, it is personal selfishness. It is seeking oneself and feeling oneself to be more just than others. "I thank you, Lord, because I'm not like that sister, like that brother, like that one there.... I thank you, Lord, that my Congregation is really catholic, observant, and not like that Congregation that goes here, there and everywhere..." This is the talk of the overly strict.[28]

Even if this person is living a seemingly coherent and moral life, he or she is still living what Pope Francis calls "a double life." It is still a sort of "hypocritical attitude: behind the good they do, there is pride."[29] Just like the scrupulous person of the previous chapter, the person imbued with this spirit has neither the joy, nor the freedom of the children of God. They wear a mask of "mourning," and they "believe that Christian life" must be taken "so seriously," they end "confusing solidity and firmness with rigidity."[30]

Here, we must make another important distinction. Just because this person is living a "double life," does not mean that this person is not being honest about it. They may sincerely believe that they are following God's will. Francis mentions the case of Saul, who was a Pharisee before he fell off the horse and became the apostle St. Paul:

---

[28] Francis. "Address to Young Consecrated Persons."
[29] Francis. "Never slaves to the law."
[30] Francis. "Christians of action and truth."

Saul, a "rigid young man, was honest". He was "wrong! — but honest"... "He believed and he acted"... I think —when I say this, about many young people who have fallen into the temptation of rigidness, today, in the Church —some are honest; they are good. We must pray that the Lord help them grow on the path of gentleness.[31]

One problem we face is that "double life" (rightfully) evokes the word "hypocrisy," and hypocrisy is a loaded word, with negative denotations just like the word "Pharisee." But can we limit ourselves to applying the word hypocrite to those who use religion to cover up their own sins, or to gain power and wealth? Let us now study what the word "hypocrite" meant during Jesus's times.

The outward mask

In common parlance, the word "hypocrite" usually means someone who says one thing and does another.[32] There are good reasons to believe that this meaning was applicable to the Pharisees of first-century Israel. After all, Jesus criticizes them thus: "for they say, and do not."[33]

But we can go even deeper in the assessment of the word "hypocrite." This word has a Greek etymology and was used in Greco-Roman culture to describe an "actor" or "someone who gives an

---

[31] Francis. "Rigid but honest."
[32] See *Merriam-Webster.com*. "Hypocrite": "a person who acts in contradiction to his or her stated beliefs or feelings."
[33] Mt 23:3.

answer, interprets an oracle, mimics another person, or acts a part in a drama."[34] This usage probably crept into Jewish culture during the Greek and Roman occupations. In postbiblical Jewish literature, the word "hypocrite" connoted "insincerity of behavior,"[35] but also conveyed the meaning of "to pretend," in the sense that one would "pretend to be other than he really is."[36]

As we have seen, the Pharisees were hypocrites because they behaved differently than what they preached, namely to attain public praise.[37] But in another part of the gospel, Jesus calls the Pharisees hypocrites because "this people honoureth me with their lips: but their heart is far from me."[38] In other words, the discrepancy was not only at the level of behavior (which, like the preaching, was outwardly), but cut through the innermost sanctum of the human soul:

---

[34] Su. "A Study in the Significance of Jesus," 153.

[35] Ibid.

[36] Ibid., 154.

[37] See, for example, Mt 6:16-18: "And when you fast, be not as the hypocrites, sad. For they disfigure their faces, that they may appear unto men to fast. Amen I say to you, they have received their reward. But thou, when thou fastest anoint thy head, and wash thy face; That thou appear not to men to fast, but to thy Father who is in secret: and thy Father who seeth in secret, will repay thee." See also Mark 12:38-39: "Beware of the scribes, who love to walk in long robes, and to be saluted in the marketplace, And to sit in the first chairs, in the synagogues, and to have the highest places at suppers: Who devour the houses of widows under the pretence of long prayer: these shall receive greater judgment."

[38] Mt 15:7-8.

Chapter 3: Pharisaism and the Double Life

the heart. The Pharisaical hypocrisy is a "distinction between inner attitudes and outward behavior."[39]

The Pharisees are hypocrites because they "pretend." They play an outward role to which their "inner disposition does not correspond accordingly." They are not merely people who say one thing and do another. They are people who actually "do the right things, but they are not the right kind of people because their hearts are wrong."[40] In other words, they do not have a behavior problem, but an attitude problem.[41]

It is interesting to note that, when Jesus condemned the Pharisees for honoring God with their lips and not their hearts, He did so in the context of the controversy of the washing of the hands and of the cups. During a shared meal, the Pharisees brought to Jesus's attention that His disciples had started eating without washing their hands. The problem here was not merely lack of hygiene. It had much deeper religious connotations. The ritual handwashing had to do with a well-established purity system. Not only the hands, but cups and pots also, should be washed in a particular way, lest the food and the participants be defiled.[42] It is at this instant that Jesus rebukes the Pharisees, saying:

---

[39] Su. "A Study in the Significance of Jesus," 158. See also Loader. *Jesus' Attitude towards the Law*, 72: "[Jesus] uses it to contrast lip and heart and to attack mere human teachings. . . The implicit contrast between mere externals and the internal in 7:3-4 now becomes one of external behaviour of the lips not matching the heart."

[40] Su. "A Study in the Significance of Jesus," 184.

[41] Loader, *Jesus' Attitude Towards the Law*, 164.

[42] Mark 7:1-4.

> Well did Isaias prophesy of you *hypocrites*, as it is written: *This people honoureth me with their lips, but their heart is far from me.* And in vain do they worship me, teaching doctrines and precepts of men. For leaving the commandment of God, you hold the tradition of men, *the washing of pots and of cups*: and many other things you do like to these. And he said to them: Well do you make void the commandment of God, that you may keep your own tradition.[43]

From this point onward, Jesus clashed repeatedly with the Pharisees and the relationship between both parties progressively soured. Finally, their opposition climaxed in the Seven Woes speech. The Pharisees had accused Jesus of leading people astray, so Jesus refuted[44] them by taking recourse to a Jewish formula: the woes, a kind of Jewish prophetic speech foretelling judgment upon those who dishonor a covenant.[45] The fifth woe is of particular interest here, because it recalled the pot washing controversy:

> Woe to you scribes and Pharisees, hypocrites; because you make clean the outside of the cup and of the dish, but within you are full of rapine and uncleanness. Thou blind Pharisee, first make clean the inside of the cup and of the dish, that the outside may become clean.[46]

---

[43] Mark 7:6-9.
[44] Su. "A Study in the Significance of Jesus," 90-91.
[45] Ibid., 95.
[46] Mt 23:25-26.

In other words, the Pharisees' obsession with outer, ritual impurity caused them to neglect the inner purity, which was the most important.[47] It is a matter of misplaced priorities, perfectly illustrated by the tableware metaphor.[48] As important as the outer cleanness of the cup is, the inner purity is more important, since the inside is the part of the cup holding the food and drink. Therefore, if the insides of the cup are unclean, the person ingests impurities and pollution. The next woe (the sixth one) further developed the same logic:

> Woe to you scribes and Pharisees, hypocrites; because you are like to whited sepulchres, which outwardly appear to men beautiful, but within are full of dead men's bones, and of all filthiness. So you also outwardly indeed appear to men just; but inwardly you are full of hypocrisy and iniquity.[49]

Once again, we have a metaphor clarifying the discrepancy between outer and inner purities. Jesus alluded to tombs, whitewashed on the outside, but on the inside, containing only death. The allusion to filth is a very strong verbal indicator of the Pharisees' inner state.[50]

---

[47] Su. "A Study in the Significance of Jesus," 133.

[48] See Loader, *Jesus' Attitude Towards the Law*, 383: "Luke's version of the woes carries the same theme. Luke is not attacking the washing of cups or even tithing of minor foodstuffs, which he still has Jesus enjoin; he is attacking preoccupation with these, while neglecting love of God and justice. He can acknowledge that those who expound Torah have the key to knowledge. Attitude and orientation are all important, as the contrast between the sinner and the Pharisee illustrates."

[49] Mt 23:27-28.

[50] Su. "A Study in the Significance of Jesus," 134-136.

Or, as Pope Francis would say, "rigidity means being fundamentally schizoid: you end up appearing rigid, but inside you are a disaster."[51]

Whenever there is an incongruity between the outer and the inner parts of our self, then there is "hypocrisy" at play—in the Greco-Roman sense of the word—because the person is "pretending" to be someone he or she is not. This "mask" is not necessarily worn consciously—sometimes it can be unconscious.[52] In fact, that is one of the reasons why Jesus stressed the sins of the Pharisees so much, and why the Pharisees reacted so strongly against Him. It is not just about saying one thing and doing another. It is about sins that lie in the heart: secret sins, hidden sins. Because these sins were hidden, the Pharisees could blind others—and worse, blind *themselves*—to them.[53] Only Jesus, who could read the hearts of men, was able to see those sins and bring them to light in front of everyone, as He did when He proclaimed the seven woes to the multitudes.

Spirit vs. letter of the law

Many Catholics tend to distrust the term "spirit of the law," since it evokes the so-called "Spirit of Vatican II." The latter is an interpretative method used by the liberal wing of the Church to implement a more progressive version of the Second Vatican Council than the one contained in the actual conciliar documents.[54] This was done

---

[51] Francis. "Mediators or intermediaries."

[52] Su. "A Study in the Significance of Jesus," 156.

[53] Ibid., 166.

[54] See, for example, Novak. "The Holy Spirit did preside": "In the Church in America, at least, I was among the first purveyors of 'the spirit

through a particular hermeneutic: the council was to be interpreted according to its "spirit," not its "letter." Conservatives and traditionalists rightfully contend that the "Spirit of Vatican II" became a way to introduce measures clearly not intended by the Council Fathers, by taking recourse to an abstract, non-falsifiable "spirit of the law" that, conveniently, always aligns with the progressives' ideology. In this sense, we can see how appealing to the "spirit of the law" can become a betrayal to the legislator, if one interprets the law in a way the legislator did not intend.

However, let us recall our discussion on *epikeia* in chapter 1: interpreting the law "to the letter" can *also* be a betrayal to the legislator if the law is applied even in particular situations that the legislator did not foresee and for which he would grant exceptions, had he known. Then, how do we interpret the law without betraying the legislator? Should we interpret it according to "the spirit" or to "the letter"? Once again, a Golden Mean approach is required. The interactions between Jesus and the Pharisees provide the necessary balance for this difficult question.

During the handwashing incident with His disciples, Jesus chastised the Pharisees for upholding "traditions of men," that "make void the commandment of God."[55] He went on to exemplify what

---

of Vatican II'—to the neglect of the actual Conciliar texts, which were more balanced and exact. I deserve to be shamed for some of the extreme things I wrote about experimental liturgies, about dissent in the Church, and about that elusive 'spirit'. . . . Just in time, as I saw it unfold over the next forty years, John Paul II (who took his name from the two popes who led the Council, John XXIII and Paul VI) rescued the Council's original purposes."

[55] Mark 7:8-9.

He meant by bringing up the practice of *Corban* i.e., offerings dedicated to the Temple that could not be used for any other purpose.

> For Moses said: Honour thy father and thy mother; and He that shall curse father or mother, dying let him die. But you say: If a man shall say to his father or mother, *Corban*, (which is a gift,) whatsoever is from me, shall profit thee. And further you suffer him not to do any thing for his father or mother, making void the word of God by your own tradition, which you have given forth.[56]

In other words, the Pharisees (in cahoots with the Temple authorities) were abusing the practice of *Corban* to enrich themselves. If people spent all their money in the Temple, they would have no means to support their elderly parents—which was also a commandment of God.[57] This practice was lawful if one stuck to the letter of the law. But, in practice, it divided the people between their inner attitudes (love for their parents) and their actual behavior (giving all their money to the Temple, leaving none for their parents.)[58]

The practice of *Corban* was a voluntary act. Furthermore, oral Jewish tradition at the time addressed circumstances where one could be released from a vow such as this. On the contrary, "honoring father and mother" was one of the Ten Commandments and, therefore, obligatory. The Pharisees were enforcing the vows of *Corban* so strictly, they were forcing people to neglect their familial

---

[56] Mark 7:10-13.
[57] Grondin. "Why Did Jesus Condemn the Practice of Corban?"
[58] Loader. *Jesus' Attitude Towards the Law*, 72.

Chapter 3: Pharisaism and the Double Life

responsibility under the pretext of obeying the Torah.[59] It was a loophole in the law, encouraging abuse. Jesus did not have an argument with the law, but with a particular interpretation of the law that deliberately sought to circumvent it.[60]

Another controversy that helps us shed light on this matter is the controversy around "gleaning on the sabbath." One day, Jesus passed by a corn field and asked His disciples to glean some food. This would have been lawful, had it not happened during the sabbath, a day of obligatory rest for Jews. Once again, the Pharisees confronted Jesus, asking Him: "Why do they do on the sabbath day that which is not lawful?"[61] Once more, Jesus replied: "The sabbath was made for man, and not man for the sabbath. Therefore, the Son of man is Lord of the sabbath also."[62]

As I have mentioned in another book,[63] the quote "the sabbath was made for man, not man for sabbath" was not made up by Jesus. Rather, it was a throwback to a precedent from the Bible. When David and his men were running away from king Saul's persecution, they asked Abiathar, the high priest, to give them something to eat. However, the only food available at the time was the holy loaves of the Temple.[64] These loaves had a connection with the sabbath, for they should be changed every Saturday and could only be eaten by a priest within the sanctuary.[65] But Abiathar allowed David and his

---

[59] Pickup. "Mathew's and Mark's Pharisees," 88-87.
[60] Loader. *Jesus' Attitude Towards the Law*, 73, 261.
[61] Mark 2:23-24.
[62] Mark 2:27-28.
[63] Gabriel. *Heresy disguised as Tradition*, 264-265.
[64] 1 Sam 21:3-6.
[65] Lev 24:5-9. See also Pickup. "Mathew's and Mark's Pharisees," 78.

men to eat those loaves, as long as they were in a state of ritual purity when doing so. Abiathar was not ignoring the Torah by doing so—otherwise he would not have cared about David's ritual cleanness when eating the loaves—but properly applying the Torah to an exceptional circumstance.[66] A matter of *epikeia*, if you will. By bringing up this Davidic precedent, Jesus was asserting His continuity with king David and, therefore, His authority and kingship.[67]

However, we can also view the utterance "the sabbath was made for man, not man for sabbath" from another angle (though both are not mutually exclusive, quite the contrary.) A humanitarian angle. We can interpret it as "the sabbath was made for humankind, not humankind for the sabbath."[68]

The Mosaic law allowed the poor and the alien, who did not have fields of their own to feed themselves, to pluck grain and grapes from an Israelite's field. This was a law meant for benevolence, so that the poor and the alien would not starve.[69] Equally benevolent was the law of the sabbath, according to which Saturday was established as a day of mandatory rest. During this rest no work was to be done, including plucking fruits.[70]

But in this particular instance, the Pharisees set both laws (the law of gleaning and the law of the sabbath) against each other and, in the process, destroyed the benevolence of both. According to the Pharisees' interpretation, the poor person could not perform *any*

---

[66] Pickup. "Mathew's and Mark's Pharisees," 79.
[67] See Benedict XVI, *Jesus of Nazareth: From the Baptism*, 107.
[68] Pickup. "Mathew's and Mark's Pharisees," 78.
[69] Ibid., 77.
[70] Ibid.

Chapter 3: Pharisaism and the Double Life

work on sabbath, including gleaning. This meant that the poor would have to starve during Saturday.[71]

Here, we can see that Jesus and the Pharisees engaged in different modes of legal interpretation.[72] The Pharisees placed a greater emphasis on the letter of the law, since for them a meticulous observance of the Torah reflected the highest form of divine service.[73] For the Pharisees, service to God came before anything else: human needs should yield to divine service. Jesus, on the other hand, believed that failing to fulfill basic human needs was itself a violation of divine service.[74] The spirit of the law would not allow a legalistic, literalist interpretation, because that would bring harm to others. Such an interpretation would in effect deprive poor people of the sustenance the very same law afforded them.[75] This was, in practice, a violation of the sabbath. When Jesus said that the sabbath was made for man, not man for sabbath, what He meant was that the sabbath should be interpreted as a gift to be inwardly enjoyed, not as a demand outwardly imposed. There was no need for so much strictness,[76] for that would lessen the enjoyment of this God-given gift and, therefore, thwart its purpose. As we have seen at the beginning of this chapter, the Pharisees were "appropriating the gift," which was not theirs.

---

[71] Ibid., 78, 88.
[72] Skeel. "What were Jesus and the Pharisees talking about?" 142.
[73] Ibid., 141-2.
[74] Pickup. "Mathew's and Mark's Pharisees," 80.
[75] Ibid., 78-9.
[76] Loader, *Jesus' Attitude Towards the Law*, 45, 52.

This was the greatest difference between the Pharisees' and Jesus's views of the law. For the Pharisees, upholding the second greatest commandment of the law ("love your neighbor") could, in some instances, be done in a way that nullified the greatest commandment ("love God above all things.") But Jesus taught that when one nullifies the second greatest commandment, one is not upholding, but rather nullifying the greatest commandment as well. It all boiled down to how love of God and love of one's fellow man were to be integrated.[77]

There is a nuance here. The Pharisees believed that, if one had to choose between the greatest commandment and the second greatest, one should choose the greatest. At first glance, this seems logical. But Jesus did *not* believe that, if one has to choose between the greatest commandment and the second greatest, one should choose the second greatest. Rather, what Jesus said is that there is no need to choose: you can only fulfill the greatest commandment by fulfilling the second greatest. You cannot uphold one by breaking the other. Both commandments stand or fall together. The Pharisees subscribed to a hermeneutic of rupture, whereas Jesus engaged in a hermeneutic of continuity, even if He was accused by the Pharisees of engaging in rupture Himself.

Jesus did not reject the sabbath (or any other aspect of the law). He only rejected the Pharisees' *interpretation* of the sabbath.[78] For Jesus, the Pharisees had a problem of misplaced emphasis, which

---

[77] Pickup. "Mathew's and Mark's Pharisees," 80. See also Loader, *Jesus' Attitude Towards the Law*, 36.

[78] Pickup. "Mathew's and Mark's Pharisees," 79. See also Loader, *Jesus' Attitude Towards the Law*, 143.

ended up completely inverting the proper hierarchy of values.[79] These improper emphases were also intimately related to Jesus's charges of hypocrisy.[80] The Pharisees were considered hypocrites because, while arrogating to themselves the role of exacters of the law, they infringed the law when they interpreted it "to the letter," and not according to its "spirit." They were hypocrites because they violated the law under the pretense of defending the law.[81] As Pope Francis explains:

> [F]aced with hunger, *Jesus set the dignity of the children of God over a rigid, casuistic and self-serving interpretation of the rules.* When the doctors of the law complained with hypocritical indignation, Jesus reminded them that God desires love, not sacrifice, and explained to them that the Sabbath was made for human beings and not human beings for the Sabbath. *He confronted their hypocritical and smug thinking with the humble understanding of the heart, which always puts people first and refuses to allow certain mindsets to obstruct its freedom to live, love and serve our neighbour.*[82]

This hypocrisy is further illustrated during the aftermath of the sabbath controversy. After proclaiming that "the sabbath was made for man, not man for the sabbath," Jesus went to a synagogue and

---

[79] Pickup. "Mathew's and Mark's Pharisees," 88.
[80] Loader, *Jesus' Attitude Towards the Law*, 383
[81] Pickup. "Mathew's and Mark's Pharisees," 86. See also Loader, *Jesus' Attitude Towards the Law*, 77-8.
[82] Francis. "Address to Meeting of Popular Movements."

started preaching. A crippled man went to Him, asking to be healed. The Pharisees stood watch and observed whether Jesus would heal this man, so they could accuse Him of violating the sabbath as well.[83] They asked Jesus whether it was lawful to heal on a sabbath.[84] From what we have seen, Jesus's hermeneutic not only said that it is lawful to help a person on a sabbath, but it would be unlawful *not* to do so. But in order to avoid the trap set by the Pharisees, Jesus turned the tables on them. He asked:

> What man shall there be among you, that hath one sheep: and if the same fall into a pit on the sabbath day, will he not take hold on it and lift it up? How much better is a man than a sheep? Therefore it is lawful to do a good deed on the sabbath days.[85]

Here, once again, the Pharisees' hypocrisy was made manifest. If one of their sheep had fallen into a pit, they would not wait for sabbath to end before helping the animal, otherwise it may well perish. But the Pharisees were not willing to afford their fellow men the same compassion they would extend to their livestock. Once again, there was an inversion in the hierarchy of values. More importantly, there was hypocrisy, because the Pharisees applied the Torah inconsistently.[86] Through this inconsistency, the Pharisees failed to

---

[83] Mark 3:1-2.
[84] Mt 12:10.
[85] Mt 12:11-12.
[86] Pickup. "Mathew's and Mark's Pharisees," 91.

provide the necessary help to their brethren, further violating the Torah and descending even more into hypocrisy.

Afterwards, Jesus asked: "Is it lawful to do good on the sabbath days, or to do evil? To save life, or to destroy?" Jesus then proceeded to heal the crippled man. When they saw this, the Pharisees went out and immediately started to conspire on how to dispose of Him.[87] Jesus "worked" on sabbath to do good and to save a life, whereas the scandalized Pharisees tried to stop Him from "working" on sabbath. In doing so they *worked* evil on a sabbath, trying to destroy His life. Once again, they were acting hypocritically, for they did not mind working on sabbath to do evil—their only objections were directed at Jesus's sabbatical work to do good.[88]

With all this in mind, let us return to the seven woes that Jesus would eventually raise against the Pharisees. In the very first woe, Jesus said: "Woe to you scribes and Pharisees, hypocrites; because you shut the kingdom of heaven against men, for you yourselves do not enter in; and those that are going in, you suffer not to enter."[89] Since the Pharisees used casuistry to obfuscate the most central aspects of the law, they were effectively preventing others from following the fulness of the law. They were not leaders, but misleaders.[90] They abused their authority, as if they were gatekeepers keeping welcomed guests out. Ironically, through these actions, the Pharisees were also effectively locking themselves out of heaven.[91]

---

[87] Mark 3:4-6.
[88] Loader, *Jesus' Attitude Towards the Law*, 37.
[89] Mt 23:13.
[90] Su. "A Study in the Significance of Jesus," 123.
[91] Ibid., 125.

The third woe also dealt with casuistry. The Pharisees used to teach that, if one was to swear an oath or a vow, then the person should swear on the gold of the Temple or the gift laid out at the altar, because those were related to the *Corban* (see above). Therefore, if someone swore on the Temple or the altar *themselves*, then the oath or vow would not be binding. Jesus pronounced the third woe in relation to this debate:

> Woe to you blind guides, that say, Whosoever shall swear by the temple, it is nothing; but he that shall swear by the gold of the temple, is a debtor. Ye foolish and blind; for whether is greater, the gold, or the temple that sanctifieth the gold? And whosoever shall swear by the altar, it is nothing; but whosoever shall swear by the gift that is upon it, is a debtor. Ye blind: for whether is greater, the gift, or the altar that sanctifieth the gift? He therefore that sweareth by the altar, sweareth by it, and by all things that are upon it. And whosoever shall swear by the temple, sweareth by it, and by him that dwelleth in it: And he that sweareth by heaven, sweareth by the throne of God, and by him that sitteth thereon.[92]

Put simply, Jesus did not condemn taking oaths or vows. What he did condemn was the kind of hairsplitting the Pharisees engaged in. It was obvious that swearing by the Temple or the altar was also binding, for these were holy objects. It was better to not swear an oath at all and answer with honesty and sincerity, than to entertain

---

[92] Mt 23:16-22.

this kind of pedantic casuistry leading to loopholes in the law and, therefore, to people breaking their oaths before God.[93] Upholding the law to the letter, once again, caused it to be violated under the pretense of following it in a more exact way.

Finally, the fourth woe summarizes what we have been talking about in a magistral way:

> Woe to you scribes and Pharisees, hypocrites; because you tithe mint, and anise, and cummin, and have left the weightier things of the law; judgment, and mercy, and faith. These things you ought to have done, and not to leave those undone. Blind guides, who strain out a gnat, and swallow a camel.[94]

Tithing was the practice of giving one-tenth of each Israelite's produce to sustain the priestly class. Once again, Jesus did not condemn this lawful practice, but only the Pharisees' misplaced priorities. The Pharisees urged people to practice tithing to the finer details, even when giving one-tenth of herbs and spices such as mint, anise, and cumin. Yet, they were willing to overlook much graver violations of the law, regarding justice and mercy.[95] By being exact with minutiae, while neglecting the "weightier matters of the law," the Pharisees were filtering flies while letting whole camels pass by. The Pharisees might be abiding by the letter of the law, but they were far from its spirit. As Pope Francis explains:

---

[93] Su. "A Study in the Significance of Jesus," 128-30.
[94] Mt 23:23-24.
[95] Su. "A Study in the Significance of Jesus," 131-2.

Rigidity. This distances us from the wisdom of Jesus, from the wisdom, beauty of Jesus: it takes away your freedom. . . and this rigidity does not help us enter through the door of Jesus: observing the law as it is written or as I interpret it is more important than the freedom of moving forward following Jesus.[96]

Hardness of heart vs. fulfilling the law

As we have proven with the Pharisees' example, upholding the law to its letter can be a betrayal of the law itself. It is much better, as Jesus teaches, to abide by the spirit of the law. But then, how can we avoid abuses like the "Spirit of Vatican II," in which the "spirit of the law" means distorting the law by imputing to it meanings clearly not contemplated by the law? Once again—as always—the answer can be found in Jesus.

Jesus charged the Pharisees with hypocrisy, because there was a divorce between their inner attitudes and their outward behavior. Jesus taught that the cure for this "double life" is to heal this rift, so that outward behavior naturally reflects the inner dispositions. In other words, the cure for hypocrisy is integrity,[97] in the etymological sense of that word.

---

[96] Francis. "Attitudes that prevent us from knowing Christ." See also Francis. "Three women and three judges": "Thus, all three were corrupt: those who brought the adulteress to Jesus, the scribes, the Pharisees, those who made the law and also passed judgements, they had the corruption of rigidity in their heart. To them, everything was the letter of the law, what the law said, they felt was pure: the law says this and you must do this..."

[97] Su. "A Study in the Significance of Jesus," 201.

Chapter 3: Pharisaism and the Double Life

During the handwashing controversy, Jesus replied to the Pharisees: "Not that which goeth into the mouth defileth a man: but what cometh out of the mouth, this defileth a man."[98] The Pharisees had it backwards, thinking that by performing outward behaviors "to the letter," they were automatically pure on the inside. But Jesus taught that the direction of purity-making goes the other way around. If a person is inwardly pure in their most intimate dispositions, then the outward behavior will organically follow, without any effort on their part.

The idea that one becomes good by following moral norms is actually a part of many non-Christian ethical models,[99] but is completely foreign to a Christian morality inspired by Thomist-Aristotelian principles.[100] In Thomism, the choice to act in a certain way results from an interplay between *reason* and *will*. On the other hand, *virtue* is not an act, but a habit, an inclination towards the good—what is called "ordered towards reason." Sometimes, the person wills something that their reason understands not to be good. If the person follows reason instead of their will, then the person does it out of a sense of duty, to uphold a certain moral law.[101]

From all that was said we can conclude, quite counterintuitively, that a person has the more sense of duty the less virtuous they are. If they are not virtuous, they are not inclined to the good, which means that will and reason are going to clash more often, and the person will act with a sense of duty. A virtuous person is going to be

---

[98] Mt 15:11.
[99] Soba. "Ética y Teología Moral," 101-4.
[100] Luño. "La Novedad de la Fe," 240.
[101] Luño. "Características y Temas Fundamentales."

naturally inclined towards the good, so their will and reason are more perfectly attuned—they will act morally not because they have a duty to do so, but because they *want* to act as such.[102]

So, the Christian ethics is not an ethics of duty, but an ethics of virtue. Morality cannot simply be reduced to evaluating each single individual act with relation to moral norms. Rather, it must be concerned with the good of the human person as a whole.[103] In *Veritatis Splendor*—Pope St. John Paul II's groundbreaking encyclical on moral theology—morality is "not so much about rules to be followed, but about the *full meaning of life.*"[104] The law, therefore, has a "pedagogic function."[105] Its role is to point where the good lies, so that the person may reorder their passions towards that good, thereby forming virtue. An act is not immoral because it breaks a moral norm, rather there is a moral norm against it because it is immoral. In the end, more important than following the law to the letter is to form the inner dispositions so that the law is followed, not compulsively, but lovingly.

This is the reason why Jesus placed the greatest priority on changing the "heart." It is also why the Pharisees—whose lips honored God, while their hearts were far away from Him[106]—are said to be "hard of heart." The term "hardness of heart" was frequently

---

[102] Ibid.
[103] Ibid., 240. See also Soba. "Ética y Teología Moral," 114-115.
[104] John Paul II. *Veritatis Splendor*, 7.
[105] Ibid., 23.
[106] Mt 15:8.

Chapter 3: Pharisaism and the Double Life

employed in the Old Testament to refer to the Israelite people whenever they went astray from God's law.[107]

Against this hardness of heart, the prophet Ezekiel foretold how God would cause Israel to walk in His commandments by "taking away its stony heart and giving it a heart of flesh."[108] Prophet Jeremiah talked of a "new covenant" with Israel where God was going to write the law "in their hearts."[109] In other words, the perfection of the commandments rests not on legalistic religious observance, but in following them interiorly, in one's own heart.[110]

This brings us to the zenith of Jesus Christ's ministry: the Sermon on the Mount. The reason why this sermon was so important is because this is where Jesus taught how to align inner dispositions with outward behaviors. From atop the mountain, Jesus issued a new Torah, where He proclaimed the "beatitudes." Those who fulfilled these beatitudes would be "blessed." In this sense, the Sermon of the Mount stood as the reverse of the coin of the seven woes with which Jesus rebuked the Pharisees.[111] In fact, at the beginning of this sermon, Jesus said:

> Do not think that I am come to destroy the law, or the prophets. *I am not come to destroy, but to fulfill. . .* For I tell you, that *unless your justice abound more than that of the*

---

[107] Gabriel. *Heresy disguised as Tradition*, 264-9.
[108] Ezek 36:26.
[109] Jer 31:31-33.
[110] Vilijoen, "Jesus' Teaching on the 'Torah,'" 149-50.
[111] Su. "A Study in the Significance of Jesus," 75.

scribes and Pharisees, you shall not enter into the kingdom of heaven.[112]

This crucial part of the sermon tells us two things. First, it once again confirms that Jesus does not have an issue with the law itself, but only with the Pharisees' interpretation of the law.[113] Whereas the Pharisees accused Him of destroying the law, Jesus is salvaging the law from the Pharisees' grasp, thereby in effect fulfilling the law. Jesus did this by interpreting the law according to the purpose for which it was given—in other words, by interpreting the law according to "its spirit." Second, it said that, if people abide by Jesus's interpretation of the law, their justice will even exceed the one of the Pharisees, the ones boasting of practicing the law to its most exact detail.

The sermon then proceeded by explaining how people can achieve this, through a series of antitheses. Whereas the law of the Pharisees ordained "Thou shalt not kill," Jesus's followers should surpass them by not even being angry at their brothers.[114] If the

---

[112] Mt 5:17,20.

[113] Loader, *Jesus' Attitude Towards the Law*, 143.

[114] Mt 5:21-22. See Francis. "The holiness of negotiation": "Essentially, Jesus says that 'it is not only a sin to kill', but also 'to insult and scold' our brothers. It is good for us to hear this. . . during this time when we are so accustomed to descriptions and we have a very creative vocabulary when it comes to insulting others. Offending others, therefore, is also a sin, it is murder. To make statements like: 'pay him no mind, he is crazy, he is stupid', and 'the many other bad words that we say when we do not show much charity to others', is 'to slap the soul of our brother, the true dignity of our brother'. This is a sin."

Chapter 3: Pharisaism and the Double Life 95

Pharisees' law commanded "Thou shalt not commit adultery," Jesus invited the multitudes to not even "look on a woman to lust after her."[115] Jesus recapitulated the controversy on oath-taking, so that people would simply respond honestly instead of taking oaths.[116] What we see here is an attempt to interiorize the law, so that people should not only restrain themselves from committing acts of murder and adultery, but that they would guard their hearts even against the thoughts that could potentially lead them to murder and adultery.[117]

Jesus continued. If someone was to offer a sacrifice at the altar while someone else held a grudge against them, they were to seek reconciliation before performing the religious ritual.[118] Divorce was now to be disallowed.[119] And even the famous *lex talionis*, that allowed "an eye for an eye and a tooth for a tooth" was now to be replaced with "turn the other cheek."[120] In short, Jesus's new law was much more radical than the Pharisees' law.[121] Interpreting the law through "its spirit" was not an excuse for laxity. Quite the contrary,

---

[115] Mt 5:27-28.

[116] Mt 5:33-34.

[117] Loader, *Jesus' Attitude Towards the Law*, 260.

[118] Mt 5:23-24. See Francis. "The holiness of negotiation": "Jesus settles the doubts of this people, who are disoriented and imprisoned, looking upwards: the law close up. He goes on, linking the conduct of the people with the worship of God and says: 'If you go to the altar to make an offering, and you have a problem with your brother, or your brother has a problem with you, first go to your brother and be reconciled'. This is to go beyond the law, and what he says is a higher justice than that of the scribes and Pharisees."

[119] Mt 5:31-32.

[120] Mt 5:37-40.

[121] Benedict XVI. *Jesus of Nazareth: from the Baptism*, 122-123.

it was infinitely more demanding than what the Pharisees were proposing.[122] Ironically, for all their strictness and rigidity, the Pharisees were the ones watering the law down.

It is important once again to note that Jesus was not abolishing the old law to introduce a new and more demanding law. Jesus was very clear, at the beginning of His sermon, that He came not to abolish, but to fulfil. Obviously, "thou shalt not murder" and "thou shalt not commit adultery" are to remain in place. However, as we have seen, that was not enough. Jesus wanted to get to the root of the problem, to the inner dispositions that caused murder and adultery. He wanted people to not live a "double life," but to have "integrity" between their hearts and behaviors. The Pharisees saw the law as an end, but Jesus saw it as a beginning. The Pharisees considered the law as a series of limits set to define moral behavior, whereas Jesus saw the law as a starting point for a deeper conversion.[123] Jesus did not want people to transgress the law, but to show them that they can achieve a far greater righteousness than if they simply adhered to the letter of the law and left it at that.[124] As Pope Francis explains:

> [Jesus] is the real legislator, who teaches us how the law must be in order to be just. However, the people were somewhat disoriented, a bit in disarray, because they did not know what to do and the ones who taught the law were not coherent. It is Jesus himself who says to them: "Do what they say, but not what they do". Moreover, they [the Pharisees] were

---

[122] Vilijoen, "Jesus' Teaching on the 'Torah,'" 143-144.
[123] Su. "A Study in the Significance of Jesus," 48.
[124] Vilijoen, "Jesus' Teaching on the 'Torah,'" 145.

Chapter 3: Pharisaism and the Double Life

not coherent in their lives, they were not a testimony of life. In this way, Jesus in this Gospel passage speaks of overcoming: "Your righteousness must exceed that of the scribes and Pharisees". Therefore, these people were a bit imprisoned in this cage, with no escape, and Jesus showed them the way to get out: it is to always get up, overcome, move on... generosity, holiness, is to go out, but always, always upwards: to move up. This is liberation from the rigidity of the law.[125]

In summary, Jesus said that He was fulfilling the law by interpreting it to its spirit (meaning, by finding the divine rationale behind the law)[126] and then, reorienting the law to where it was pointed to, bringing the law to its full intended meaning.[127] This is not a betrayal of the legislator. Quite the contrary, it is the only way that honors and takes the legislator seriously. In fact, Jesus acted like this because He is a "champion of the law."[128] Furthermore, we can never forget how hypocrisy does not only damage the hypocrite, but also the people who are turned away from the righteous path due to the scandal caused by the hypocrite.[129] Hypocrisy turns other people

---

[125] Francis. "The holiness of negotiation."
[126] Vilijoen, "Jesus' Teaching on the 'Torah,'" 150.
[127] Ibid., 148.
[128] Loader, *Jesus' Attitude Towards the Law*, 383.
[129] See Su. "A Study in the Significance of Jesus," 166: "The hypocritical behavior decimates their [the Pharisees'] relationship with God and causes a stumbling block for others to embrace the Gospel of the kingdom of heaven." See also Francis. "The holiness of negotiation": "So often we hear these things in the Church, so often!... That priest, that man, that woman of Catholic action, that bishop, that Pope who always tell us 'you have to

away from the law. It is Jesus's "unrelenting concern for holiness that makes Him a sworn enemy of hypocrisy."[130]

Jesus fulfilled the law, not by limiting it, but by showing its proper application.[131] He brought the law to its correct understanding by refocusing it, not on the letter, but on its spirit. And the spirit of the law is mercy: "I desire mercy, not sacrifice."[132] Unlike the Pharisees, Jesus demonstrated this mercy, not only with His teaching and ministry, but with His life.[133] We are going to talk more about mercy in chapter 5.

As for the Pharisees, they in effect appropriated God's gift of mercy by reducing it to a "moralistic ideology," a list of precepts that were nothing but "sophisticated arguments for everything."[134] This is the reason behind Jesus's woes to the Pharisees of his day, this is why He condemned them so strongly: because they appropriated the gift.[135] As we have seen above, a person who is not virtuous will feel

---

act like this!' while he himself does the opposite. This is precisely the scandal that hurts the people and does not allow God's people to grow, to move forward. It does not free them. This people... had also seen the rigidity of these scribes and Pharisees, so much so that when a prophet came who gave them a bit of joy, they persecuted and even killed him: there was no place for prophets there."

[130] Ibid., 98.

[131] Vilijoen, "Jesus' Teaching on the 'Torah,'" 151.

[132] Mt 9:13.

[133] Vilijoen, "Jesus' Teaching on the 'Torah,'" 152.

[134] Francis. "Let us not forget the gratuitousness."

[135] See Francis. "Let us not forget the gratuitousness": "He made Himself a gift for us and we must give this, make others see this as a gift, not as our possession. Clericalism is not something that belongs only to these times. Rigidity is not something of these days. It already existed at Jesus's time. And then, Jesus goes ahead in explaining the parable - this is chapter

Chapter 3: Pharisaism and the Double Life

a greater sense of duty, because this person does not will the good, but does it out of a sense of obligation. Since the person does not do good out of love, they will be focused on their merits for having chosen well when they did not want to. In such a merits-based mentality, the person will demand compensation for acting well, and penalties for those who fail to do so. Heaven and Hell are viewed, not as the presence and absence of God whom they love, but solely as reward and punishment. There is no place for God's gift, only for justice. There is no love for good for goodness's sake, only self-interest.[136] The law will be followed to the letter, and the heart hardened.

But today as well, we are faced with this problem. Pope Francis asks us to let go of the obstacles that lead us to a "double life," chief among which is rigidity:

> As Jesus "shook" the doctors of the law to break them free of their rigidity, now also the Church is "shaken" by the Spirit in order to lay aside comforts and attachments. . . . The Lord of the Sabbath, the reason for our commandments and prescriptions, invites us to reflect on regulations when our

---

21 - He goes ahead up to chapter 23 with the condemnation, where we see God's wrath against those who take the gift as if it were a possession and reduce its richness to the ideological whims of their own mind."

[136] Luño. "Características y Temas Fundamentales." See also Francis. "Our relationship with God is gratuitous": "Our relationship with God, our relationship with Jesus is not a relationship of 'doing things': 'I do this and You give me that.' A relationship like that – forgive me, Lord – commercial. No! It is free, just like the relationship between Jesus and the disciples. 'You are my friends'. 'I do not call you slaves, I call you friends.' 'You did not choose me, but I chose you' This is gratuitousness."

following him is at stake; when his open wounds and his cries of hunger and thirst for justice call out to us and demand new responses.[137]

---

[137] Francis. Homily at Enrique Olaya Herrera airport.

Chapter 4

The Judaizers and Indietrism

Although the Galatians believed in the crucified Jesus, they heard some theologians who said to them: "No, no! The law is the law. What justifies you is the law." In so doing, they left Jesus aside. In practice, they were "too rigid" . . . this was the problem of these people: ignoring the Holy Spirit, and not knowing how to move forward. They were closed, closed within regulations.

—Francis, Morning Meditation
"Half a life"

One of Pope Francis' catchphrases is a neologism he coined himself: "*indietrismo*." It is derived from the Italian *indietro*, which means "backwards." Some have, therefore, convincingly translated it into English as "backwardsism."[1] I will, however, for the remainder of this book, continue using "indietrism," the Anglicized version of the original word.

What does indietrism mean? During a press conference on the return flight from an apostolic visit to Canada, Pope Francis explained the meaning of this term:

---

[1] Lewis. "Pope Francis, neologisms, and doctrinal development."

I think this is very clear: a Church that does not develop its thinking in an ecclesial sense, is a Church that is going backward. This is today's problem, of many who call themselves "traditional." No, they are not traditional. They are *"indietristi"* people who look to the past, going backward, without roots. "It has always been done that way, that's how it was done last century". And looking "backward" *is a sin because it does not progress with the Church*. . . Tradition is precisely the root of the inspiration to go forward in the Church. And this is always vertical. And "backwardness" is going backward, *it is always closed*. It is important to understand well the role of tradition, *which is always open*, like the roots of the tree, and the tree grows like that.[2]

This term caused discomfort among traditionalist Catholics and their sympathizers.[3] "Of course we should look backwards, we should be mindful of Tradition!"—so they would argue. For them, this was proof that Pope Francis is a progressive, with utter disregard (if not contempt) for tradition.[4]

---

[2] Francis. "Press Conference on the return flight to Rome."

[3] See, for example, Welborn. "You indietrist, you." See also Hunwicke. "Indietrism again."

[4] See, for example, Charlier. "What is 'indietrism' (backwardness) anyway?": "With this expression [indietrism], invented by himself, our holy stepfather refers to all Catholics who adhere to the Apostolic Tradition and ecclesiastical tradition even where it does not fit into his Jesuit frame -- and that is quite a lot of it. . . should the Church of Progress, proclaimed by many after the last Council (and apparently reaffirmed with Bergoglio's election), also consider the faith it once professed dead and done with?"

Chapter 4: The Judaizers and Indietrism

Of course, an attentive reading of the Pope's words shows that Francis is not discounting tradition. The problem is not tradition, but rather going backwards *without roots*, outside *an ecclesial sense*. He is not saying that following tradition is wrong. He is saying that many who call themselves traditional are not traditional at all. Far from eschewing tradition, His Holiness is showing how tradition should be properly understood. This tradition is not static but allows for doctrinal development. Elsewhere in this intervention, Francis quoted St. Vincent of Lérins—the great theologian of doctrinal development—to explain that "true doctrine, in order to move forward, to develop, must not be still, it develops *ut annis consolidetur, dilatetur tempore, sublimetur aetate*"[5] (consolidated by years, enlarged by time, refined by age.)

Traditionalists are not convinced by Francis's justifications, however. For them, it is obvious that Pope Francis is contradicting perennial tradition, both when he decries indietrism and in many other of his papal decisions (like for example, *Amoris Laetitia*, the Catechism revision on the death penalty, and so on.) I have written a whole book about how tradition, properly interpreted and developed by the Magisterium, often takes the appearance of an innovation or a contradiction, and how heresies often cloak themselves as tradition.[6] I will, therefore, not rehash these arguments here. Since I already explained elsewhere—and with significant detail—how one can reconcile all of Pope Francis's interventions with tradition, I will simply take that for granted and proceed to flesh out the phenomenon of indietrism in its own right.

---

[5] Francis. "Press Conference on the return flight to Rome."
[6] See Gabriel. *Heresy disguised as Tradition*.

How does indietrism relate with rigidity? To better understand this, we will have to explore another concept that Pope Francis often ties with rigidity: fixism. At first glance, it might seem like there is no connection between fixism and indietrism. After all, fixism denotes lack of movement, whereas indietrism indicates movement: backwards movement, but movement nonetheless. However, this depends on our reference point: are we are considering the isolated person, or the person in relation to the Church? A fixist person remains where they are. In the meantime, the Church advances and the fixist does not accompany the Church. This fixist person will then try to force the Church to move backwards to meet them at the point where they remain fixed.

Being fixed during the journey

When Pope Francis talks about tradition, he often employs two metaphors. When he seeks to describe the wrongheaded interpretation from traditionalist factions, he usually refers to it as a "museum" (meaning a dead tradition, meant only to be exhibited, not used.) But when he seeks to describe *authentic tradition*, he uses the image of a "growing tree." One instance where he used both metaphors was a press conference during a return flight from Romania:

> I feel the "juice" of the roots that comes to me and helps me to go forward. I feel this tradition of the Church which is not a museum thing, the tradition, no. Tradition is like roots, which give you juice to grow. And you won't become like the roots, no: you will blossom, the tree will grow, you will bear

fruit and the seeds will be roots for the others. The tradition of the Church is always in flux... Tradition is the guarantee of the future and not the guardian of the ashes. It's not a museum. Tradition doesn't keep the ashes, the nostalgia of the fundamentalists, going back to the ashes, no. Tradition are roots that ensure that the tree grows, flowers and bears fruit. And I repeat that piece by the Argentinean poet that I like so much to quote: "Everything that the tree has that flowers comes from what it has unearthed."[7]

On the other hand, when one studies Pope Francis's use of the tree metaphor, we can see the interplay between two other recurrent themes: "roots" and "moving forward." Like a tree, tradition is "vertical,"[8] either growing deep roots or shooting its branches towards the sky. If tradition is vertical, we must always look either up or down. By looking down, we honor the roots. But when we look up to the branches, we see the tree grow. In a sense, the tree branches are "moving forward," at least chronologically. What we cannot do is step backwards.[9] That would mean that the tree's branches would shrink back to the roots, which would, in effect, shrivel up the tree. This is why Francis criticizes indietrism.

---

[7] Francis, "Press Conference during the flight of return to Rome from Romania" (translation from the original Italian with the help of Google Translate).

[8] Francis. "Address during the Apostolic Journey to Kazakhstan."

[9] Ibid.

Everything the tree has produced comes from what it has underground. *Without roots, there is no moving forward.* It is only through roots that we become people: not statues in a museum, like certain traditionalists, who are cold, stiff, rigid, who think that being prepared for life means *living stuck to the roots*. This relationship with one's roots is necessary, but we also need to move forward. *And this is the true tradition: taking from the past to move forward.* Tradition is not static: it is dynamic, aimed at moving forward.[10]

His Holiness does not discount the importance of the roots. They are indispensable because they give the tree energy to grow. But those who draw energy from the roots will "move forward." For this reason, Pope Francis usually links the "growing tree" metaphor with the image of a "journey." Conversely, it is not surprising that those who get "stuck to the roots" are said to be "fixated during their journey."

To better illustrate what Pope Francis means, I would like to draw some biblical parallels. I will start with a journey, a journey that changed the whole world. In the Book of Genesis, God called upon a Mesopotamian shepherd to leave the house of his idol-making father. God did not tell this man where he was being led—only that, by accepting this journey, God promised to make a great nation out of him and to bless all the earth through him.[11] And the name of this man was Abram.

---

[10] Francis. "Address to Members of the Global Researchers."
[11] Gen 12:1-3

Chapter 4: The Judaizers and Indietrism

Humbly, Abram took his family, servants, and flocks, and left the idols of his father's house. In front of him there was nothing but uncertainty. However, Abram knew of this God Who had called him because of a tradition much older than himself, much older than the gods of his father. The knowledge of this One God dated back to Noah and even Adam! Knowing his roots, Abram could go forward on this journey, and bring many with him, because he had faith in this One God. As Pope Francis explains: "The humble give life, attract others and push onwards towards the unknown that lies ahead."[12] And elsewhere: "The humble allow themselves to be challenged. They are open to what is new, since they feel secure in what has gone before them, firm in their roots and their sense of belonging. Their present is grounded in a past that opens them up to a hope-filled future."[13]

This humble attitude before the unknown contrasts with the posture of the proud. A proud person could never embark on such a journey guided only by faith, without any reassurances. Perhaps, some of Abram's kin refused to leave their beloved city of Ur and the idols of their fathers. They would go on with their daily lives, repeating their everyday actions, growing rigid as bone joints bereft of activity. The proud "simply repeat, grow rigid. . . and enclose themselves in that repetition, feeling certain about what they know and fearful of anything new because they cannot control it; they feel destabilized... because they have lost their memory."[14] The humble, unlike the proud "know that their existence is not based on their

---

[12] Francis. "Address to the Members of Communion and Liberation."
[13] Francis. "Address to the Roman Curia."
[14] Francis. "Address to the Members of Communion and Liberation."

merits or their 'good habits.' As such, they are able to trust, unlike the proud."[15]

Eventually, after many years wandering the desert, Abram had God entering a covenant with him. By establishing this covenant, God changed the very name of Abram (symbol of his essence and identity) into Abraham. As an external sign of this covenant, Abraham was asked to circumcise his foreskin, and also to circumcise all males of his people, both born and yet to be born.[16] As Pope Francis teaches, "*the word of God changes us*. It penetrates our soul like a sword. If, on the one hand it consoles us by showing us the face of God, on the other, it challenges and disturbs us, reminding us of our inconsistencies. It shakes us up."[17] Rigidity, on the other hand, does "*not change us, it hides us.*"

Centuries later, Abraham's descendants were enslaved by Egypt. Once again, God sent for someone to free them. This time, the choice fell upon Moses. After God crushed Egypt with ten plagues, the Hebrew people were released. Their toil was not over, though. Again, a journey awaited them in the desert, which is recounted in the Book of Exodus and the remainder books of the Torah. Once again, Francis tells us that "mission and service lead you to take on the dynamics of *exodus* and giving, of coming out of yourselves, of walking and sowing."[18]

---

[15] Francis. "Address to the Roman Curia."
[16] Gen 17.
[17] Francis. "Homily." January 23, 2022.
[18] Francis. "Address to the Little Missionary Sisters of Charity."

Chapter 4: The Judaizers and Indietrism

Of course, the road was not without challenges, or even falls. Many times, the desert's harshness made the people rebel against Moses and God:

> Let us reflect, though, on the history of the people of Israel: they suffered under the tyranny of the Pharaoh, they were slaves and then the Lord set them free. Yet to experience true freedom, not simply freedom from their enemies, they had to cross the desert, to undertake an exhausting journey. Then they began to think: "Weren't we better off before? At least we had a few onions to eat..." This is the great temptation: better a few onions than the effort and the risk involved in freedom. This is one of our temptations... Sometimes in the Church too this idea can take hold. Better to have everything readily defined, laws to be obeyed, security and uniformity, rather than to be responsible Christians and adults who think, consult their conscience and *allow themselves to be challenged*. This is the beginning of casuistry, trying to regulate everything. In the spiritual life and in the life of the Church, we can be tempted to seek an ersatz peace that consoles us, rather than the fire of the Gospel that unsettles and transforms us. *The safe onions of Egypt prove more comfortable than the uncertainties of the desert. Yet a Church that has no room for the adventure of freedom, even in the spiritual life, risks becoming rigid and self-enclosed.*[19]

---

[19] Francis. "Address on the Occasion of the Concluding Mass of the 52nd International Eucharist Congress."

However, even when this People of God—a stiff-necked people[20]—turned repeatedly away from Him, not even then did He forsake them. "The path of our redemption is a road on which there is no shortage of failures... that history, which begins with a dream of love and continues with a history of failures, ends in the victory of love: the Cross of Jesus."[21] We too, must "not forget this path," though it is a "difficult path."[22] To be a disciple, "a pilgrim" must be "on the way of the Gospel and of life, facing the threshold of the mystery of God and *on the holy ground of the people entrusted to him.*"[23]

It was during this journey in the desert that God gave His law to the Hebrew people and their descendants. Just like with Abraham, God established a covenant with Moses and the people he was guiding. *Just like circumcision was the external sign of the Abrahamic covenant, God's Mosaic law was the sign of the Mosaic covenant.* It was this law that, as we have seen in this last chapter, the Pharisees tried to pit against Jesus.

The error of the Pharisees was that they did not see this law, this tradition they inherited from their forebears, as a way to "move forward," or to "go on a journey." Unlike their ancestors, the Pharisees were already established in the nation of Israel. They had become sedentary, used to their everyday repetitions, just like those who preferred to remain in Ur instead of accompanying Abram. "The

---

[20] Exod 33:5.

[21] Francis. "Salvation is drawn from rejection."

[22] Ibid.

[23] Francis. "Address to Participants in the Plenary Session of the Congregation for the Clergy."

doctors of the Law knew all the laws, all of them, all of them. *But they were fixed there.* They did not understand when God was passing by. They were rigid, attached to their habits. Jesus Himself says so, in the Gospel: attached to habits. And if in order to conserve these habits, they had to commit an injustice, it wasn't a problem."[24]

But in doing so, they were not following the tradition of their ancestors. When Abraham and the Exodus people received the law, they were on a journey. "The law is for walking, and the kingdom of God is on its way. The kingdom is not stagnant, but, even more, the kingdom of God 'is built' each day. . . [unlike] the attitude of the person who observes the law but does not walk, who was fixated, and that being fixated, was an attitude of rigidity."[25]

Peter and "the God of surprises"

After Jesus's ascension to heaven—or more accurately, after the Holy Spirit's descent at Pentecost—the apostles started spreading the good news. Still, the apostles were observant Jews, just like Jesus before them. It is not strange that they would initially preach to the Jewish people.[26]

As we have seen in the last chapter, there was a division among the Jewish people between the "separatist" Pharisees and the Hellenists.[27] The Hellenists were Jews that had absorbed at least some of the Hellenistic culture and customs during the Greek conquest of

---

[24] Francis. "What happens when Jesus passes."
[25] Francis. "Flour and yeast."
[26] Acts 2-4.
[27] Mullin, *A Short World History of Christianity*, 4—5.

Israel. On the other hand, the Jews of the diaspora, living in foreign lands, also fell under the Greek sphere of influence during Alexander the Great's expansion. For two hundred years before Christ, Hellenized Jews had exposed many Gentiles (i.e., non-Jews) to Judaism, converting them. A debate arose between Hellenists and purists on whether these converts (also named "proselytes") should undergo circumcision, just like the Abrahamic covenant demanded.[28]

Now, this debate was about to be imported to the emerging Christian movement. The Pharisees had largely rejected Jesus's message, even playing a role in His execution. As for the Hellenists, they were much more amenable to the gospel—though even in the newborn Church, they were butting heads with the more traditionalist faction early on.[29] Soon, the apostles themselves would cross paths with willing Gentiles, eager to convert.

The first of such occurrence recorded in scripture is the case of the apostle St. Philip's exchange with an Ethiopian eunuch, ending

---

[28] Hirsch, "Circumcision", 93—95.

[29] Acts 6:1: "And in those days, the number of the disciples increasing, there arose a murmuring of the Greeks against the Hebrews, for that their widows were neglected in the daily ministration." See also Francis. "Address to the Faithful of the Diocese of Rome": "To return to the Acts of the Apostles, we see the emerging problem of how to organize the growing number of Christians, and particularly how to provide for the needs of the poor. Some were saying that their widows were being neglected. The solution was found by assembling the disciples and determining together that seven men would be appointed full time for *diakonia*, to serve the tables (Acts 6:1-7). In this way, though service, the Church advanced, journeyed together, was 'synodal', accompanied by discernment, amid the felt needs and realities of life and in the power of the Spirit."

Chapter 4: The Judaizers and Indietrism

with his baptism.[30] But we will now take a deeper look into another episode: St. Peter and the Roman centurion Cornelius.

The Book of the Acts of the Apostles tells us of Cornelius, a Roman man who, despite his pagan origins, feared the One God. One day, Cornelius received a vision of an angel, telling him that his prayers and alms had found favor with God, and that he should send for a certain Simon Peter.[31] Peter, as we all know, was the one entrusted by Jesus to "feed His sheep."[32] He was the "rock" upon which Jesus said He would build His Church, and to whom He gave the keys of heaven and earth.[33] For this reason, Peter is traditionally understood to have been the first pope.

After Cornelius's vision, Peter received a vision of his own. He saw a great linen sheet coming down from heaven, wherein all kinds of animals were laid down. Peter then heard a great voice telling him to kill and eat those animals. This posed a problem: the Mosaic law forbade the Jewish people from eating certain kinds of meat, namely of many animals present in that sheet. Peter, as a faithful Jew, was scandalized by this command. He replied to the voice: "Far be it from me; for I never did eat any thing that is common and unclean." But the voice answered: "That which God hath cleansed, do not thou call common."[34]

This was certainly a throwback to that handwashing incident I have mentioned in the last chapter, when Jesus said: "Not that which

---

[30] Acts 8:26-39.
[31] Acts 10:1-8.
[32] John 21:15-17.
[33] Mt 16:18-19.
[34] Acts 10:10-15.

goeth into the mouth defileth a man: but what cometh out of the mouth, this defileth a man."[35] However, Peter was still much enclosed in his own perceptions to understand this—and therefore, to understand what the voice was trying to teach him. Another great theologian of doctrinal development, St. Cardinal Henry Newman, used this episode to showcase how the mere appearance of contradiction is not enough to determine whether a certain doctrinal development is legitimate or not:

> [W]e cannot determine whether a professed development is truly such or not, without some further knowledge than an experience of the mere fact of this variation. Nor will our instinctive feelings serve as a criterion. *It must have been an extreme shock to St. Peter to be told he must slay and eat beasts, unclean as well as clean, though such a command was implied already in that faith which he held and taught*; a shock, which a single effort, or a short period, or the force of reason would not suffice to overcome.[36]

Interestingly, this "shock" of St. Peter according to St. Newman perfectly mirrors what Pope Francis teaches when discussing another recurring theme of his pontificate—"the God of surprises." We will return to this point shortly.

The voice insisted with St. Peter for three times, and for three times the apostle declined (it seems that Peter had a penchant for triple denials!) Eventually, the sheet was brought back to heaven,

---

[35] Mt 15:11.
[36] Newman, *Development of Christian Doctrine*, 176-177.

Chapter 4: The Judaizers and Indietrism

leaving Peter behind, befuddled and perplexed. At that moment Cornelius's emissaries knocked on his door. After they relayed their master's message, Peter went out to meet the Roman centurion.[37]

The apostle crossed the threshold of the Gentile's house—an act that, as he himself admitted, was viewed as "abominable," because Jews should neither "keep company or come unto one of another nation."[38] However, Cornelius recounted the vision he had received and, as he did, knelt before Peter.[39] This was a subversive act, for a high rank officer of a conquering army to kneel before a fisherman hailing from an occupied country. At that moment, Peter understood what the vision was trying to show him: that God was "not a respecter of persons,"[40] and no man should be called common or unclean.[41]

The Holy Spirit then descended upon Cornelius and all his household, and they all started speaking in tongues and praising God. Peter gazed upon this sight and acknowledged that, if the Holy Spirit Himself had come down to dwell among those Gentiles, then the apostle could not deny them the waters of baptism.[42] As Pope Francis teaches:

Peter had the courage to be surprised by the novelty of the Holy Spirit, to break the rigid response of "this is the way it

---

[37] Acts 10:16-23.
[38] Acts 10:28.
[39] Acts 10:21-25.
[40] Acts 10:34.
[41] Acts 10:28.
[42] Acts 10:44, 46-48.

has always been done". He was not afraid of creating "scandal" or of not fulfilling his mission as the "rock". He had the freedom not to hinder "God's grace", and not to "silence the din that the Spirit makes when he comes to the Church"... The Holy Spirit descends, disrupts everything and Peter baptizes: he understands God's sign and is capable of making a brave decision; he is capable of accepting *God's surprise*...

Though Cornelius was an influent man, he was marginalized and despised, because he was a Gentile. Peter, however, had the courage to go to the existential "outskirts," not allowing himself to "be impeded by prejudice, by habit, by *an intellectual or pastoral rigidity*, by the famous 'we've always done it this way!'"[43]

But while Peter was indeed open to this God of surprises, the same cannot be said of some who had accompanied him, which the Bible calls "the faithful of the circumcision." The Acts tell us that they were "astonished" that the grace of the Holy Spirit was being poured out on the Gentiles as well. Their astonishment, however, did not bear fruit. When Peter returned to Jerusalem, those "that were of the circumcision contended with him."[44] Pope Francis explains:

[T]he Apostles, the brothers who were in Judea came to know that the Gentiles had also accepted God's word. Referring to them as "the uncircumcised", they wondered: "How

---

[43] Francis. "Address in a Meeting with the Clergy"
[44] Acts 11:2.

Chapter 4: The Judaizers and Indietrism

can this happen? Peter and the others must be mistaken; they went beyond searching for a novelty"... [and thus] "mistrust began" and it reached the point that "when Peter went up to Jerusalem, the circumcised faithful scolded him, saying: 'You went into the homes of uncircumcised men and ate with them!'". It was as if to say, "look at the scandal you are causing! You, Peter, the rock of the Church, where are you taking us?"[45]

Scripture tells us that Peter answered these charges by merely describing what had transpired, "in all simplicity." He told them of his own vision, of Cornelius's revelation and actions, and of the outpouring of the Holy Spirit he witnessed:

Peter "excuses himself" saying these words: "if then God gave the same gift to them as he gave to us when we believed in the Lord Jesus Christ, who was I that I could withstand God?"... [This] is "truly the word of the apostolic instrument, of that Apostle who feels as an instrument of God: who am I to stop God's grace, to silence the din of the Holy Spirit when he comes to the Church?"[46]

---

[45] Francis. "God of surprises."
[46] Ibid. See also Francis. "Address to the Faithful of the Diocese of Rome"

When they heard this, those who were of the circumcision are said to have "held their peace and glorified God."[47] Nevertheless, this controversy was far from over...

Paul's geography of salvation

Peter would not be the only one surprised by God. An unlikely man would also be struck by God's unfathomable designs. He was a pious Pharisee, who "made progress in the Jewish religion above many of [his] equals... being more abundantly zealous for the traditions of [his] fathers."[48] His name was Saul, and he suffered from the same rigidity as his Pharisee peers (see last chapter).

As the Church kept expanding, even among the Gentiles, a concerned Saul tried to quell the emerging religion, becoming a fierce persecutor of Christians. He was tasked to go to Damascus, to hunt down Christians there and bring them to justice. However, along his way to destroy Christianity, he was *surprised* by Christ. As Saul went on his *journey*, a light from heaven dazzled him and knocked him out of his horse. The Pharisee heard a voice, introducing itself as "Jesus, whom you persecutest." When Saul arose, he was completely blind.[49]

In due course, Saul found a Christian community... not to hound them anymore, but to find healing. He was miraculously cured of his blindness and converted to that same Christianity which

---

[47] Acts 11:18.
[48] Gal 1:14
[49] Acts 9:1-8.

Chapter 4: The Judaizers and Indietrism 119

had completely overturned his expectations.[50] On his end, Saul would also overturn expectations and surprise others. The change of his religious convictions would be nothing short of radical. Even though he had been a Pharisee, he would become a preacher to the Gentiles. And even though he had been a legalist, he would teach a new message, giving primacy to God's grace over His law. Thus, so says Pope Francis, "the rigid youth, who had become a rigid —but honest! —man, became as a child, allowing himself to be led where the Lord had called him."[51]

When Saul came to Jerusalem to officially join the other disciples, many were afraid that his conversion would be fake and that he may be a spy. But Saul—now known by his Romanized name "Paul"—found a friend and ally in a certain disciple called Barnabas, who took him under his wing.[52] Pope Francis explains that Barnabas "had the patience of accompaniment: he knew how to accompany and allow growth to occur. He did not overwhelm the fragile faith of the newcomers by taking a rigorous and inflexible approach, or by making excessive demands about the observance of precepts... He accompanied them, taking them by the hand and dialoguing with them. Barnabas was not scandalized; he was like mothers and fathers who are not scandalized by their children, who accompany them and help them to grow... Barnabas is the man of patience."[53]

Maybe Barnabas's friendship explains Paul's profound change. After all, Barnabas is said to have "spoken also to the Gentiles and

---

[50] Acts 9:10-20.
[51] Francis. "Rigid but honest."
[52] Acts 9:26-27.
[53] Francis. "Address in Meeting with Movements of Cyprus."

disputed with the Greeks."[54] Paul would set out with Barnabas on another journey: not to quell the gospel, but to spread it. They started at Antioch and from there they moved on to many cities in the Hellenized world, founding churches wherever they passed. Once again, Pope Francis picks up on this journey to instruct us:

> The Book of Acts is the story of a journey that started in Jerusalem, passed through Samaria and Judea, then on to the regions of Syria, Asia Minor, Greece, ending up in Rome. A journey that reveals how God's word, and the people who heed and put their faith in that word, *journey together. The word of God journeys with us.* Everyone has a part to play; no one is a mere extra... *Yet that story, that journey, was not merely geographical*, it was also marked by a constant inner restlessness. This is essential: if Christians do not feel a deep inner restlessness, then something is missing. That inner restlessness is born of faith; it impels us to consider what is best to do, what needs to be preserved or changed. History teaches us that it is not good for the Church to stand still. *Movement is the fruit of docility to the Holy Spirit, who directs this history, in which all have a part to play, in which all are restless, never standing still...*
>
> [Peter and Paul] were capable of reassessing things in the light of events, witnesses of an impulse that led them to stop and think – that is another expression we should remember: to stop and think. An impulse that drove them to be daring,

---

[54] Acts 9:29.

Chapter 4: The Judaizers and Indietrism

to question, to change their minds, to make mistakes and learn from those mistakes, but above all to hope in spite of every difficulty. *They were disciples of the Holy Spirit, who showed them the geography of salvation,* opening doors and windows, breaking down walls, shattering chains and opening frontiers. This may mean setting out, changing course, *leaving behind certain ideas that hold us back and prevent us from setting out and walking together.*[55]

From this quote we learn that, for Pope Francis, being docile to the Holy Spirit is not merely setting out on a journey. It is not just about walking, but about *walking together*, as a Church. This would become extremely important later on, since Paul and Barnabas would soon clash with "those who were of the circumcision." In other words, with some converts from the Jewish religion.

These converts—heretofore referred to by the name "Judaizers"—visited Paul and Barnabas's Gentile churches. From Peter, the Judaizers had accepted that the Gentiles could be baptized and belong to the Church. However, they were scandalized to know that Paul's proselytes did not obey all the precepts of the Mosaic law. Namely, they were not circumcised. Coming from Judea, the

---

[55] Francis. "Address to the Faithful of the Diocese of Rome". See also, from the same address: "You see, we cannot understand what it means to be 'catholic' without thinking of this large, open and welcoming expanse. Being Church is a path to enter into this broad embrace of God. . . When the Church is a witness, in word and deed, of God's unconditional love, of his welcoming embrace, she authentically expresses her catholicity. And she is impelled, from within and without, to be present in every time and place. That impulse and ability are the Spirit's gift."

Judaizers began to teach at the Pauline churches: "That except you be circumcised after the manner of Moses, you cannot be saved."[56]

The Judaizers were "uniformists." They wanted to "make everything uniform: everyone as equals." If the Jewish converts had to undergo circumcision, the Gentile converts should as well. However, "uniformity goes hand in hand with rigidity." These Christians "confused what Jesus preached in the Gospel [with] their doctrine of equality," when "Jesus never wanted His Church to be rigid." Jesus wanted to make a more wonderful work out of these Gentiles, through which the Word could reach all corners of the earth. However, the Judaizers did "not have the freedom that the Holy Spirit bestows"[57] (see chapter 2):

> These Christians, who had been pagans, believed in Jesus Christ and had received baptism. And they were happy: they had received the Holy Spirit. They went from paganism to Christianity without any intermediary stage. Instead, those People who were called "Judaizers" sustained that you could not do that, that if someone had been a pagan they had to become Jews first, a good Jew, and then become a Christian, so as to be in line with the election of the People of God. And these Christians did not understand this. "But why? Are we second-class Christians? We cannot go directly from paganism to Christianity? Didn't Christ's resurrection dissolve the ancient law and bring it to an even greater fullness?" They were disturbed and there were a lot of discussions among

---

[56] Acts 15:1.
[57] Francis. "A house not for rent."

them. And those who wanted this were people who had pastoral arguments, even some moral ones. They sustained that no, you had to make the passage in this way! And this put into question the freedom of the Holy Spirit, and the free gift of Christ's resurrection and grace. They were methodical, and also rigid. . .

[It was a] religion of prescriptions, and thus they took away the Holy Spirit's freedom. And the people who followed them were rigid people, people who did not feel comfortable, they did not know the joy of the Gospel. The way of following Jesus to perfection was through rigidity: "You have to do this, this, this, and this". These people, these doctors, "manipulated" the consciences of the faithful, or they made them become rigid, or they would go away.[58]

The Acts of the Apostles tell us, quite euphemistically, that Paul and Barnabas "had no small contest"[59] with the Judaizers. But how should this question be settled? Who was right, the Judaizers or Paul? At a first glance, it would seem like the Judaizers had the better point: if the Gentiles wished to convert to Christianity, they should obey all the precepts of the Mosaic law, for Jesus Himself had been an observant Jew (see previous chapter). But sticking too rigidly to these precepts seemed to endanger the growing wave of converts outside the Jewish faith. What to do?

Here is where that concept of "walking together" comes in handy. . .

---

[58] Francis. "Our relationship with God is gratuitous."
[59] Acts 15:2.

Synodality and the Council of Jerusalem

Another favorite concept of Pope Francis is "synodality." Throughout his whole pontificate, Francis tried to establish a more synodal Church.[60] His critics, however, have tried to resist this process every step of the way.[61]

If we look at the etymology of this word, "synod" means "journeying together"[62] in Greek. And the first instance of "synodality" in the Church was the apostolic Council of Jerusalem. Paul and Barnabas returned to Jerusalem, to give account of the thriving Church of the Gentiles. But they were opposed by the "sect of the Pharisees that believed" i.e., the Judaizers, who proclaimed: "They must be circumcised, and be commanded to observe the law of Moses."[63] So, Scripture tells us that the apostles and the presbyters gathered to discuss this matter. It is said that there was "much disputing,"[64] (which is actually a good thing, as long as it is done *as a Church* and *within the Church*.)[65] They debated at length, but the arguments seemed

---

[60] Grech. "Synodality at the core of Pope Francis' ministry."

[61] See, for example, Altieri. "'Synodality' means whatever Pope Francis wants it to mean."

[62] Francis. "Address to the Faithful of the Diocese of Rome"

[63] Acts 15:4-5.

[64] Acts 15:9-7.

[65] Francis. "Address to the Faithful of the Diocese of Rome": "There was also the clash of differing visions and expectations. We need not be afraid when the same thing happens today. Would that we could argue like that! Arguments are a sign of docility and openness to the Spirit. Serious conflicts can also take place, as was the case with the issue of circumcision for pagan converts, which was settled with the deliberation of the so-called Council of Jerusalem, the first Council."

irreconcilable.⁶⁶ They were faced with a crossroads that would define the very soul of Christianity:

> In every movement one strongly feels a twofold need: faithfulness to the original charism and the need for change and novelty in order to respond to and transform situations. The question was: "*How to maintain harmony between these two tensions? How to discern the novelty that the Holy Spirit suggests from the novelty that instead moves away from the charism? How to understand whether a certain faithfulness to the original charism is more rigidity than true loyalty to the Holy Spirit?*". This is important. To understand and know souls: "Do not trust, beloved ones, in every Spirit", the Apostle says to us. Know when an inspiration is in harmony with the original charism and when it is not. This going forth leads you to *find different situations, different cultures, and the original charism must be interpreted for that culture. Not betrayed! Interpreted.* It must be the charism, but interpreted! "I don't want problems, I follow the original charism…" This way you will become a beautiful display, a museum. You will make of your movement a museum of things that are not useful today. Each charism is called to grow! Why? *Because it carries the Holy Spirit inside, and the Holy Spirit makes it grow!* Each charism must confront different cultures, with different ways of thinking, with different values. What does this do? It leaves the door open to the Holy Spirit.⁶⁷

---

⁶⁶ Francis. "Address to the Faithful of the Diocese of Rome"
⁶⁷ Francis. "Address to the Cursillos de Cristiandad movement"

As Pope Francis explained, this discussion among the apostles was not about betraying their original charism but interpreting it so that it could go forth and expand to every culture on the globe, becoming truly "catholic" i.e., "universal." The discernment undergone at the Council of Jerusalem was a "return to the sources of our charism," and thus a rediscovery of "the driving force needed to respond to challenges."[68] Returning to the sources is not anti-traditional. On the contrary, it is the very essence of a truly traditional thought.[69] On the other hand, if "forms and methods become ends in themselves," as the Judaizers intended, they become "removed from reality which is constantly developing; closed to the newness of the Spirit, such rigid forms and methods will eventually stifle the very charism which gave them life."[70]

During the council, the apostles did not rely on the apparently simpler—albeit arguably reductive—answer of simply repeating what they had always done. Rather, they *discerned*. "Discernment is a remedy to the immobilism of 'it has always been so' or 'let us take time'. It is a creative process that is not limited to applying schemas. It is an antidote to rigidity, because the same solutions are not valid everywhere."[71]

In the end of this discernment process, the time was ripe for Peter to speak his mind. Pope Francis has always been very explicit that

---

[68] Francis. "Address to the Third World Congress of Ecclesial Movements."

[69] See Gabriel. *Heresy disguised as Tradition*, 37-50.

[70] Francis. "Address to the Third World Congress of Ecclesial Movements."

[71] Francis. "Address to the Bishops ordained over the past year."

Chapter 4: The Judaizers and Indietrism

any synodal process must happen *cum Petro et sub Petro* ("with Peter and under Peter.") This "is not a limitation of freedom, but a guarantee of unity." After all, if "synodality" means "walking together," then there must be a "visible source and foundation of the unity both of the bishops and of the whole company of the faithful."[72] Otherwise, how would we know if we are really walking together, or if we are just walking on our own? There must be a point of reference, a shepherd, a beacon that determines when we have fallen astray and started walking alone.

The first pope stood up amid the first council and delivered an impassioned speech. Drawing from his experience with Cornelius, Peter proclaimed that God had "put no difference" between the apostles and the Gentiles, for in all the hearts were purified by faith. Therefore, putting upon the proselytes' shoulders the yoke of the law (which neither the apostles, nor their forefathers had been able to bear) would be to "tempt God." It is said that when Peter finished his speech, "all the multitude held their peace."[73]

It was St. James's turn to speak. Indeed, Peter was the first pope, but the council was held in Jerusalem and therefore fell under the jurisdiction of James, bishop of that city. James was partial towards the Judaizer party,[74] but in the end, he was docile to the promptings

---

[72] Francis. "Address on the 50th Anniversary of Institution of the Synod of Bishops."

[73] Acts 15:7-12.

[74] See, for example, Matthews, "The Council at Jerusalem", 340: "The multitude were impressed, and listened again to Barnabas and Paul as they related more particularly the signs and wonders which God had wrought among the Gentiles. Thereafter even an extreme legalist like James could

of the Holy Spirit.[75] The bishop acquiesced to Peter's decision, but sought to add a few conditions, as a way of concession to the Judaizer party. Proselytes were not to be disquieted but should nonetheless refrain from four things: 1) pollution of idols, 2) fornication, 3) meat of strangled animals, and 4) blood.[76]

I have explained elsewhere the basis for these prohibitions.[77] But for now, I would like to focus on how the council's final decision was worded. At the end of the proceedings, the apostles wrote a letter to Antioch, saying: "For it hath *seemed good to the Holy Ghost* and to us, to lay no further burden upon you than these necessary things." Please note that, *at the end of this synodal path, the apostles did not speak out of their own accord, but on what pleased the Holy Spirit.*[78]

---

see the difference between a Jewish and a Gentile denomination of Christians"

[75] Francis. "Resistance vs. docility": "Today I would like to say something about this docility. James, the Apostle, in the first chapter of his letter advises us to receive the Word with meekness, welcoming it as it comes: the Word that the Holy Spirit brings. And to do so we must be open, not closed, not rigid: open. The first step is to welcome the Word. The first step in the journey of meekness is to welcome the Word: to open our heart, receive it, allow it to enter like a seed that will sprout. . . I have to receive the Spirit who leads me to the Word with meekness, and this docility, that is, not resisting the Spirit, will lead me to this way of living, to this way of acting."

[76] Acts 15:19-20

[77] Gabriel. *Heresy Disguised as Tradition*, 105-106.

[78] Francis. "God of surprises": "The only way is to ask for the grace of discernment. . . The instrument that the Spirit himself gives us is discernment: to discern, in any case, as one must do. Indeed, this is what the Apostles did. They met, they spoke and they saw that this was the path of the Holy Spirit."

Indeed, the final "document" presented the Spirit as the protagonist in the process of decision-making and reflected the wisdom that He is always capable of inspiring.[79] Without the presence of the Holy Spirit, that assembly would not have been a synod, but a mere parliament,[80] where certain matters would be discussed from a human perspective. If it were so, there could be a temptation to assume a certain "ecclesiology of substitution," wherein we "do things on our own," as if "once ascended to heaven, the Lord had left a void needing to be filled, and we ourselves have to fill it." This is not so. God has left us His Spirit, and this Spirit is to be "the protagonist of Church's life."[81]

This brings us to a final overtone in Francis's thoughts on this matter. Francis often says that rigid Catholics are *enclosed* within themselves. If they are self-enclosed, then they are also closed to the action of the Holy Spirit. Closing oneself off from the Holy Spirit means not only a lack of freedom; it is a sin.[82] However, they do not stop there. Not only are they closed off to the Holy Spirit, but they also try to enclose the Holy Spirit as well. This was the mistake of the Judaizers. As Catholics, we are called to not "cage the Holy Spirit", but rather trying to "let him fly, to let him breathe in his soul."[83]

---

[79] Francis. "Address to the Faithful of the Diocese of Rome."
[80] Ibid.
[81] Ibid.
[82] Francis. Homily on the Solemnity of Pentecost. See also: "The world needs men and women who are not closed in on themselves, but filled with the Holy Spirit. Closing oneself off from the Holy Spirit means not only a lack of freedom; it is a sin. There are many ways one can close oneself off to the Holy Spirit, [namely by] *by rigid legalism*."
[83] Francis. "Address to the Newspaper Avvenire."

This is the reason why the Church must continuously journey. Our current synodal journey did not begin with Pope Francis's synodality, or even with the Second Vatican Council, but "with the first Apostles and has continued ever since. *Once the Church stops, she is no longer Church, but a lovely pious association, for she keeps the Holy Spirit in a cage.*" We need a "pilgrim hermeneutic capable of persevering in the journey begun in the Acts of the Apostles. Otherwise, the Holy Spirit would be demeaned."[84]

By being open to undergo this journey and let the Holy Spirit guide them, the apostles allowed the gospel to become truly "catholic," reaching everywhere on earth. This only happened because they were open to go to the peripheries, which at their time were the Gentiles all over the world. The Council of Jerusalem shows us that we "can only go to the outskirts if we carry the Word of God in our hearts and if *we walk with the Church*," as the apostles did.[85]

Paul corrects Peter's indietrism

However, as conclusive as the Council of Jerusalem might have seemed, the controversy was still not finished. It seems like not all Judaizers accepted the synod's conclusions. Or they might have accepted them in theory but did not assimilate the "spirit" of those conclusions (see chapter 3): they tried to reinterpret the synod's instructions in ways that ran counter to what was intended. Maybe— so they reasoned—the Gentiles might not have to be circumcised

---

[84] Francis. "Address to the Faithful of the Diocese of Rome."
[85] Francis. "Address in a Meeting with the Clergy"

Chapter 4: The Judaizers and Indietrism

and follow the totality of the Mosaic law; however, they were still to be deemed ritually impure and, therefore, as someone with whom a Jewish convert could not share a meal. This way, they denied the Council of Jerusalem in practice, even if they did not do so in theory.

We know that this is not what the synod intended, because St. Peter had made it very clear that God was "not a respecter of persons." In fact, one of the earlier sources of the controversy was Peter staying and eating at Cornelius's house for some days.[86] But the Judaizers were "fixed" on their journey and would not budge, even if the Church had moved along through the Council of Jerusalem. Since they would not walk together with the Church, they would demand the Church to turn backwards to where they were fixed. They would not adapt to the Church but would rather pressure the rest of the Church—namely the Gentiles—to adapt to *them*. And since Peter had been one of the engines of the new *status quo*, they would put pressure on Peter as well.

So it happened that one day, Peter came to visit Antioch[87] to see that astonishing Gentile wonder for himself—a church made up almost exclusively of proselytes! In the beginning, everything seemed to go well. Peter would eat with the Gentiles, just like he had done before with Cornelius. But then, an entourage came from Jerusalem and started sowing confusion. From that moment on, Peter "withdrew and separated himself, fearing them who were of the circumcision."[88] He would no longer eat alongside the Gentiles to avoid ritual impurity. In his epistle to the Galatians, Paul laments that even

---

[86] Acts 10:48.
[87] Gal 2:11
[88] Gal 2:12

his good friend Barnabas eventually succumbed and did the same![89] Paul was not going to take it. He recounted that he went up to Peter and "withstood him to the face, because he was to be blamed."[90] This is Paul's famous correction to Peter.

Some of Pope Francis's current critics use this incident of Paul's correction to Peter as precedent for their resistance to the Holy Father's magisterial teachings. Sometimes, they even accuse the pontiff of promoting heresy on those grounds.[91] In my book *Heresy disguised as Tradition*, I explain why that precedent does not hold, since Paul was not correcting Peter's magisterium. Paul's correction was directed at Peter's behavior as an individual person, which was undermining his own authoritative teachings in the Council of Jerusalem. Paul was upholding Peter's magisterium, even if Peter himself was betraying it!

---

[89] Gal 2:13

[90] Gal 2:11. Here I will accept the generally accepted position that the Cephas mentioned by Paul really refers to the apostle St. Peter. For a better overview of the various interpretations of this incident, see Gabriel. *Heresy disguised as Tradition*, 103-104.

[91] See van den Aardweg et al. *Correctio filialis*, 1: "We are permitted to issue this correction . . . by the law of Christ: for His Spirit inspired the apostle Paul to rebuke Peter in public when the latter did not act according to the truth of the gospel (Gal. 2). St Thomas Aquinas notes that this public rebuke from a subject to a superior was licit on account of the imminent danger of scandal concerning the faith (Summa Theologiae 2a 2ae, 33, 4 ad 2), and 'the gloss of St Augustine' adds that on this occasion, 'Peter gave an example to superiors, that if at any time they should happen to stray from the straight path, they should not disdain to be reproved by their subjects' (ibid.)."

However, in this book, I wish to go even further. Paul was not only correcting Peter's behavior, but more than that, he was correcting Peter's *indietrist* behavior. The Church had moved forward thanks both to Peter and the Council of Jerusalem. This forward movement had even been touted as a fruit of the Holy Spirit! But now, Peter had caved into the demands of a particular party within the Church and tried to put the genie (or rather, the Holy Spirit) back inside the bottle. Peter, who had always accepted the Gentiles on the grounds that he could not block something the Holy Spirit clearly favored, was now trying to "cage" this same Spirit within the human preconceptions of rigid people. The first pope was moving backwards to meet those who had stayed behind because they were fixed during their journey—and he was rightfully corrected for it.

Nowadays, most of the Church's members are what could be categorized as Gentiles, so we know that Peter accepted Paul's correction. Some, like the Judaizers, could wonder: "if these Gentiles were sinners and were damned and then they changed, then does faith change?" The answer is "no." Faith never changes. Faith is the same, though it moves; it grows; it broadens,[92] according to the principles delineated by St. Vincent of Lérins, as we have seen above. Nevertheless, we cannot forget that our God is a "God of surprises. . . because he is a living God, a God who abides in us, a God who moves our heart, a God who is in the Church and walks with us; and he always surprises us on this path." Thus, *"just as he had the creativity to create the world, so He has the creativity to create new things every day."*[93] "It is always the perennial today of the Risen One who

---

[92] Francis. "God of surprises."
[93] Francis. "God of surprises."

demands that we not resign ourselves to the repetition of the past and have the courage to ask ourselves whether the proposals of the past are still evangelically valid."[94]

Therefore, the Judaizer controversy was—as St. Cardinal Newman explained—the first instance of proper doctrinal development in the Church. "Doctrine cannot be preserved without allowing it to develop, nor can it be tied to an interpretation that is rigid and immutable without demeaning the working of the Holy Spirit. 'God, who in many and various ways spoke of old to our fathers' (Heb 1:1), 'uninterruptedly converses with the bride of His beloved Son' (Dei Verbum, 8). We are called to make this voice our own by 'reverently hearing the word of God' (ibid., 1), so that our life as a Church may progress with the same enthusiasm as in the beginning, towards those new horizons to which the Lord wishes to guide us."[95]

As Pope Francis continuously reminds us, tradition cannot be like a museum. "It is not about guarding ashes, but about keeping a fire burning... Tradition is like a mass of leavened dough; we can see it growing and in that growth is communion: *journeying together brings about true communion.*"[96]

The Judaizer controversy was also, in a way, the first great moment of internal crisis in the Church—at least since Pentecost. But from this crisis, we have achieved a better understanding of the interplay between God's law and His grace. Pope Francis tells us that experiencing crises is a necessary way to grow. Even with moments

---

[94] Francis. "Address to the Bishops ordained over the past year."
[95] Francis. "Address to the Pontifical Council for Promoting New Evangelization."
[96] Francis. "Address to the Faithful of the Diocese of Rome."

of crisis and resurrection, the "garment of faith is not starched, but develops with us." If it grows with us, it cannot be rigid.[97]

"The Church always needs renewal – *Ecclesia semper renovanda* ('Church always being renewed.') She does not renew herself on her own whim, but rather does so 'firm in the faith, stable and steadfast, not shifting from the hope of the gospel' (Col 1:23) . . . The Lord of the Sabbath, the reason for our commandments and prescriptions, invites us to reflect on regulations when our following him is at stake; when his open wounds and his cries of hunger and thirst for justice call out to us and demand new responses."[98]

---

[97] Francis. "General Audience," April 14, 2021.
[98] Francis. Homily at Enrique Olaya Herrera airport.

Chapter 5

Donatism and Lack of Mercy

We cannot run the risk that a penitent not perceive the maternal presence of the Church, which welcomes and loves each one. Should this perception fail, due to our rigidity, it would do serious harm in the first place to the faith itself, because it would impede the penitent from feeling included in the Body of Christ.

—Francis, Address during the Meeting
With the Missionaries of Mercy

One of the hallmarks of Francis's pontificate is his insistence on "mercy." To make this even clearer, the Holy Father chose as his papal motto the sentence *Miserando atque eligendo*. It is a play of words using "mercy" as a verb, instead of as a noun.[1] It clumsily translates as "mercying, He chose him," a reference to Bede the Venerable's commentary on St. Matthew's call to discipleship: "Jesus therefore sees the tax collector, and since He sees *by having mercy and by choosing*, He says to him, 'follow me.'"[2]

---

[1] Ivereigh. *The Great Reformer*, 12.

[2] Dicastery for Communication, "The Coat of Arms": "This has particular significance in the life and spirituality of the Pope. In fact, on the Feast of St Matthew in 1953, the young Jorge Bergoglio experienced, at the age of 17, in a very special way, the loving presence of God in his life. Following confession, he felt his heart touched and he sensed the descent of

Pope Francis often returns to this gospel episode to teach on divine mercy. Even so, many of the pontiff's critics misunderstand these teachings, believing that Francis's emphasis on mercy obscures God's justice, or the graveness of sin.[3] Nothing could be further from the truth.[4]

For Francis, the act of God's "mercying" unfolds through three stages. Once again, the Pope uses St. Matthew as a case-study. The first stage is *calling*. Jesus called Matthew to follow Him *while he was still living a sinful life*. But how did He call him? By looking upon the publican with love. This was paramount. Matthew was socially ostracized because of his sins. Matthew had never felt loved until that moment. For him, it would be impossible for someone like Jesus to love him. Jesus's love was the flame that thawed the tax collector's cold heart to His calling.[5]

---

the Mercy of God, who with a gaze of tender love, called him to religious life, following the example of St Ignatius of Loyola."

[3] See, for example, Browne, "*Misericordiae Vultus*": "For Francis extolls the glory of God's mercy, but with nary a mention of the reason man needs his mercy—sin. In order to call man to embrace God's mercy, it is necessary first to call him to repentance... But Francis avoids mention of the consequence of the failure of man to show mercy to man—Divine punishment, and even condemnation."

[4] See, for example, Francis. "Angelus," March 24, 2019: "Today, let us each think: what must I do before this mercy of God who awaits me and who always forgives? What must I do? We can have great trust in God's mercy *but without abusing it. We must not justify spiritual laziness*, but increase our commitment to respond promptly to this mercy with heartfelt sincerity."

[5] Vatican Radio. "Pope Francis: if you want mercy, know that you are sinners."

Chapter 5: Donatism and Lack of Mercy

Therefore, it was precisely "that sinful conscience which opened the door to the mercy of Jesus . . . This is the first condition of salvation: feeling oneself in danger. It is the first condition of healing: feeling sick. Feeling sinful is the first condition for receiving this gaze of mercy."[6] In other words, a proper understanding of mercy *presupposes the existence of sin*. If sin is not present, there is no need for mercy at all.

"There is a struggle between mercy and sin."[7] The nature of this struggle was presented during the Extraordinary Jubilee of Mercy, called by Pope Francis a mere couple of years after his election. One of his most iconic photos is him opening the Holy Door of Mercy at St. John Lateran's Basilica, symbolically opening the door of mercy at every cathedral in the world, so that pilgrims passing through them could receive a plenary indulgence.[8] At the end of this jubilee,

---

[6] Vatican Radio. "Pope Francis: if you want mercy, know that you are sinners."

[7] Ibid.

[8] See Francis. Homily of the Holy Mass and Opening of the Holy Door: "We have opened the Holy Door, here and in all the Cathedrals of the world. Even this simple sign is an invitation to joy. The time of great forgiveness begins. It is the Jubilee of Mercy. It is time to rediscover the presence of God and his fatherly tenderness. God does not love rigidity. He is Father; he is tender. . . Before the Holy Door that we are called to pass through, we are asked to be instruments of mercy, knowing that we will be judged on this. Those who are baptized know that they have a greater task. Faith in Christ leads to a lifelong journey: to be merciful like the Father. The joy of passing through the Door of Mercy is accompanied by a commitment to welcome and witness to a love that surpasses justice, a love that knows no boundaries. It is for this infinite love that we are responsible, in spite of our contradictions."

Francis issued an apostolic letter titled *Misericordia et Misera*, meaning "mercy with misery." Again, there is a contrast between Jesus's mercy and the misery of our sin:

> A woman and Jesus meet. She is an adulteress and, in the eyes of the Law, liable to be stoned... This Gospel account, however, is not an encounter of sin and judgement in the abstract, but of a sinner and her Saviour. Jesus looked that woman in the eye and read in her heart a desire to be understood, forgiven and set free. *The misery of sin was clothed with the mercy of love.* Jesus' only judgement is one filled with mercy and compassion for the condition of this sinner.[9]

Nonetheless, the sinner's calling is not the end of the "mercying" process. There are two more stages involved. The second stage is a *party*. Whenever a sinner turns away from his sin to follow Jesus, there is much rejoicing in heaven,[10] which is translated as a feast here on earth. Matthew felt happy and invited Jesus to come home to eat with him. Matthew also invited his friends, "those of the same trade," sinners and publicans.[11]

---

[9] Francis. *Misericordia et Misera*, 1. See also Francis. Homily on the Feast of Our Lady of Guadalupe: "The word 'mercy' [*misericordia*] is composed of two words: misery and heart [*miseria* and *cuore*]. The heart indicates the capacity to love; mercy is that love which embraces the misery of the human person."

[10] Luke 15:10.

[11] Vatican Radio. "Pope Francis: if you want mercy, know that you are sinners."

Chapter 5: Donatism and Lack of Mercy

But then comes the third stage, a stage extrinsic to the process of mercy itself, but inexorably caused by it: *scandal*. Scripture tells us that the Pharisees were scandalized whenever Jesus ate with sinners.[12]

> The Pharisees saw that publicans and sinners were at table with Jesus, and said to His disciples, "How is your Master eating with publicans and sinners?" A scandal always begins with this phrase: "But how come?" When you hear this sentence, it smells, and scandal follows. They were, in essence, scandalized by the impurity of not following the law. They knew "the Doctrine" very well, knew how to go on the way of the Kingdom of God, knew better than anyone how things ought to have been done, but had forgotten the first commandment, of love...
>
> That "how come?", which we've heard so many times from Catholics when they saw works of mercy. How come? Jesus is clear, He is very clear: "Go and learn." He sent them to learn, right? "Go and learn what mercy means. [That's what] I want, and not sacrifices, for I did not come to call the righteous but the sinners." If you want to be called by Jesus, recognize *yourself* a sinner...[13]

---

[12] Luke 5:27-30.

[13] Vatican Radio. "Pope Francis: if you want mercy, know that you are sinners." See also chapter 3 of this book.

Church history is filled with examples of this hard truth: Christ's mercy always produces scandal. I believe one particularly illustrative case can be found in the Novatian and Donatist schisms.

Mortal sins and communion

Baptism was held in the highest regard at the onset of the third century AD. Among other important graces, this sacrament granted plenary forgiveness of all sins committed before, no matter how severe. This, however, posed a problem. Baptism could be administered only once, meaning that this amnesty was also a once-in-a-lifetime event. What about those who had relapsed into sin *after* baptism?[14]

Sins of a lesser nature could still be absolved through acts of charity, prayer, and fasting.[15] The thorny issue pertained the three gravest sins: adultery/fornication, murder, and idolatry. These were the so-called *peccata mortalia* (mortal sins or "sins unto death")[16] or *peccata aeterna* (eternal sins).[17] As the name suggests, they were deemed irremissible. Committing one of these mortal sins after baptism would effectively end the sinner's prospect for salvation, as it would mean the departure of the Holy Spirit gifted during the sacrament.[18] Such sinners were, of course, also excluded from

---

[14] Newman, *Development of Christian Doctrine*, 195.
[15] Bryant. "Decius & Valerian, Novatian & Cyprian, Part I", 145.
[16] Ibid.,147.
[17] Bryant. "Decius & Valerian, Novatian & Cyprian, Part II", 161.
[18] Ibid.

Chapter 5: Donatism and Lack of Mercy

Eucharistic communion.[19] St. Cardinal Newman remarked that, as venerable as this ancient sacramental discipline was, it soon became unsustainable:

> But such a system of Church discipline, however suited to a small community, and even expedient in times of persecution, could not exist in Christianity, as it spread into the *orbis terrarum*, and gathered a net of every kind. A more indulgent rule gradually gained ground; yet the Spanish Church adhered to the ancient rule even in the fourth century, and a portion of Africa in the third, and in the remaining portion there was a relaxation only as regards the crime of incontinence (i.e., adultery or fornication).[20]

One of the proponents of a more lenient approach was Pope St. Callixtus, who allowed for priestly absolution of sins of the flesh, provided the sinner had displayed proper signs of repentance and atonement.[21] Not everyone was happy with this reform, though.

---

[19] See Chapman. "Novatian and Novatianism": "In general, it was a well-established principle in the Church of the second and beginning of the third century that an apostate, even if he did penance, was not again taken into the Christian community, or admitted to the Holy Eucharist. Idolatry was one of the three capital sins which entailed exclusion from the Church."

[20] Newman, *Development of Christian Doctrine*, 195.

[21] Bryant. "Decius & Valerian, Novatian & Cyprian, Part I", 147. Some critics may object that, in this instance, repentance is necessary, whereas Francis seems to extend mercy even to unrepentant sinners, like the divorced and remarried not living in continence in *Amoris Laetitia*. Such a criticism fails to take two points into account: 1) the novelty of Callixtus's

Tertullian, a respected author and apologist, resisted the pope's "innovation."[22] A learned presbyter called Hippolytus of Rome led a schism against the pope's "laxism" and became the first antipope of Church history.[23] Though Hippolytus would likely die reconciled with the Church, Tertullian died as a Montanist heretic. Eventually, the resistance to this new discipline fizzled away.

The situation, however, would repeat itself, now as regards another mortal sin. A catastrophe was about to befall the Church and submit the olden discipline to a proof of fire as never seen before.

When Decius became Roman Emperor in 249 AD, he inherited an empire in shambles. The Romans had been cursed with a succession of military defeats and natural catastrophes during the preceding decades. Decius knew he had to renew the empire and boost the populace's morale. Furthermore, there was a widespread perception

---

proposal, which certainly scandalized many of the faithful then, just like Francis's today; and 2) Francis does not extend mercy to unrepentant sinners in *Amoris Laetitia*. The great philosopher Rocco Buttiglione explains that the resolution to not sin again is "certainly necessary," but this means the sinner must have "the desire of leaving his irregular situation and strive to perform acts that will allow him to effectively leave such a situation. It is possible, however, that the sinner will not be in a stage where he can realize this detachment and reconquer his own sovereignty in an immediate way... He must strive, so *as to keep the resolution*, to leave the situation of sin." In other words, the resolution to not sin again means an "*endeavor to remove, in an opportune way and timing, the objective impediments.*" See Buttiglione. *Risposte amichevoli*, 181 (my translation from the original Italian).

[22] Chapman. "Novatian and Novatianism."

[23] Bryant. "Decius & Valerian, Novatian & Cyprian, Part I", 147.

that Rome's misfortunes might be due to divine wrath: the gods needed be appeased.[24]

Decius conceived a strategy to unify the empire under the banner of a common religion, while simultaneously placating the gods. The emperor ruled that every governor of every province should see to it that everyone offered a sacrifice to the pagan idols. Imperial commissions were established to supervise and enforce the decree, even in remote villages. The sacrificants would need to sign two certificates after the deed: one certificate to be held by the sacrificants as proof, exempting them from further scrutiny; another certificate to be archived by the local authorities.[25] Furthermore, these certificates—also called *libelli*—were meant to have retrospective value: by signing one of those papers, the sacrificants acknowledged not only that they had made a one-time sacrifice to the gods, but that they had held a *long-standing devotion* to the pagan deities. This was not merely a *performative* policy, but an *inquisitorial* one as well.[26]

These orders were inherently incompatible with Christian faith and practices. Of course, this was a feature of Decius's decrees, not a bug. His idea was not merely to revitalize the empire, but also to ferret out the religious deviants who had brought about the wrath of the gods.[27] This policy was meant to force Christians to choose one of two outcomes: 1) either to apostatize their Christian faith, returning to their pagan roots or at least severely demoralizing other Christians; or 2) to refuse to comply and be martyred, thus being removed

---

[24] Bryant. "Decius & Valerian, Novatian & Cyprian, Part I", 131.
[25] Ibid.
[26] Ibid., 135-6.
[27] Ibid., 136.

from the empire's fabric. Whatever their choice, it was a win-win situation for the emperor.[28]

A cruel persecution ensued, bringing about a mass wave of apostasies. Across the empire, Christians flocked and queued to the pagan temples to fulfill their civic duty, albeit reluctantly.[29] They were driven by fear of losing their office, their property, their freedom (there were sentences to forced labor in mines for men or in brothels for women) and even their lives.[30] Martyrdoms also multiplied. Pope St. Fabian was killed, alongside many high-ranking clerics. The whole situation did not allow for the safe election of a successor for the Roman See until the persecution had died down.[31]

After an initial onslaught, the persecution began to relax after a year, as local authorities were not enforcing the decrees so strictly anymore.[32] Furthermore, Decius's reign lasted only two years. After his death in 251 AD, the persecution also subsided. The Church, however, had suffered a severe blow. A great proportion of the surviving faithful could now fall into two categories. The confessors or *stantes* were the ones who had "confessed Christ" or "stood faithful," enduring exile, imprisonment, and torture, until their miraculous survival at the end of the persecution. Some of these confessors had also survived by refusing to appear before the authorities (*privatae*

---

[28] Ibid., 137.
[29] Ibid., 139.
[30] Ibid., 143.
[31] Chapman. "Novatian and Novatianism."
[32] Bryant. "Decius & Valerian, Novatian & Cyprian, Part I", 144.

Chapter 5: Donatism and Lack of Mercy

confessiones).[33] The other category, however, the one of the *lapsi* or "lapsed", far outnumbered the *stantes*.

Not all *lapsi* were the same. The *sacrificati* were the ones who had actually offered a sacrifice to the Roman idols. The *thurificati* had burnt a pinch of incense before the pagan altars. The *libellatici* had forged their *libelli* or had bribed the authorities to receive their certificates, as if they had performed a sacrifice without ever having done so. Some others had sent their slaves to offer sacrifices in their stead or had paid off pagans to impersonate them performing the required sacrifices.[34]

Interestingly, the *stantes* often did not harbor bad feelings towards the *lapsi*. There are reports of apostates who, while kept in prison awaiting release, repented of their previous lapse because of the kind treatment they received from their steadfast counterparts.[35] But this merciful behavior on the confessors' part was to soar to further heights at the end of the Decian persecution.

When the persecution waned, the multitudes of apostates sought readmission to the Church and her communion.[36] They were

---

[33] Ibid., 146.

[34] Kirsch, "Lapsi."

[35] See, for example, Kirsch, "Lapsi": "The letter of the Christians of Lyons, concerning the persecution of the Church there in 177, tells us likewise of ten brethren who showed weakness and apostatized. Kept, however, in confinement and stimulated by the example and the kind treatment they received from the Christians who had remained steadfast, several of them repented their apostasy, and in a second trial, in which the renegades were to have been acquitted, they faithfully confessed Christ and gained the martyrs' crown"

[36] Bryant. "Decius & Valerian, Novatian & Cyprian, Part I", 146.

opposed by the clerics, who sought to exalt the confessors' example by enforcing the strict discipline of excluding relapsing idolaters from communion, as it was an irremissible sin. Remarkably, in this instance, the lapsed were going to find their greatest allies, not in the clergy, but in the confessors, who seemed to reject exaltation to the detriment of their brethren. As Pope Francis likes to say, quoting St. Ambrose of Milan: "Where there is the Lord, there is mercy. Where there is rigidity, His ministers alone are there."[37]

The confessors picked up on the task of distributing mercy with great zeal. They were second only to martyrs in honor: their opinion carried significant weight. Some *stantes* claimed the privilege of anticipated intercessory prayer, others issued their own *libelli pacis* nullifying the apostasy certificates. Some even issued blanket reconciliations to all expressing remorse—even the infamous *sacrificati*. This, in effect, forced the bishops to yield to mercy and readmit the lapsed to communion.[38]

---

[37] See Francis. "Mercy first and foremost." See also Francis. Homily at the Celebration of Vespers.

[38] Bryant. "Decius & Valerian, Novatian & Cyprian, Part I", 149. See also Chapman. "Novatian and Novatianism": "Feeling secure against further persecution, they now wished to attend Christian worship again and to be readmitted into the communion of the Church, but this desire was contrary to the then existing penitential discipline. The *lapsi* of Carthage succeeded in winning over to their side certain Christians who had remained faithful, and had suffered torture and imprisonment. These confessors sent letters of recommendation in the name of the dead martyrs (*libella pacis*) to the bishop in favor of the renegades. On the strength of these 'letters of peace', the *lapsi* desired immediate admittance into communion with the Church."

The rigorist clerics would not stand for such laxism, though. They would decry the "false mercy" of these practices and feared the "lethal contagion" of those who had offered sacrifice to Satan and his demons.[39] They also claimed the backing both of scripture and tradition. After all, they defended the oldest discipline and could quote the gospels, where it was written: "Every one therefore that shall confess me before men, I will also confess him before my Father who is in heaven. But he that shall deny me before men, I will also deny him before my Father who is in heaven."[40]

Even the moderates were alarmed by the prospects of laxism. The Roman See was, at the height of the persecution, more favorable to the rigorists. St. Cyprian, bishop of the venerable city of Carthage (current-day Tunisia) also tried to side with the more traditional discipline. But one of those moderates who would soon rise to greater prominence was a presbyter named Novatian.

Submission to the urgencies of the times

To deter the spread of laxism, St. Cyprian issued provisional guidelines affirming that apostasy was beyond the priestly powers of absolution. The *lapsi* were to hold a life of penance, hoping for God's mercy during the Last Judgment, or that they might restore their honor if they would suffer the martyrdom they had avoided with their lapse. They were to refrain from partaking from the Eucharist, except maybe—if they had displayed proper penance—on their deathbeds. These instructions applied to all kinds of *lapsi*, *sacrificati*

---

[39] Bryant. "Decius & Valerian, Novatian & Cyprian, Part I", 149.
[40] Mt 10:32—33.

and *libellatici* alike, for the latter had practiced in their hearts what the former had done outwardly.[41]

The Roman clergy issued similar interim directives,[42] to be upheld until societal conditions would allow for the election of a new pope and the assembling of synods to address the topic.[43] Novatian, a presbyter in Rome, wrote two letters to Cyprian concerning the *lapsi*, sharing with the Carthaginian bishop a moderate attitude towards the issue.[44] Until a pope was elected and councils were convened, severity of discipline was to be preserved, all the while avoiding cruelty towards the repentant.[45] An anonymous author who would set out to refute Novatian, praised him, saying that: "so long as [Novatian] was in the one house, that is in Christ's Church, he bewailed the sins of his neighbours as if they were his own, bore the burdens of the brethren, as the Apostle exhorts, and strengthened with consolation the backsliding in heavenly faith."[46]

Though these guidelines seemed moderate at the time, they would prove unsustainable when the dust of the persecution settled. The numbers of apostates knocking on the Church's doors were far too great.[47] The scale of the catastrophe was such, it threatened the

---

[41] Bryant. "Decius & Valerian, Novatian & Cyprian, Part I", 150-1.

[42] Ibid., 150.

[43] Chapman. "Novatian and Novatianism": "The Roman clergy agree with Cyprian that the matter must be settled with moderation by councils to be held when this should be possible; the election of a new bishop must be awaited."

[44] Editors of the Encyclopaedia Britannica. "Novatian."

[45] Chapman. "Novatian and Novatianism."

[46] Ibid.

[47] Bryant. "Decius & Valerian, Novatian & Cyprian, Part I", 151.

very organizational viability of the Church. The clergy, now at freedom to gather in synods, was faced with a difficult choice: should they conform rigidly to traditional norms and disciplines, or should practical aspects allow for tactical adjustments to face unprecedented challenges?[48] Choosing the latter due to an organizational imperative was also not an easy task: it required Church leaders to find ways to legitimize this course of action within the limits set by scripture and tradition.[49]

The African churches were the first to convene synods. Here, and despite the rigorist leanings of the influential Cyprian, it was already possible to grasp the social pressure for a more lenient approach. Since not all *lapsi* were the same, penitential practices should also be different. The *libellatici* had committed a lesser offense, so they might be readmitted after a reasonable penance, whereas the *sacrificati* and *thurificati* could only be reconciled on their deathbeds. But even towards these grave offenders, case-by-case discernment was required. While setting proper penance, it was necessary to consider the circumstances in which the apostasy had taken place: whether the lapsed had offered sacrifice willingly or after torture, or whether the sacrificant had led the family into apostasy or, on the contrary, had obtained the certificate to save the rest of the family from performing the deed, etc.[50]

Though this was obviously not the outcome sought by Cyprian, the saintly bishop abided by the decisions of the synod,

---

[48] Ibid., 146.
[49] Ibid., 148-9.
[50] Chapman. "Novatian and Novatianism."

commending the new consensus for its "healthy moderation."[51] In Rome, however, the situation was direr. Sixteen bishops had gathered at the Imperial City and, with the consent of nearly all the clergy and people present, elected a certain Cornelius as pope against his will.[52] There was a problem with this election, though. During the Decian persecution, Cornelius had been a *libellaticus*.

This was too much for Novatian to bear. It is said that the presbyter "suffered an extraordinary and sudden change."[53] Abjuring all pretense of moderation, Novatian became the champion of the rigorist party.[54] A few days after Cornelius's election, Novatian set himself up as the competing pope.

Novatian was a worthy contender, to be sure. During the one-year period of *sede vacante* left by Fabian's martyrdom, Novatian had written letters on behalf of the Roman clergy,[55] a sign of high status. He was also a gifted theologian.[56] Cornelius would derisively call him: "that maker of dogmas, that champion of ecclesiastical learning."[57]

Obviously, all rigorists sided with Novatian and all laxists with Cornelius. Now, both parties were to compete for the hearts of the moderates. Both contenders sent envoys and letters to moderate bishops, vying for their support.[58] Surprisingly, and despite his

---

[51] Bryant. "Decius & Valerian, Novatian & Cyprian, Part I", 152.
[52] Chapman. "Pope Cornelius."
[53] Chapman. "Novatian and Novatianism."
[54] Editors of the Encyclopaedia Britannica. "Novatian."
[55] Chapman. "Novatian and Novatianism."
[56] Bryant. "Decius & Valerian, Novatian & Cyprian, Part I", 152.
[57] Chapman. "Novatian and Novatianism"
[58] Bryant. "Decius & Valerian, Novatian & Cyprian, Part I", 153.

previous backing of the rigorist cause, St. Cyprian sided with Pope St. Cornelius, bringing with him the whole African church. The Carthaginian bishop justified himself with the different circumstances of each stance: during Decius's persecution, his job was to exhort the faithful not to succumb, but now the most pressing matter was "healing the wounds" of the *lapsi*, as a "necessary submission to the urgencies of the times" (*necessitati temporum succubuisse*).[59] Novatian's followers, on their end, decried placing expediency above sacred principle.[60]

St. Cornelius convened an Italian synod which excommunicated Novatian. Novatian responded by unilaterally consecrating replacements for bishops who might have been *lapsi*. At some point, Novatianists could claim an estimated 20-30% of *all* the faithful.[61] Thus, the *Catholic Encyclopedia* rightfully tells us that there "could be no more startling proof of the importance of the Roman See than this sudden revelation of an episode of the third century: the whole Church convulsed by the claim of an antipope."[62]

Purity, Mercy, and Unity

It is fascinating to study the rhetoric issuing from both sides of the divide. Novatian's followers named themselves *Katharoi* (i.e.,

---

[59] Ibid., 155. I argue that a similar situation happened with *Amoris Laetitia* and the divorced and remarried controversy. See Gabriel. *The Orthodoxy of Amoris Laetitia*, 137-51.

[60] Bryant. "Decius & Valerian, Novatian & Cyprian, Part I", 154.

[61] Bryant. "Decius & Valerian, Novatian & Cyprian, Part II", 171.

[62] Chapman. "Novatian and Novatianism"

"Pure,")⁶³ and called for the renewal of a "Holy Church of the Pure" (*ecclesia pura*).⁶⁴ While Novatian had refused absolution to apostates and idolaters, his followers would eventually extend this logic to all mortal sins, including adultery and fornication⁶⁵ (an act of indietrism bringing them back to the position advocated by Hippolytus of Rome.) For the *Katharoi*, readmitting adulterers and apostates to communion would bring "contagion to the virgin bride of Christ." The Pure accused their opponents of "irreligious laxity," "mistaken compassion," and of overturning the "ancient faith" and "evangelical discipline."⁶⁶ Thus, Novatianists called the Church in communion with the pope an "Apostate Church" and a "Synedrium."⁶⁷

The other faction called itself "Catholic," and invoked divine mercy as the "overriding principle of pastoral care."⁶⁸ Catholics accused the Novatianists of being "destroyers of charity," of "denying the Father's mercy," of refusing to extend the "healing medicine of penance" to their wounded brethren, and of setting up a "counterfeit altar," thereby being "renegades against the peace and unity of Christ."⁶⁹

St. Cyprian—who had sided with the rigorists before—now reviled them for *inclementia* (lack of clemency) and *acerbia*

---

[63] Chapman. "Novatian and Novatianism"
[64] Bryant. "Decius & Valerian, Novatian & Cyprian, Part I", 153.
[65] Chapman. "Novatian and Novatianism"
[66] Bryant. "Decius & Valerian, Novatian & Cyprian, Part II", 161-62.
[67] Chapman. "Novatian and Novatianism"
[68] Bryant. "Decius & Valerian, Novatian & Cyprian, Part II", 160.
[69] Ibid., 161-2.

Chapter 5: Donatism and Lack of Mercy

(bitterness), calling them *castra diaboli* (camp of the Devil).[70] According to Cyprian, "no one is to be denied the fruits of penance and the hope of reconciliation. . . reconciliation may be granted through His priests, bestowable to all who mournfully implore and call upon His mercy."[71]

The most eloquent response from the Catholic side was an anonymous treaty titled *Ad Novatianum*. In this document, a nameless bishop lamented:

> What sort of folly is thine, Novatian, *only to read what tends to the destruction of salvation, and to pass by what tends to mercy*, when Scripture cries, and says, "Repent, ye who err: be converted in heart;" and when the same prophet also exhorts, and says, "Be converted unto me with all your heart, in fasting, and weeping, and mourning; and rend your hearts, and not your garments; be ye converted to the Lord your God: *for He is merciful, and one who pities with great compassion?*" . . . [Novatian] *labours more readily in the destruction of those things which are built and standing, than in the building up of those which are prostrate.*[72]

This anonymous writer set out to refute the mishandling of that biblical passage so often repeated by the Novatianists: "But he that shall deny me before men, I will also deny him before my Father who is in heaven." For the Novatianists—so he argued—"heavenly

---

[70] Bryant. "Decius & Valerian, Novatian & Cyprian, Part I", 151.
[71] Ibid.
[72] "A Treatise Against Novatian," 9, 13.

Scriptures are read rather than understood... if they are not interpolated."[73] The author then explained that the biblical quote had an eschatological purpose, referring to the Last Judgment. It was not meant to be applied to the present age.[74] By invoking this biblical passage to exclude the *lapsi* from communion, the Novatianists were usurping a judging role belonging to God alone.[75]

The writer then presented scriptural precedent for God's mercy, including the woman washing Jesus's feet[76] and St. Peter's triple denial.[77] Scripture revealed that God's mercy was given even to wicked pagans, including the Ninevites and—for a time—Pharaoh, when he implored Moses for clemency.[78] If God's wrath was immediately

---

[73] Ibid., 2.

[74] Ibid., 8: "For that He says, 'Whosoever shall deny me before men, him will I also deny before my Father which is in heaven,' its meaning is assuredly with respect to future time—to the time at which the Lord shall begin to judge the secrets of men—to the time at which we must all stand before the judgment-seat of Christ—to the time at which many shall begin to say, 'Lord, Lord, have we not prophesied in Thy name, and in Thy name cast out devils, and in Thy name done many wonderful works?' And yet they shall hear the voice of the Lord saying, 'Depart from me, all ye that have worked iniquity: I know you not.' Then shall it be fulfilled that He says, 'I also will deny them.'"

[75] Ibid., 8: "[T]his they judge from that utterance of the Lord, where He says, 'Whosoever shall deny me before men, him will I deny before my Father which is in heaven.' Oh grief! why do they strive against the Lord's precepts, that this offspring of Novatian, following the example of his father the devil, *should now endeavour to put in force those things which Christ will do in the time of His judgment?* that is, when Scripture says, 'Vengeance is mine; and I will repay, saith the Lord.'"

[76] Ibid., 11.

[77] Ibid., 8.

[78] Ibid., 12.

Chapter 5: Donatism and Lack of Mercy

placated after they had repented, why would the *lapsi* not be offered the same mercy?

But while searching for scriptural grounds for the new discipline, the author of *Ad Novatianum* interestingly flipped the tables on the Novatianists. For this purpose, he used Noah's Ark as an allegory:

> [T]he desire of schismatics is not in the law; *which law points out to us the one and only Church* in that ark to wit, which was fashioned, by the providence of God, under Noah before the deluge, in which—to answer you quickly, O Novatian—we find that there were shut up *not only clean animals, but also unclean.*[79]

He developed this metaphor by bringing up the dove and the crow that Noah released to ascertain whether the flood waters had receded. Both animals went out of the ark, but only one returned. The dove, not having found "rest for its feet," "bearing in its mouth an olive leaf,"[80] symbolized the lapsed, who also returned to the Church, bearing in their repentance a sign of peace. But the crow, who did not return, symbolized those who went out of the Church and did not come back.[81] Those would include the schismatics.

The nameless bishop also dug up scriptural precedent to accuse those guilty of schism. St. John had called them "antichrists," the evangelists called them "chaff," and Christ would say that those

---

[79] Ibid., 2.
[80] Ibid., 2, 5-6.
[81] Ibid., 2.

"who entereth not by the door into the sheep-fold, but goeth down by some other way, the same is a thief and a robber."[82] The author also contrasted Jesus Christ, the Good Shepherd, Who leaves ninety-nine sheep to find the lost one, with the wicked shepherds who "have not visited the weak, have not healed the halting, and have not recalled the wandering."[83] In other words, the Novatianists were accusing the Catholics of error when *they* were the ones in error.

> [L]et not the abrupt madness of that perfidious heretic move disturb us however, beloved brethren, who, although he is placed in such great guilt of dissension and schism, and is separated from the Church, with sacrilegious temerity does not shrink from hurling back his charges upon us: for although he is now by himself made unclean, defiled with the filth of sacrilege, he contends that we are so.[84]

Likewise, the Novatianists were using a scriptural passage against the *lapsi*, when that citation accused them more than the lapsed, for their sin was of a greater magnitude:

> *Behold how glorious, how dear to the Lord, are the people whom these schismatics do not shrink from calling "wood, hay, stubble." the equals of whom, that is, those who are even still placed in the same guilt of their lapse, they presume must not be admitted to repentance. This they judge from*

---

[82] Ibid., 2.
[83] Ibid., 14-5.
[84] Ibid., 1.

that utterance of the Lord, where He says, "Whosoever shall deny me before men, him will I deny before my Father which is in heaven"...

And yet [the Novatians] shall hear the voice of the Lord saying, "Depart from me, all ye that have worked iniquity: I know you not." Then shall it be fulfilled that He says, "I also will deny them." *But whom will the Lord Christ chiefly deny, if not all of you heretics, and schismatics, and strangers to His name?* For ye who were some time Christians, but now are Novatians, no longer Christians, have changed your first faith by a subsequent perfidy.[85]

In other words, the schismatic Novatianists were in greater need of mercy than the *lapsi* yet dared look down on God's mercy. The irony was not lost on this wise bishop: the Novatianists were sawing the branch where they were sitting on. He ended his masterful treatise by exhorting the Novatianists to the same repentance the *lapsi* had demonstrated, for Christ "rejoices, who once again with full and merciful moderation exhorts us... saying, 'Turn ye, and return from your impieties, and your iniquities shall not be to you for a punishment.'"[86]

The anonymous author of *Ad Novatianum* was not the only one to use this gambit. Many other Church Fathers tried bringing to light the satanic trap the Novatianists had fallen prey to. In dire need of mercy, they were denying mercy to others. St. Gregory Nazianzen called them the "new Pharisees... pure in title, but not in purpose..

---

[85] Ibid., 7-8.
[86] Ibid., 18.

. setting laws beyond humanity's reach"[87] (see chapter 3). St. Dyonisius, bishop of Alexandria, also inveighed against antipope Novatian:

> If it was against your will, as you say, that you were led, you will prove it by retiring of your free will. For you ought to have suffered anything rather than divide the Church of God and to be martyred rather than cause a schism would have been no less glorious than to be martyred rather than commit idolatry, nay in my opinion it would have been a yet greater act; *for in the one case one is a martyr for one's own soul alone, in the other for the whole Church.*[88]

St. Cyprian would apply the same logic. Schism was now to be viewed as a sin greater than apostasy, as apostasy affected one soul while schism affected many. In an ironic twist of faith, Cyprian added schism to the list of *peccata mortalia*. To discredit them even further, the Carthaginian bishop would often equivocate schism with the other mortal sins, calling Novatianists "heretics," "apostates," and "adulterers" (since they had abandoned the Church, the Bride of Christ, to pursue other religious venues.)[89]

However, Cyprian did not stop at equating schism with the other irremissible sins: he turned it into a sin even more irremissible than the others. Whereas the "moderate position" prior to Cornelius's election was that martyrdom could wash away the sin of apostasy, Cyprian now argued that martyrdom could not expiate the sin of

---

[87] Bryant. "Decius & Valerian, Novatian & Cyprian, Part II", 178.
[88] Chapman. "Novatian and Novatianism"
[89] Bryant. "Decius & Valerian, Novatian & Cyprian, Part II", 172-3.

schism. For one to be saved, one should be in unity with the Catholic Church. It is in this context that the traditional sentence "*extra Ecclesiam nulla salus*" ("outside the Church there is no salvation") emerged for the first time.[90]

I am certain that this double standard must have been received with confusion and even derision by the Novatianists: why was so much mercy extended to apostates and adulterers, while schismatics were shown only rigidity? Similar bewilderment exists today, when papal critics ask why Pope Francis talks about "mercy," "accompaniment," "dialogue," when dealing with those they deem sinners, but not with them.[91] But it is a very traditional principle in Church history, since at least the Novatian crisis, to place the criterion of unity above everything else. It is important not to forget that the pope is the "guarantor of unity,"[92] and that schism is "the refusal of submission to the Roman Pontiff or of communion with the members of the Church subject to him."[93] Schism is the worse sin, because by refusing to submit to the pope, the schismatic is endangering Church unity. By rejecting communion with Cornelius, even if he had formerly been a *libellaticus,* Novatian was incurring a greater sin than the ones he judged guilty.

---

[90] Ibid.

[91] See, for example, Williams. "The Tragedy of Traditionis Custodes": "This is the on-the-ground reality of [*Traditionis Custodes*]. The MostMercifulPopeEver™ and the papacy of self-described #listening, #synodality, and #accompaniment is nothing but brutality, ideology, and devastation."

[92] John Paul II. *Ut Unum Sint*, 88.

[93] CCC, 2089.

Leniency vindicated

The relative peace inherited after Decius's death was short-lived. In 257 AD, emperor Valerian restarted the campaign to wipe out Christianity from the Roman Empire. His method was more strategic than his predecessor's. Whereas Decius had tried to brute force the suppression of Christianity by enforcing his decrees on the whole population, Valerian hit surgically at the elites of the Christian movement. Clergymen were to sacrifice to the pagan gods or face banishment or death. High-ranking officials and nobles should also abide or risk losing their office and property. By doing this, Valerian sought to decapitate the Christian movement, depriving Christians from the clergy that led the Church and from the wealthier members who financed her activities.[94]

This renewed persecution led to the martyrdom of the reigning pope, of St. Cyprian, and of Novatian. Though the former two are nowadays revered as saints in the Catholic Church, Novatian is not.[95] This vindicates Cyprian's aphorism that "outside the Church there is no salvation." Though Novatian died a martyr, his martyrdom did not erase the sin of schism, insofar as he died outside of unity with the Catholic Church.

---

[94] Bryant. "Decius & Valerian, Novatian & Cyprian, Part II", 164—165.

[95] The schismatic Hippolytus of Rome is also revered as a saint by the Catholic Church, but there are two crucial differences: 1) it is believed that Hippolytus reneged his schism and died in communion with Rome, and 2) Hippolytus lived before St. Cyprian's doctrinal developments on the importance of Church unity.

Chapter 5: Donatism and Lack of Mercy

Valerian's persecution ended in 260 AD, after his death in battle. His successor relented of persecuting the Christians, as he could not afford to sustain an undertaking with so much resistance.[96] Valerian's persecution did not wound the Church as much as Decius's. The Novatian crisis had, unexpectedly, strengthened the Church. The lenient approach had been vindicated.

It is true that, at a certain point, the Novatianists could claim 20-30% of the whole Church. Not only that, but their rigorist stance also attracted those seemingly most committed to follow the tenets of the Christian faith.[97] However, in the end, the Catholic Church triumphed over this battle of numbers, as she endures to this day while the Church of the Pure is no more. This is not just because the Catholic Church, being the original one, had a greater initial following, or because she was the one in possession of greater material resources, but because her disciplinary flexibility allowed her to reabsorb back into the fold the swathes of Christians who had formerly apostatized. Also, her gentle and moderate position was more appealing to the general population, allowing access to a greater pool of potential converts.[98]

The Valerian persecution also produced an abundance of martyrs, namely among the clergy. This helped the Catholic hierarchy reclaim some of the credibility lost through its lenient discipline.[99] It was now hard for the Novatianists to keep shunning the Catholic

---

[96] Bryant. "Decius & Valerian, Novatian & Cyprian, Part II", 166.

[97] Ibid., 168, 171. See also Bryant. "Decius & Valerian, Novatian & Cyprian, Part I", 129.

[98] Bryant. "Decius & Valerian, Novatian & Cyprian, Part II", 164, 170.

[99] Ibid., 174.

Church as an Apostate Church, when so many Catholics were receiving the crown of martyrdom. Furthermore, just like the confessors of Decius's time had asked for mercy for the *lapsi* before, now confessors of the Valerian persecution were urging the Novatian schismatics to renounce their heretical beliefs and return to unity with the Church.[100]

The Catholic Church's leniency was also vindicated through the fruitful doctrinal developments resulting from the whole calamity. The most important of these was, obviously, the acknowledgment of the sacrament of Penance. St. Cardinal Newman, the great theologian of doctrinal development, credited the Montanist and Novatian crises—and the subsequent need for mercy for post-baptismal sin—as the catalysts for a better understanding of many Catholic teachings we take for granted today, namely the doctrine of Purgatory[101] and the sacrament of Reconciliation[102]

Baptized Catholics did not need to despair anymore if they relapsed into sin. On the contrary, they could find forgiveness by going to a priest for absolution, while displaying a sincere and contrite heart. And this was not a once-in-a-lifetime event, like baptism, but could be sought repeatedly after each fall. Certainly, a Novatianist would see here a source of moral laxism susceptible to exploitation from unscrupulous sinners. But the sacrament of Reconciliation is currently a fundamental, consensual, and inextricable part of Catholic tradition. The great Father of the Church St. John Chrysostom would exhort the sinners under his care:

---

[100] Ibid., 174-5.
[101] Newman, *Development of Christian Doctrine*, 388-93.
[102] Ibid., 385-6.

"Have you sinned? Then enter the Church and wipe away your sin. . . [A]s often as you sin, repent your sin. . . Come then, repent, for here there is a hospital, not a courtroom, not a place where punishment for sins is exacted, but where forgiveness of sins is granted."[103]

The parallels with Pope Francis's rhetoric are striking. One of Francis's trademark sentences is the Church as "a field hospital for sinners."[104] Following through with the medical metaphors, it is noteworthy how, in his controversial *Amoris Laetitia* footnote, Francis says that "the Eucharist is not a prize for the perfect, but a powerful medicine and nourishment for the weak."[105] This view of the sacraments as "medicine" was also common in Catholic arguments against Novatian heresy.[106]

---

[103] Bryant. "Decius & Valerian, Novatian & Cyprian, Part II", 179.

[104] See, for example, Francis. "Homily for the Opening of the Synod of Bishops": "And the Church is called to carry out her mission in charity, not pointing a finger in judgment of others, but – faithful to her nature as a mother – conscious of her duty to seek out and care for hurting couples with the balm of acceptance and mercy; to be a 'field hospital' with doors wide open to whoever knocks in search of help and support."

[105] Francis. *Amoris Laetitia*, n351.

[106] See Bryant. "Decius & Valerian, Novatian & Cyprian, Part II", 161—162, 176: "Pacian of Barcelona composes a lengthy epistolary defence of the Catholic Church against Katharist criticisms, insisting God's spirit-reviving gifts to the baptized—the 'medicines' of confession and penitence—shall be needed and utilized until such time as 'the serpent retires from this world'. . . In callously refusing to extend the 'healing medicines of penance' to their wounded brethren, the Katharoi are 'rebels against the saving sacrifice of Christ' and duly marked for damnation as partisans of the 'brother-hating heresy of Cain.'"

History repeats itself

Neither schisms nor persecutions were over. In 303 AD, emperor Diocletian initiated what would be the Roman Empire's last antichristian persecution. This one would be, however, unprecedented in scope—so much so it became known as "the Great Persecution."[107] Diocletian also tried to force Christians to offer incense to the gods under pain of death. Besides that, the emperor ordered Christian sacred books to be confiscated and burned, and churches to be destroyed.[108] Again, the Church sought compromises, so that she could "ride the waves of the crisis and not drown in martyrdom."[109] Once more, this attitude scandalized faithful of a more rigorous bent.

Besides the categories of apostasy seen earlier in this chapter, a new class emerged: the *traditores* (meaning "traitors"), the clerics who had given up the sacred books to the authorities to be burned. However, not all *traditores* delivered actual sacred books. Some had used clever ruses, taking advantage of the authorities' ignorance of Christian scripture, offering fakes to be burned instead. These were still considered *traditores*, though.[110]

One such case involved Mensurius, successor of Cyprian as bishop of Carthage. In a letter to a fellow bishop, Mensurius admitted that he hid the sacred books in his house and gave up heretical

---

[107] Mullin, *A Short World History of Christianity*, 47—48, 53.
[108] Chapman. "Donatists."
[109] Mullin, *A Short World History of Christianity*, 72.
[110] Kirsch, "Lapsi."

Chapter 5: Donatism and Lack of Mercy

writings to the authorities instead.[111] Also, Mensurius had cooperated with the authorities by not holding public services during the period of persecution.[112]

Knowing this, some of the faithful—who would later be martyred for their faith—disowned Mensurius and broke communion with him.[113] This did not sit well with Caecilian, a deacon and the bishop's right-hand man. It is said that Caecilian "raged more furiously against the martyrs than did the persecutors themselves."[114] Though the objectivity of these accounts is contested (for they come from the schismatic side,) it is important to note that going against the unity of one's rightful bishop was a grave sin, as we have seen in the previous sections of this chapter.

Mensurius died after the persecution abated. Caecilian was elected his successor. Nevertheless, some faithful of his diocese did not recognize his legitimacy, because he had been consecrated by a *traditor*. A council was called by bishops of a more rigorous disposition to judge the whole affair, which ended declaring Caecilian's ordination invalid and consecrating a certain Majorinus as bishop of Carthage in his place.[115]

---

[111] Chapman. "Donatists."
[112] Mullin, *A Short World History of Christianity*, 72.
[113] Chapman. "Donatists."
[114] Ibid.
[115] Mullin, *A Short World History of Christianity*, 72—73. See also Kaufman. "Donatism Revisited," 131—132: "Perhaps as early as 305 CE, although more likely in the next decade, neighboring prelates objected to the incumbent's alleged disdain for confessors, questioned the validity of his consecration, and elected Majorinus to replace him. Caecilianus and his partisans refused to step aside."

This council did more than that: it ventured into the doctrinal realm. While Mensurius before them had held that a *traditor*'s ordination was valid, the council affirmed that a *traditor* could never be a bishop. Moreover, those who were in communion with Caecilian were to be deemed as excommunicated. Those resisting Caecilian called themselves a "Church of the Martyrs."[116]

Novatian had already laid out the seeds for this kind of thinking. According to him, the *lapsi* had irreversibly forfeited the Holy Spirit's presence in themselves. Therefore, lapsed clerics could not impart sacramental grace, and the baptisms conferred by those clerics were invalid. Those who were to be received into the "Pure" Church would have to repeat their baptism to be sure of their belonging to the Body of Christ.[117]

Now, the followers of Majorinus picked up where the Novatianists had left. Very soon, dioceses began having two bishops, one in communion with Caecilian and the other with Majorinus.[118] The latter would eventually be succeeded by a certain Donatus,[119] and his followers would be known as "Donatists."

In the meantime, Diocletian's persecution was the death rattle of the pagan empire. One year after Diocletian's abdication, Constantine was crowned emperor, after winning a battle at the Milvian Bridge under the sign of the cross. Constantine became the first Christian Roman Emperor, thus ending Roman persecution against Catholicism. In 313, Constantine issued the Edict of Milan, granting

---

[116] Chapman. "Donatists."
[117] Bryant. "Decius & Valerian, Novatian & Cyprian, Part II", 162.
[118] Chapman. "Donatists."
[119] Kaufman. "Donatism Revisited," 132.

Chapter 5: Donatism and Lack of Mercy

religious toleration across the empire. He also restored churches and property, paid compensations, and even donated money to the Church. However, he was faced with a problem: how could he support the Church if there were two contending factions, each claiming to be the one true Church?

This was particularly problematic in Africa, where Donatist bishops had created a veritable parallel church. Rome relied on the African province to produce much of its grain: this region was even dubbed the "breadbasket of the empire."[120] If Constantine wanted to avoid strife and conflict, he needed to find a way to restore unity.

Constantine appealed to the Pope for judgment. After hearing both Caecilian and Donatus's case, the Pope decided that the accusations against Caecilian were anonymous and unproven. Therefore, Caecilian was the true Catholic bishop, whereas the Donatists were the ones in schism. Since Donatus and his followers did not accept the Pope's decision, Constantine asked a council to be gathered in Arles. This council issued a series of canons forbidding re-baptism and decreeing that false accusations would be punished with excommunication until the hour of death. The council tried to pursue some moderation, declaring that *traditores* should also be refused communion, as long as their betrayal had been properly proven with due process. Those who had been ordained by the *traditores*, however, had been validly ordained and should retain their clerical offices.[121] This was unacceptable for the Donatists.

Exasperated by the Donatists' constant appeals, Constantine ordered their churches to be transferred to Catholics, confiscated the

---

[120] Mullin, *A Short World History of Christianity*, 73.
[121] Chapman. "Donatists."

rest of their property, and evicted Donatist clergy. The Donatists, on their end, felt proud of this "persecution of Caecilian," which "the Pure" suffered at the hands of the "Church of the *Traditores*."[122]

As the resistance grew fierce, Constantine relaxed his measures and asked Catholics to suffer the Donatists with patience. The latter, however, were not exempt from aggressive behavior. For several times, the Donatists broke out in violence, forcefully occupying Catholic cathedrals. Since they did not recognize the validity of the sacraments administered by the *traditores*, the Donatists would take possession of Catholic churches and then cast the Eucharist to the dogs,[123] thus incurring a greater sacrilege than the ones distributing communion to those deemed sinners by the Donatists.

The Donatists were also joined by bands of uncouth ruffians, called Circumcellions, who "converted" to the Donatist faith and terrorized Catholic populations. These brigands were even capable of measuring forces with the imperial military. Though attracted by the Donatists' simplistic tenets of purity, the Circumcellions often indulged in the vices of gambling, drunkenness, and prostitution. Sometimes, the Circumcellions sought martyrdom by unnecessarily endangering their lives and even through suicide. The Donatist clergy was not proud of their crude followers but did not mind using their services to wreak havoc in the Church and empire. For example, the Donatists would halfheartedly reprimand their followers, explaining that suicide was a grave sin. Yet, they would revere suicidal Circumcellions as martyrs.[124] Thus, those accusing Catholics of

---

[122] Ibid.
[123] Ibid.
[124] Ibid.

bowing down to expediency would not hesitate to do the same to attain their own ends.

Suspicion and lack of love

The greatest Catholic champions against Donatism were St. Optatus and St. Augustine. Optatus was the first to formulate the doctrinal principle according to which the grace of the sacraments is derived, not from the worthiness of the minister, but from the *opus operatum* ("from the work performed") of Jesus Christ.[125] The unworthiness of the priest or bishop did not hinder the validity of the sacraments they ministered. This validated the canons of the Council of Arles, forbidding second baptisms.

But Augustine was the one who put the final nail in Donatism's theological coffin. The Donatists had not stopped at excommunicating Caecilian and those consecrated by him. They also believed that anyone associated with Caecilian was guilty by association.[126] Since the universal Church, including the Church of Rome, had decided to commune with Caecilian, then the Church in the rest of the world had perished. The Donatists were the last remnant of the true Church. So fearful were they of contaminating their purity, they

---

[125] Ibid. Augustine would pick up on Optatus' reasoning. See Viss. "Augustine and the Donatists Controversy": "Petilian, a Donatist priest and rival to Augustine, argued that the priest's conscience, if pure, could cleanse a believer through the receiving of baptism. But Augustine insisted that the conscience of the priest was irrelevant because the power of the sacraments was administered through Christ alone." See also Mullin. *A Short World History of Christianity*, 73—74.

[126] Kaufman. "Donatism Revisited," 132.

would drive off any Catholic who would come to their churches and then wash the floor with salt.[127]

This attitude was a grave sin against Church unity. Just like Cyprian before him, Augustine argued that the Church should retain her *Catholicity* (i.e., "unity") all over the world, including in Africa.[128] Jesus had foretold that the gospel would reach all parts of the world, not be confined to a particular African sect.[129] The Donatists' views on a holiness exclusive to them made it impossible for this unity to come to fruition.[130]

According to Augustine, this lack of unity worked against the Donatists' own claims. The New Testament had instructed the churches on how to address common problems. These problems were known only because those churches were "in communion" ("unity") with one another. But the Donatists were not united with the universal Church. Therefore, they could not condemn the Church, for they would have to be in communion with those they had accused.[131] Whereas the Donatists emphasized *purity* (even if such purity was exclusivist), Catholics stressed *connection*: regional churches like the African church were a part of a larger network of churches. Donatists said they were the true Church because they were the purer church. Catholics countered that they were the true Church because they were universally recognized, namely by Rome

---

[127] Chapman. "Donatists."
[128] Viss. "Augustine and the Donatists Controversy," 5.
[129] Ibid., 7-8.
[130] Ibid., 5.
[131] Ibid., 6.

and Jerusalem.[132] Augustine appealed to the See of Rome, with an uninterrupted succession of bishops since St. Paul and, most especially, St. Peter, "the rock against which the proud gates of Hell shall not prevail."[133]

These different conceptions had implications on the definition of Church holiness. Donatists had an individualistic view of holiness, whereas for Catholics, the Church's holiness was organizational and communal: it was not "empirical, but structural."[134] The Church was indeed holy, but she was also messy. Noah's Ark, a type of the Church, was an ark of salvation in spite of being dark and dirty.[135] Augustine, as other Catholics, would often take recourse to the parable of the wheat and tares, in which the good wheat and the wicked tares were bound to grow together, side-by-side, until the end of the world (not until the Donatists or the Circumcellions decided to wipe them out).[136]

The true Church was to be the one vine, whose branches grow all over the earth.[137] The Church was the Body of Christ, a body united in its members in a framework of love. "By God's grace and through His love, our division and enmity have been restored to unity with Himself, in the local church and the universal (Catholic)

---

[132] Mullin, *A Short World History of Christianity*, 73.

[133] Chapman. "Donatists."

[134] Mullin, *A Short World History of Christianity*, 73. I am reminded of Pope Francis's statement (so controversial at the time), that "no one is saved alone, as an isolated individual." See Francis. *Gaudete et Exsultate*, 6.

[135] Mullin, *A Short World History of Christianity*, 73.

[136] Viss. "Augustine and the Donatists Controversy," 7.

[137] Chapman. "Donatists."

church."[138] Herein lied the main issue. It was not just a matter of unity, but of love. Or rather, unity existing through love.

Augustine was very clear that the dispute between Catholics and Donatists was not so much doctrinal, but attitudinal. Donatists entered schism first and became heretics only later.[139] At first, their doctrinal principles seemed indistinguishable from the ones held by Catholics. But Donatists had yielded to intense doubt and suspicion regarding their brethren.[140] This groundless suspicion had evolved to a lack of love and peace, which eventually broke unity with the Church.[141] The greatest problem of the Donatist sect was not their view on rebaptism or the nature of the Church. It was not doctrinal or dogmatic. Rather, the root of their error was a "distorted Christian conduct and practice, namely *lacking love*": "You do not have love . . . so for your own honor you divide unity."[142] Donatists had fallen "into the darkness of schism, losing the light of Christian charity" because "Christian charity cannot be preserved except in the unity of the Church."[143] Augustine quoted St. Paul's magnificent anthem to charity: "If I speak with the tongues of men, and of angels,

---

[138] Viss. "Augustine and the Donatists Controversy," 7.

[139] This was also what happened with the Novatians. See Chapman. "Novatian and Novatianism": "there was no heresy until it was denied that the Church has the power to grant absolution in certain cases. This was Novatian's heresy." See also Park. "Lacking Love or Conveying Love?" 111: "In this sense, Newman, Lewis, and Pérez's argument—i.e., the early stage of Donatism was close to a schism, not a heresy, but the latter stage transformed into a heresy—could be right."

[140] Park. "Lacking Love or Conveying Love?" 105-6.

[141] Ibid., 107-8.

[142] Ibid., 110-1.

[143] Park. "Lacking Love or Conveying Love?" 108.

Chapter 5: Donatism and Lack of Mercy

and have not charity, I am become as sounding brass, or a tinkling cymbal."[144]

The Donatists' warrantless suspicion was so great, it endangered charity and unity *among themselves*. According to the Donatists, by flirting with the world, the Catholic Church had become indistinguishable from the world.[145] But when emperor Constantine's persecution of the Donatists subsided, some of them welcomed the new *status quo* and became accustomed to it. The most rigid among the Donatists then seceded from their gentrified counterparts.[146] Thus, the Donatist church was fractured with schism even within itself, on account of its lack of charity and unity. As Augustine pointed out, if the Donatists had love and tolerance, the Church would not have been divided by their suspicion.[147]

In this sense, Augustine once again flipped the tables on the Donatists, telling them that, while they condemned the *traditores* as "betrayers," *they* were the true "betrayers of the sacred books."[148] Once again, the greatest sinners were the ones eschewing mercy. Augustine also raised some *ad hominem* arguments, bringing up the Donatists' own inconsistencies.[149] After all, they allowed full fellowship to miscreants like the Circumcellions, and several of the "Pure" had been found to be *traditores* themselves.[150]

---

[144] 1 Cor 13:1. See Park. "Lacking Love or Conveying Love?" 110.
[145] Kaufman. "Donatism Revisited," 139.
[146] Ibid.
[147] Park. "Lacking Love or Conveying Love?" 111.
[148] Ibid., 108.
[149] Chapman. "Donatism."
[150] The *Catholic Encyclopedia* mentions the case of a certain Donatist bishop named Silvanus who had not only been a *traditor*, but had

I am once again reminded of Pope Francis's insightful teachings on the eldest son from the Merciful Father parable:

> But the elder son, who does not accept the father's mercy, withdraws; he makes a greater mistake. He thinks he is just; he presumes he has been betrayed and he judges everything on the basis of his concept of justice. Thus he becomes angry with his brother and rebukes the father.[151]

> In the parable, the elder son does not say "my brother" to the Father. No, he says "that son of yours," as if to say: he is not my brother. In the end, he risks remaining outside of the house. In fact, the text says: "he refused to go in," because the other one was there.[152]

Like the Novatians, the Donatists, and the elder son, rigid people may end up refusing their own salvation by not extending mercy to their lapsed brethren. In the face of such "outward rigidity" sometimes it is better—so says Francis—when God "throws down a banana peel in front of him, so he takes a good slip, is ashamed of being a sinner and thus encounters" the Savior.[153] Unfortunately, it does not seem like the Donatists' sinfulness softened their hearts towards mercy.

---

participated in a theft of goods from the church's treasury. See Chapman. "Novatian and Novatianism"

[151] Francis. "Angelus." September 15, 2019.
[152] Francis. "Angelus." March 27, 2022.
[153] Francis. "Darkness of the Heart."

Chapter 5: Donatism and Lack of Mercy

In 411 AD, emperor Honorius decided to settle the issue once and for all. He sent an official named Marcellinus to adjudicate the Donatist cause with complete impartiality. Of course, Augustine was the chief speaker on the Catholic side. The *Catholic Encyclopedia* described the Donatists' strategy as raising "technical objections, to cause delay, and by all manner of means to prevent the Catholic disputants from stating their case. The Catholic case was, however, clearly enunciated. . . It was then evident that the unwillingness of the Donatists to have a real discussion was due to the fact that they could not reply to the arguments and documents brought forward by the Catholics. The insincerity as well as the inconsequence and clumsiness of the sectaries did them great harm. The main doctrinal points and historical proofs of the Catholics were made perfectly plain."[154]

In the end, Marcellinus judged in favor of the Catholic party. Honorius issued a final law against the Donatists, exiling all their bishops and clerics from Africa. The Circumcellions tried some last-ditch resistance, but overall Donatism had heard its death knell.[155]

---

[154] Chapman. "Donatism."
[155] Ibid.

Chapter 6

Pelagianism and Self-Sufficiency

[It's the] self-absorbed promethean neopelagianism of those who ultimately trust only in their own powers and feel superior to others because they observe certain rules or remain intransigently faithful to a particular Catholic style from the past. A supposed soundness of doctrine or discipline leads instead to a narcissistic and authoritarian elitism, whereby. . . instead of opening the door to grace, one exhausts his or her energies in inspecting and verifying.

—Francis, *Evangelii Gaudium*, 94

One of the controversial points in *Amoris Laetitia* is its pastoral implementation of St. John Paul II's "law of gradualness."[1] This

---

[1] See Francis. *Amoris Laetitia*, 295: "Along these lines, Saint John Paul II proposed the so-called 'law of gradualness' in the knowledge that the human being 'knows, loves and accomplishes moral good by different stages of growth.' This is not a 'gradualness of law' but rather a gradualness in the prudential exercise of free acts on the part of subjects who are not in a position to understand, appreciate, or fully carry out the objective demands of the law." See also John Paul II. *Familiaris Consortio*, 9: "What is needed is a continuous, permanent conversion which, while requiring an interior detachment from every evil and an adherence to good in its fullness, is brought about concretely in steps which lead us ever forward. Thus a dynamic process develops, one which advances gradually with the

document acknowledges the difficulties that some divorced and civilly remarried Catholics may find in their attempts to follow Church teaching on this matter and asks for a pastoral accompaniment that more fully recognizes the *progressive* character of their spiritual path. Some of *Amoris Laetitia*'s critics, on the contrary, posited that the exhortation contradicted the following infallible canon from the Council of Trent[2]: "If any one saith, that the commandments of God are, even for one that is justified and constituted in grace, impossible to keep; let him be anathema."[3] Since God does not command us to do something impossible, *Amoris Laetitia* would be heretical[4] or, at least, minimizing sin.[5]

---

progressive integration of the gifts of God and the demands of His definitive and absolute love in the entire personal and social life of man."

[2] As an example, see the section "Inconsistency with the teaching of Trent on grace" from Brugger, "Five Serious Problems with Chapter 8 of *Amoris Laetitia*."

[3] Trent, 6th Session, c. XVIII.

[4] See the first alleged heretical proposition "corrected" by the *Correctio filialis*: "A justified person has not the strength with God's grace to carry out the objective demands of the divine law, as though any of the commandments of God are impossible for the justified; or as meaning that God's grace, when it produces justification in an individual, does not invariably and of its nature produce conversion from all serious sin, or is not sufficient for conversion from all serious sin."

[5] See, for example, Tranzillo. "*Amoris Laetitia*, the Human Person, and the Meaning of Marital Indissolubility": "Many people who have resigned themselves to evil are at peace with themselves about it. The examination of conscience must, therefore, be based on one concrete fact: Do I, or Do I not obey God's commandments to the full? For God does not command the impossible. He gives us all the help we need to obey him. In fact, his commands are not even burdensome, but light (Mt 11:30; 1 Jn 5:3). Often,

As I argued in my book *The Orthodoxy of Amoris Laetitia*, Pope Francis was not contradicting Trent at all. Rather he reaffirmed the Tridentine canon, while at the same time seamlessly weaving it together with another reference from John Paul II's *Familiaris Consortio*:

> For the law is itself a gift of God which points out the way, a gift for everyone without exception; it can be followed with the help of grace, *even though each human being "advances gradually with the progressive integration of the gifts of God and the demands of God's definitive and absolute love in his or her entire personal and social life."*[6]

As I argued in that book, *Amoris Laetitia* does not contradict Trent, but only a personal interpretation of Trent by people in modern times. According to this personal interpretation of Trent, a sinner would never sin if he really wanted to stop sinning, for God would always provide enough grace for the sinner to immediately achieve this. This erroneous interpretation of Trent flies in the face of reality; otherwise, people would not struggle with their sins.[7] Also, it contradicts Trent itself, for in another canon, the council decrees: "If any one saith, that a man . . . is able, during his whole life, *to avoid*

---

we find the commandments burdensome, or are not keeping them at all, because of our own sorry condition."

[6] Francis. *Amoris Laetitia*, 295. The non-italics part of this citation is a reference to the Council of Trent's canon, whereas the italics part is a direct quote from *Familiaris Consortio*, 9. See also my argument at Gabriel. *The Orthodoxy of Amoris Laetitia*, 181—182.

[7] Gabriel. *The Orthodoxy of Amoris Laetitia*, 80.

all sins, even those that are venial,—except by a special privilege from God, as the Church holds in regard of the Blessed Virgin; let him be anathema."[8]

This interplay between sin, grace, and gradualness is also a hallmark of Francis's thought. Right at the beginning of his pontificate, in his programmatic exhortation *Evangelii Gaudium*, Francis warned about two different—albeit interrelated—ways that can fuel spiritual worldliness: Neognosticism and Neopelagianism.[9] We will come back to the topic of spiritual worldliness in the next chapter. For now, let us focus a bit more on what Francis means by Neopelagianism.

His Holiness fleshes out his thoughts with significant more detail in his apostolic exhortation on holiness *Gaudete et Exsultate*. Here, Francis dedicates a whole section of the document to "Contemporary Pelagianism." Some Catholics, believing that what makes us saints is the kind of life we lead, began to attribute the power of sanctification to the human will, or personal effort.[10] In other words, Neopelagianism is the mistaken belief that holiness depends on one's actions, through individual determination and sheer strength of will.

This belief is wrongheaded, because it leaves no room for God's mystery or for the workings of His grace.[11] An often-overlooked Church teaching is that we are justified not by our own works or

---

[8] Trent, 6th Session, c. XXIII.
[9] Francis. *Evangelii Gaudium*, 94.
[10] Francis. *Gaudete et Exsultate*, 47-8.
[11] Ibid., 47.

Chapter 6: Pelagianism and Self-Sufficiency

efforts, but by the grace of the Lord, who always takes the initiative.[12] Quoting from the Second Council of Orange, Francis teaches that even "the desire to be cleansed comes about in us through the outpouring and working of the Holy Spirit."[13] Also, by citing the Catechism, Francis reminds us that the gift of grace "surpasses the power of human intellect and will."[14]

Of course, the critics may not recognize themselves in these words. They may reply that it is precisely their respect for God's grace that makes them take this stand.[15] They are the ones—so they argue—acknowledging grace's effectiveness, so that a sinner who truly wants to stop sinning can do so with the help of grace. Otherwise, God's grace would be powerless to lead a sinner away from a life of sin.

However, the opposite is true. Pope Francis admits that Neopelagianism can "speak warmly of God's grace," but "ultimately trust only in their own powers and feel superior to others because they observe certain rules or remain intransigently faithful to a particular Catholic style."[16] "Underneath our orthodoxy, our attitudes

---

[12] Ibid., 52.

[13] Ibid., 53.

[14] Ibid., 54.

[15] See, for example, Ferrara. "Pope Pelagius?": "A 'sanctifying grace' presumed to be more or less universal among men who are generally presumed to be in good conscience, dissociated from any act of faith in Christ or even basically moral behavior, would not be sanctifying grace at all—a divine gift superadded to fallen nature. It would, rather, be an intrinsic attribute of Pelagian man, who has never fallen in the first place. Pelagian man, able to save himself without faith, baptism or the Catholic Church, is precisely the man of the Bergoglian vision."

[16] Francis. *Gaudete et Exsultate*, 49.

might not correspond to our talk about the need for grace, and in specific situations we can end up putting little trust in it."[17]

This erroneous view of grace is caused or aggravated by a certain aversion to human frailty:

> *When some of them tell the weak that all things can be accomplished with God's grace, deep down they tend to give the idea that all things are possible by the human will, as if it were something pure, perfect, all-powerful, to which grace is then added.* They fail to realize that "not everyone can do everything", and that in this life human weaknesses are not healed completely and once for all by grace . . .
>
> Ultimately, the lack of a heartfelt and prayerful acknowledgment of our limitations prevents grace from working more effectively within us, for no room is left for bringing about the potential good that is part of a sincere and genuine journey of growth. Grace, precisely because it builds on nature, does not make us superhuman all at once. That kind of thinking would show too much confidence in our own abilities. . . . Grace acts in history; ordinarily it takes hold of us and transforms us progressively. If we reject this historical and *progressive reality, we can actually refuse and block grace, even as we extol it by our words.*[18]

As the name suggests, Neopelagianism appears as a resurgence of an older heresy: Pelagianism. However, Neopelagianism is not a

---

[17] Ibid., 50.
[18] Ibid., 49-50.

pure reiteration of its ancient counterpart. Rather, Francis uses this term to refer to mistaken attitudes that mirror, in their hearts, what was wrong with that heresy. As Bishop Serratelli of Paterson, New Jersey, explains: "Francis detects traces of this type of thinking in those people today who act as if salvation depends on human strength or on merely human means."[19]

But what is Pelagianism exactly? And how can we learn from it, so that we detect these traces of Pelagianism in our day and age? More importantly for the purpose of this book: were Pelagians rigid, as Pope Francis often says they were?[20]

Moral athletes and frail humans

By becoming both emperor and Christian, Constantine created the conditions for a Church boom. The number of baptisms skyrocketed. Being a Christian was no longer a drawback for a Roman citizen, but an advantage. Being the same religion as the emperor improved one's life prospects. This, of course, also increased the number of insincere conversions.[21] Many Christians fled this new Catholic worldliness by seeking refuge in an ascetic life.[22]

---

[19] Serratelli. "The faith confronting Neo-Pelagianism and Neo-Gnosticism."

[20] See Francis. Homily at *Domus Sanctae Marthae*: "Let us think of the Pelagians, of those… those famously rigid people." See also Francis. Homily at the Sunday of the Word of God: "I spoke of rigidity, that modern pelagianism that is one of the temptations of the Church."

[21] Mullin, *A Short World History of Christianity*, 59.

[22] Ibid., 60-1.

One such Christians was Pelagius, a British monk. After moving to Rome at around 410 AD, he became renowned for his morals and asceticism.[23] Pelagius was concerned about the slack moral standards among Christians, and hoped to improve their conduct by his teachings.[24] For him, this rushed Christianization of the empire was not making people true Christians, but rather "conforming pagans."[25]

Pelagius focused on attaining purity, just like the Donatists did.[26] According to the monk, the holiness of the Church was related to the holiness of the individual faithful (see chapter 5).[27] Whereas for the Donatists, one could attain this purity by "walling oneself off" in a "pure" community, Pelagius believed that this purity was achieved by each individual through sheer determination of will.[28] For Pelagius, sin was an act of the human will, in that every person is free to choose whether to sin or not. If that were not the case, people would

---

[23] Lamberigts. "Recent Research into Pelagianism," 178.

[24] Editors of the Encyclopaedia Britannica. "Pelagianism." See also Squires. "Reassessing Pelagianism," 117: "In fact, [Pelagius] was uncomfortable with laxity that had been increasing since the early fourth century."

[25] Ó Riada. "Pelagius to Demetrias."

[26] Squires. "Reassessing Pelagianism," 116, 120: "We can see here that there are some important similarities between the Donatists and Pelagius. Both placed purity at the center of their thought. While it was Petilian who said that 'you should not call yourselves holy, in the first place, I declare that no one has holiness (*sanctitas*) who has not led a life of innocence (*innocens*),' this could easily have been said by Pelagius... As both [Donatists] and Pelagius laid claim to a purity superior to their opponents."

[27] Lamberigts. "Recent Research into Pelagianism," 183.

[28] Mullin, *A Short World History of Christianity*, 75.

not be responsible for their actions.²⁹ Furthermore, this would detract from God's goodness, since God commanded people to act righteously, and He does not ask us to do the impossible.³⁰ In a letter to the virgin Demetrias, Pelagius wrote: "The best incentive for the mind consists in teaching it that it is possible to do anything which one really wants to do."³¹

Therefore, Pelagius hated any appeals to human frailty when dealing with God's commandments. As he taught to Demetrias:

> [O]n the contrary, with a proud and casual attitude of mind, in the manner of good-for-nothing and haughty servants, we cry out against the face of God and say, "It is hard, it is difficult, we cannot do it, we are but men, we are encompassed by frail flesh." What blind madness! What unholy foolhardiness! We accuse God of a twofold lack of knowledge, so that he appears not to know what he has done, and not to know what he has commanded; as if, forgetful of the human frailty

---

²⁹ Lamberigts. "Recent Research into Pelagianism," 181: "[Pelagian] considered Manichean determinism as a danger to authentic Christian ethics, which he maintained could only exist in so far as components such as freedom and responsibility were safeguarded. Precisely because of the fact that he took such freedom and responsibility seriously, Pelagius thus insisted that the human person, who had received their *posse* from God, had a *duty* to live a life without sin."

³⁰ Bray. "Augustine and the Pelagian Controversy." See Pelagius. "A letter from Pelagius": "Moreover, the Lord of Justice wished man to be free to act and not under compulsion; it was for this reason that 'he left him free to make his own decisions.'"

³¹ Pelagius. "A letter from Pelagius."

of which he is himself the author, he has imposed on man commands which we cannot bear...

The prime device of this most evil of all enemies, his most cunning stratagem, is to employ notions as a means of wearing down souls inexperienced in coping with them and to assail minds newly embarked on their chosen vocation with that feeling of depression which sometimes results from their conduct itself, so that a mind may be easily deterred from making progress with a project as it begins to realize how harsh are the first steps involved.[32]

Pelagius rejected the arguments of those who claimed they sinned because of human weakness.[33] For him, the reason why it seemed difficult to do good was because of long-standing habits of sin. "Habit is what nourishes both vices and virtues, and it is strongest in those with whom it has grown bit by bit from the start of their lives."[34] The bad old habits would attack the convert's newfound freedom of will through sloth and idleness. On the contrary, the way to oppose this inclination to evil was through moral training, applied by Pelagian as if he were training an athlete.[35]

On this basis, one can easily ascribe to Pelagius a certain tendency for pride in one's own capacities, or a downplaying of the

---

[32] Ibid.

[33] Editors of the Encyclopaedia Britannica. "Pelagianism."

[34] Pelagius. "A letter from Pelagius."

[35] See, for example, Pelagius. "A letter from Pelagius": "The first five years are the best for moral training, for there is a flexible, yielding quality in them which can easily be shaped and directed according to the wishes of the instructor."

Chapter 6: Pelagianism and Self-Sufficiency

importance of grace. However, just like the Neopelagians of today, Pelagius would reject both charges. For one thing, humility is a virtue and, therefore, something that Pelagius valued highly. As he himself taught: "Before God there is nothing more exalted than humility, and he himself speaks through the prophet: On whom shall I look, unless it be he that is humble and quiet and trembles at my word."[36] Furthermore, this humility was necessary to obtain moderation during one's moral training, so that the flesh "would be controlled but not broken," and so that the soul would not be "weighed down by the labour involved in this task. . . [so that it will not] immediately collapse under its weight."[37]

As for grace, Pelagius also spoke warmly of it.[38] Pelagius knew that temptation is too strong for mere humans to resist it without God's grace. However, his concept of grace was different from what we read in the Catechism. Pelagius believed that grace was a *power* given to us so that we can choose what is good.[39]

Pelagius has also been accused of viewing grace as a mere "external assistance, whereby the Law, the Gospels and the example of Christ were 'offered' to the human person, who was free to accept

---

[36] Ibid.

[37] Ibid.: "Therefore, let holiness be sought in moderation, and fastings, which so weaken the body, be practised in uncomplicated ways and with all humility of mind, lest they inflate the spirit and lest a matter calling for humility create pride instead and vices be born of virtue."

[38] cf. Francis. *Gaudete et Exsultate*, 49: "Those who yield to this pelagian or semi-pelagian mindset, even though they speak warmly of God's grace, "ultimately trust only in their own powers."

[39] Bray. "Augustine and the Pelagian Controversy."

their assistance or reject it without restraint or hindrance."[40] Whether this accusation holds true or not, Pelagius certainly viewed Jesus as an "example to be followed"[41] —this will be important later on.

The monk's thought system possessed many theological ramifications, namely as regards to original sin and infant baptism, eventually leading to its condemnation as heretical. For the purpose of this book, however, what interests us most—besides Pelagius's views on grace—are his ideas of sinlessness.

The Possibility of Sinlessness

Sinlessness is but a logical conclusion of Pelagius's thought. If sin is a free choice, and if humans have free will to avoid sin, then it is possible—at least theoretically—for a person to live a sinless life. Though Pelagianism, as a movement, gathered a heterogeneous group of people with diverse beliefs in many points, what seemed to tie them all together was this belief on the possibility of sinlessness.[42] For this reason, St. Jerome, one of Pelagianism's greatest adversaries, would scorn at them by derisively calling them "preachers of sinlessness."[43]

---

[40] Lamberigts. "Recent Research into Pelagianism," 177.

[41] Ibid., 152.

[42] Squires. "Reassessing Pelagianism," 5—6: the author of this article does not seem to disagree that this tenet was what united the Pelagian movement, but rather on whether this was *the* central tenet of that movement.

[43] Rackett. "What's wrong with Pelagianism?" 223.

Chapter 6: Pelagianism and Self-Sufficiency

There was an obvious fault with this line of reasoning: even if sinlessness was possible in theory, in practice, there seemed to be no record of any sinless person besides Jesus Christ.[44] But the Pelagians were unfazed by this objection. As Dr. Gerald Bray, Professor for Beeson Divinity School in Birmingham, says: "Jesus was the exception that proved the rule. He had kept the law perfectly and was therefore sinless. The fact that He achieved this shows that it is possible, and it makes those who fail to live up to the standard guilty of their sin."[45]

Pelagius also tried to claim that some other biblical figures had been sinless, like Job or St. Elizabeth.[46] The Catholic authors who set out to refute him would take him to task on this, leaving only the case of the Virgin Mary as open for debate—or without daring to address this particular case at all.[47] So, for the rest of this chapter, any argument against the possibility of a sinless life should not be construed as including the dogma of the Immaculate Conception[48] since, as the Council of Trent admits, that was "a special privilege from God."[49]

---

[44] Ibid., 229: "Finally, Jerome... chided the Pelagians for their inability to produce any examples of sinless people."

[45] Bray. "Augustine and the Pelagian Controversy."

[46] Squires. "Reassessing Pelagianism," 37.

[47] Ibid., 36 (for St. Augustine) and 91 (for St. Jerome).

[48] It is good to remember that the aforementioned canon of the Council of Trent that anathematizes the belief of the possibility of a sinless life, makes the following exception: "... except by a special privilege from God, as the Church holds in regard of the Blessed Virgin" See Trent, 6th Session, c. XXIII.

[49] Trent, 6th Session, c. XXIII.

Besides Pelagius, the greatest expounder of his philosophy was Caelestius, a eunuch and noble lawyer, whom the British monk befriended during his stay in Rome. Though St. Augustine admitted that Pelagius was a "saintly man," he called Caelestius "incredibly loquacious."[50] Attracted to the ascetic life of Pelagius's teachings, Caelestius would boast of "doing more than what is prescribed in the law and the gospel."[51] He also boldly asserted that "human beings cannot be called sons of God unless in every manner they have come to be without sin."[52] Caelestius then endeavored to propose an intellectual framework proving the possibility of a sinless life almost syllogistically. His propositions were as follows:

1) "If sin cannot be avoided, it is not sin; if it can be avoided, one can live without sin."
2) "If sin is an essential part of human nature, it ceases to be sin; if an accidental part, it can be avoided."
3) "The injunction to live without sin implies its possibility."
4) "Each of us can be without sin, though we are not. But if we examine why, we freely admit that the fault is ours."[53]

Among the Catholic writers who sought to refute this Pelagian framework, two giants stand out: St. Augustine (whom we have followed in the previous chapter already) and St. Jerome. While Augustine preferred to disprove Pelagianism on the grounds of grace

---

[50] Pohle. "Pelagius and Pelagianism."
[51] Squires. "Reassessing Pelagianism," 150.
[52] Rackett. "What's wrong with Pelagianism?" 226.
[53] Ibid.

Chapter 6: Pelagianism and Self-Sufficiency

and original sin, it was Jerome who most systematically dismantled Pelagius's concept of sinlessness.[54]

For Jerome, the theory of sinlessness was blasphemous, as it implied equality between God and Man,[55] since Man could achieve this sinless state without any further help from God.[56] Whereas Pelagius wished to create a Church "without spot or wrinkle,"[57] Jerome affirmed such a state to be only attainable in heaven: before that, every human perfection was relative.[58]

The Father of the Church would acquiesce that humans could potentially achieve perfection in the exercise of *one or two* virtues, but not for the *totality* of human action (except, of course, in the case of Jesus.)[59] Furthermore, Jerome acknowledged that people can indeed avoid sin altogether, but only for *a short period of time*. Just like a person can fast, walk, or sleep for a short while, but not perpetually, so humans cannot be sinless but momentarily. Perpetual sinlessness was reserved for God alone,[60] and this was a wide chasm separating God from Man.

Jerome also tried undermining Pelagianism by tying it to all sorts of heresies. For the purpose of this book, it is particularly important to note how Jerome linked Pelagius's idea of potential sinlessness

---

[54] Squires. "Jerome on sinlessness," 697, 701.
[55] Ibid., 701.
[56] Squires. "Reassessing Pelagianism," 159-60.
[57] Ibid., 117.
[58] Rackett. "What's wrong with Pelagianism?" 230.
[59] Squires. "Jerome on sinlessness," 701.
[60] Ibid., 702.

with the Stoic concept of *apatheia* ("passionlessness").[61] Scholars today argue whether this comparison is accurate or fair.[62] But either way, the fact that such a luminary of orthodox Catholic thought as Jerome rejected Stoic rigidity must be analyzed in its own right, if we are to gauge how faithfulness does not necessarily entail rigidity.

Stoicism was a philosophical system, started in Greece at around 322 BC. Later, it became fashionable among the Roman Empire's elites. As a school of thought, it rivalled with the Aristotelians who, as we have seen in chapter 1, would be integrated into Catholic theology by St. Thomas Aquinas during the Middle Ages. Let us leave Jerome for a bit and briefly lean on Aquinas to understand how a

---

[61] Rackett. "What's wrong with Pelagianism?" 229—230. See also Squires. "Reassessing Pelagianism," 105.

[62] For a succinct summary of the diversity of views on this matter, see Squires "Reassessing Pelagianism," 106. The author eventually agrees that, though Pelagius's views might not be outright Stoic, they were certainly influenced by Stoicism. See Squires "Reassessing Pelagianism," 107—108: "While it is outside the scope of this dissertation to offer a detailed analysis of the relationship between Pelagius and the Stoics, I would argue that he was, in fact, influenced by them. One does not read in Pelagius any direct quotation from them, but Jerome correctly detects some similar foundational assumptions. Pelagius most likely had stewed in the Stoic *milieu* during the years he was among the Roman elite before. Stoicism had been popular in Rome before Constantine and many of the first Christians after Constantine, especially ascetics engaged in the life of *otium*, had been influenced by it. Staniforth has said that Stoicism was 'a code which was manly, rational, and temperate, a code which insisted on just and virtuous dealing, self-discipline, unflinching fortitude, and complete freedom from the storms of passion [that] was admirably suited to the Roman character.' Such a statement could have been made about Pelagius' thought."

more developed Catholicism came to reject Stoicism, so that we will appreciate Jerome's reaction better.

As far as acts are concerned, Aristotle subdivided them into two categories: 1) human acts and 2) acts of Man. Human acts are voluntary, proceeding directly from the will. The will, in its turn, choses the best course of action after reason deliberately apprehends the end of the action.[63] On the contrary, the acts of Man are conditioned by external factors, thereby reducing the voluntariness of the act.[64] These are also termed *passions*, meaning motions of the sensitive appetites, so that a person tends towards attaining some good or avoiding some evil[65] (here not considered necessarily as a *moral* good or evil, but as a *practical* good or evil). Passions, therefore, are *inclinations* and are not completely voluntary, as they depend on the senses and not on the will.

The Stoics and the Aristotelians disagreed on this matter since the Stoics did not make a distinction between intellectual and sensitive appetites. In other words, they did not discriminate between the passion of the soul (sensitive appetite) and the movements of the will (intellectual appetite). For the Stoics, passions are "diseases of the soul."[66] Since, for the Stoic, every passion of the soul is evil, then the moral goodness of an act was necessarily diminished by the

---

[63] Ming. "Human acts." See also Aquinas. *Summa Theologiae*, I-II, q. 6, a. 1.

[64] Ming. "Human acts."

[65] Devine. "Passions." See also Aquinas. *Summa Theologiae*, I-II, q. 22, a. 3.

[66] Aquinas. *Summa Theologiae*, I-II, q. 24, a. 2, co.

passions.[67] Therefore, the Stoics would try to attain a state of passionlessness, or *apatheia*.

Not so for the Aristotelians—and therefore, for Catholics imbibed with Thomistic theology. Passions are not necessarily evil, rather they are motions of the sensitive appetite. They belong to human nature since the senses are also a part of the person. What makes passions good or evil is whether they are ordered towards reason or not.[68] If passions are contrary to the order of reason, they incline us to sin. However, if passions are controlled by reason, they incline us to virtue.[69]

Since the good of a human being is to be found in reason, then a person is the more perfect, the more he or she is ordered towards reason. This means that it is more perfect for a person to order his or her passions to reason, than to extirpate passions altogether.[70] It is folly and unnatural to attain a state of pure passionlessness. According to Catholic theology, it is much better to order our passions to reason through virtuous habits, so that we may become more naturally inclined to do good.

---

[67] Ibid., I-II, q. 24, a. 3, co. This is not completely accurate, since the Stoics did believe that there were some "good" passions, the eupathic passions. See Gleason. "Review of Stoicism and Emotion": "The Stoic sage is not without feeling. He does make a sharp distinction between ordinary affective responses, directed at externals, and eupathic responses. . . The normative wise man, of course, has no defects of character, but Garber makes an appealing case for his genuinely eupathic forms of emotion: a yearning for what is good, manifested in friendship or (even) erotic love."

[68] Ibid., I-II, q. 24, a. 2, co.

[69] Ibid., I-II, q. 24, a. 2, ad 3.

[70] Ibid., I-II, q. 24, a. 3 co.

Instilling virtuous habits does indeed require us to exercise good moral training, so that we may gradually grow in virtue. But this framework also allows for human frailty, since not all acts are completely voluntary. It is a better explanation for the reality we live in and eschews excessive moral rigidity as the one the Stoics allegedly defended.

Returning to Jerome, we can now appreciate why he felt he was significantly undercutting Pelagianism by asserting its influence by Stoicism. For the Stoics, the individual must remove his passions through either practicing or meditating on virtue. But for Jerome, attaining this goal would turn the person into "either a stone or a god."[71] Pelagius and his followers were overestimating the power of free will,[72] and at the same time underestimating the influence of the flesh on the soul. Though Pelagius certainly acknowledged this influence of the flesh, he also believed that the flesh could be conquered through sheer determination of the will.[73] For Jerome, free will was indeed preserved, but "according to the *circumstances, time, and state of human frailty*."[74]

Redefining grace

In 411 AD, Pelagius and Caelestius traveled to North Africa. They docked near Hippo, St. Augustine's diocese. The good bishop was absent at the time, busy with the Donatists elsewhere in Africa

---

[71] Squires. "Jerome on sinlessness," 700.
[72] Rackett. "What's wrong with Pelagianism?" 230.
[73] Squires. "Reassessing Pelagianism," 160.
[74] Squires. "Jerome on sinlessness," 702.

(see chapter 5). Pelagius moved on to Palestine, but Caelestius stayed in Carthage, where he asked to be ordained a priest.[75] This brought his writings and teachings into greater scrutiny. Caelestius had opposed the doctrine of original sin as this was the only way to reconcile Christianity with his Pelagian tenets.[76] A deacon submitted to his bishop a letter containing six theses of Caelestius that should be deemed heretical. A synod was convened at Carthage to examine the whole matter. Caelestius refused to recant any of the six theses, alleging that original sin was still an open question and hence its denial was no heresy. The synod at Carthage, however, excluded Caelestius from ordination and condemned the six theses as heretical.[77] Pelagius defended himself by distancing from his pupil, saying that he did not subscribe to the six heresies.[78]

Though most of these six theses dealt with Adam, one of them (the sixth) did pertain to the typical Pelagian idea of possible sinlessness.[79] This statement, condemned as heretical at Carthage, stated: "even before the advent of Christ there were men who were without sin."[80]

At first, Augustine was wary of censuring the possibility of sinlessness. The bishop cautioned that those "who say that human beings are able to be without sin in this life must not be immediately opposed with incautious rashness," lest we challenge human free

---

[75] Pohle. "Pelagius and Pelagianism."
[76] Rackett. "What's wrong with Pelagianism?" 225.
[77] Pohle. "Pelagius and Pelagianism."
[78] Squires. "Reassessing Pelagianism," 150.
[79] Ibid.
[80] Pohle. "Pelagius and Pelagianism."

Chapter 6: Pelagianism and Self-Sufficiency 199

will or divine mercy.[81] At this point, Augustine did believe it was theoretically possible for a human being to live a sinless life, though in practice only Jesus had achieved this. For him, the theoretical possibility of sinlessness was neither erroneous nor dangerous, as long as no one would claim that *they* were sinless, for such would boost their pride.[82]

However, as Pelagian ideas kept spreading through North Africa, Augustine understood he had to step in. Though he was willing to grant the point of theoretical sinlessness, Pelagius's view on grace was universes away from Augustine's perception. Therefore, the bishop of Hippo sought to refute Pelagianism, not on the basis of sinlessness, but of grace.[83]

To be fair, St. Jerome *also* disputed Pelagianism on grace. Jerome acknowledged that Pelagius did indeed recognize the importance of grace: the problem was that Pelagius had redefined the meaning of grace in a narrower sense. Pelagius had defined grace as the commandments of God, free will, and creation.[84] Those were all free gifts from God, which allowed everyone to live a sinless life if they so

---

[81] Rackett. "What's wrong with Pelagianism?" 231.
[82] Ibid., 232.
[83] Ibid.
[84] Squires. "Reassessing Pelagianism," 157. See also Rackett. "What's wrong with Pelagianism?" 229. See also Ogliari. *Gratia et Certamen*, 236: "[W]e perceive again Pelagius' understanding of grace as being primarily a 'fundamental' grace inherent in human nature and not extrinsically added to it. Bestowed by God through the creation of man, this grace is an integral part of the latter's nature, and as such it cannot be thought to affect, from without, the autonomous exercise of human free will."

chose. But Jerome correctly noted that God's grace is needed in every single moment for every single act.

Augustine saw other ways in which Pelagius had redefined grace. Whereas for Augustine, Adam's sin had been passed on to the rest of humankind by way of *propagation,* for Pelagius this happened through *imitation.*[85] Furthermore, whereas Pelagius viewed grace as a power given to us so we can choose what is good, Augustine saw it as something we need to deliver us from a spiritual condition we can do nothing about.[86] Pelagius's most "fatal error" was, for Augustine, that he asserted that one can live without sin *while also without divine grace, properly understood.*[87]

In the meantime, Pelagius had stayed in Palestine, protected under the wing of the bishop of Jerusalem, who "dearly loved" his guest. The bishop had tried to exonerate Pelagius in a local council, but since the controversy would not die out, a new synod was convoked in Diospolis (modern-day Israel).[88]

During the Synod of Diospolis, Pelagius rejected some of the more controversial statements from his disciples, including Caelestius. Pelagius's most important objective was to salvage his favorite tenet: the possibility of sinlessness. To appease the council, the monk agreed to deny that anyone had lived a sinless life, as long as he could continue to maintain its theoretical possibility on these terms: human beings "are able to be without sin by their own labor

---

[85] Squires. "Jerome on sinlessness," 704.
[86] Bray. "Augustine and the Pelagian Controversy."
[87] Rackett. "What's wrong with Pelagianism?" 233.
[88] Pohle. "Pelagius and Pelagianism."

Chapter 6: Pelagianism and Self-Sufficiency

and God's grace."[89] This, however, was duplicitous: when Pelagius said "God's grace," what he meant was "God's creation."[90] This ruse was enough to deceive the synod and grant him acquittal of all charges.

This created a major problem for Augustine, since a group of bishops had just proclaimed Pelagius to be orthodox. How could he now extirpate Pelagius's wicked teachings from his flock? It was precisely at this time that Augustine understood that the hypothesis of theoretical sinlessness could not be sustained, if the good bishop wanted to salvage a proper understanding of God's grace.[91]

Soon, Augustine found out about Pelagius's deception. In a letter, the monk had written about how the bishops at Diospolis had approved his statement that "human beings are able to be without sin and *easily* to keep the commandments of God, if they wish." Augustine noted that the word "easily" did not figure in Pelagius's actual testimony during the synod. Also, there was no longer any reference to grace in that statement. Augustine alleged then that, through this assertion, Pelagius was still affirming that people can become sinless without any intervention from divine grace.[92] In other words, Pelagius had spoken "warmly of God's grace" in the synod, but "ultimately, trusted only in his own powers."[93]

---

[89] Rackett. "What's wrong with Pelagianism?" 233.

[90] Pohle. "Pelagius and Pelagianism."

[91] Squires. "Reassessing Pelagianism," 43—44. To see a summary of how much Augustine's position on theoretical sinlessness changed over the years, see Squires. "Reassessing Pelagianism," 28—29, 32.

[92] Rackett. "What's wrong with Pelagianism?" 232. See also Squires. "Reassessing Pelagianism," 42—43.

[93] Francis. *Gaudete et Exsultate*, 49.

Augustine and the Northern African bishops gathered together in a synod to condemn Pelagius and then appealed to the Roman See. Starting from the principle that the resolutions of provincial synods have no binding force until they are confirmed by the supreme authority of the Apostolic See, the pope developed the Catholic teaching on original sin and grace. Pursuant to a papal decree, another council was held in Carthage in 418, in the presence of 200 African bishops.[94]

This Council of Carthage issued 8 (or 9, according to the source) canons, later confirmed by the pope, thus becoming articles of faith.[95] Among these canons, the one dealing a death blow to Pelagius's concept of sinlessness was: "Without God's grace it is not merely more *difficult*, but absolutely *impossible* to perform good works."[96]

The canons of the Council of Carthage also exposed Pelagius's false humility. Catholic authors had argued that Pelagianism would inevitably lead to pride, but Pelagius countered by saying that humility was a virtue to be held in the highest regard. However, this was a false humility: the individual might, for example, pray "forgive us our trespasses" during the Our Father, not because he or she might have any trespasses to be forgiven, but out of a forced humility with no connection with reality. To address this, the Council of Carthage issued the following canons:

---

[94] Pohle. "Pelagius and Pelagianism."
[95] Ibid.
[96] Ibid. See also Squires. "Reassessing Pelagianism," 45.

Chapter 6: Pelagianism and Self-Sufficiency

1. Not out of humility, but in truth must we confess ourselves to be sinners.
2. The saints refer the petition of the Our Father, "Forgive us our trespasses", not only to others, but also to themselves.
3. The saints pronounce the same supplication not from mere humility, but from truthfulness.[97]

The implications of these canons were obviously anti-Pelagian: it was impossible to be sinless, even for those considered "holy persons."[98] Pelagius was exiled from Jerusalem and settled in Egypt, where he would later die. Caelestius sought refuge with bishop Nestorius of Constantinople, who would also become a heretic, albeit of a different kind. A few decades later, Pelagianism would be definitely condemned as a heresy (alongside Donatism) at the ecumenical Council of Ephesus in 431 AD.[99] As the *Catholic Encyclopedia* affirms, Pelagius's gravest error was that he "did not submit to the doctrinal decisions of the Church."[100]

The victorious law of love

While triumphant over Pelagianism, Augustine's views on grace were not easy to accept. Augustine's pessimism about human nature and the central role ascribed to grace as always taking initiative over

---

[97] Pohle. "Pelagius and Pelagianism." See also Squires. "Reassessing Pelagianism," 45.
[98] Squires. "Reassessing Pelagianism," 45.
[99] Pohle. "Pelagius and Pelagianism."
[100] Ibid.

Man's will, was too much for many to accept. For this reason, some thinkers tried to find a "middle way" between Pelagius's heresy and Augustine's uncanny opinions.

An older Augustine would call these thinkers "relics of the Pelagians." In more modern times, the term "Semipelagians" was adopted, since these views were clearly not Augustinian, but "half Pelagian." However, most scholars nowadays dislike this term, since it was produced in connection with later debates on grace during the 16th century (see chapter 8). It is, therefore, an ideologically loaded expression. Currently, scholars prefer the designation Massilians, as these thinkers were known in their time, since many of them were monks from Marseilles.[101]

The Massilians tried to find a balanced perspective. On the one hand, they accepted the decisions of the Council of Carthage, duly ratified by the pope. On the other hand, they tried to preserve the concept of human free will by allowing Man to *initiate* the process of conversion (the *initium fidei*).[102] Its major tenets were, as listed by the *Catholic Encyclopedia*:

1. In distinguishing between the beginning of faith (*initium fidei*) and the increase of faith (*augmentum fidei*), one may refer the former to the power of the free will, while the faith itself and its increase is absolutely dependent upon God;
2. The gratuity of grace is to be maintained against Pelagius in so far as every strictly natural merit is excluded; this,

---

[101] Pohle. "Semipelagianism."
[102] Ogliari. *Gratia et Certamen*, 295.

Chapter 6: Pelagianism and Self-Sufficiency

however, does not prevent nature and its works from having a certain claim to grace;

3. As regards final perseverance in particular, it must not be regarded as a special gift of grace, since the justified man may of his own strength persevere to the end.[103]

Among the Massilians monks, the most highly regarded—even today—was John Cassian, "a celebrated and holy man."[104] Certainly, Cassian had Semipelagian tendencies, namely 1) his optimistic view of human nature; 2) a certain Stoic conviction that vice is not intrinsic to Man and can, therefore, be effectively extirpated;[105] and also 3) the notion that a person can "start" the process of conversion (*initium fidei*), through a desire for a new life, repentance of the previous one, and hope for salvation.[106]

However, since he was only "half" Pelagian, Cassian also had some points of contact with Augustinian philosophy, namely vis-à-vis grace. It is instructive to explore these points of contact, since Massilianism was an attempt to find middle ground between Pelagianism and Augustinianism. Consequently, Massilianism highlights the errors of Pelagianism wherever it departs from Pelagian doctrine.

Though he shared the optimism of Pelagianism and Stoicism, Cassian also understood that Man cannot accomplish any good

---

[103] Pohle. "Semipelagianism."
[104] Ogliari. *Gratia et Certamen*, 278-82, 288, 291.
[105] Ibid., 282.
[106] Ibid., 296.

work or save himself by his own efforts alone.[107] For Cassian, complete freedom of will could only be achieved through a complete submission to God's will: "He who becomes truly free, becomes prisoner of the Lord."[108]

Cassian also distanced himself from Pelagius on the issue of possible sinlessness. Perfectly mirroring the rhetoric of Augustine and Jerome, Cassian claimed that one could only avoid sin for a short time, not perpetually: "Can I fast, watch, walk, sing, sit, sleep perpetually?"[109] However, Cassian added an interesting twist to the ongoing debate on sinlessness. As an ascetic monk, Cassian took the concept of sinlessness to another level. For Cassian, *perfect virtue was defined as continuous and undistracted contemplation of God*. Even the most fleeting break from this contemplation would be a grave offense against God. Not even the most virtuous of monks could sustain such perfection continuously, for eventually the needs of the flesh would lead the mind to lose focus. In this sense, no one could be sinless, for no one could remain forever vigilant in prayer. One may be holy (*sanctus*), but not immaculate (*immaculatus*).[110]

Furthermore, Cassian showed how Pelagius's teachings effectively undermined Christ's salvific nature. Pelagius believed that Jesus had saved humankind yes, but by being an example we should emulate. But Cassian knew this to be a dangerous teaching with profound Christological implications: just like the heretical Nestorius had posited that there were, in effect, two Christs (one the same

---

[107] Ibid., 280.
[108] Ibid., 298.
[109] Squires. "Reassessing Pelagianism," 70.
[110] Ibid., 65-7, 84.

Chapter 6: Pelagianism and Self-Sufficiency

Person as He Who is God, another who was born of the Virgin Mary), likewise Pelagius had insisted on the existence of two Christs (one teacher and the other redeemer.) To say that Christ is simply an example is to call into question Christ's role as mediator between God and humanity.[111]

However, as correct as Cassian was in all these points, Augustine also tackled Massilian theology in his later writings. For Augustine it is vital that grace be, as the name implies, "gratuitous." In other words, grace must precede any good work on Man's part, even the initiative of faith: the *desire* to will and do good comes from God, not from Man.[112] After the Fall, free will is too corrupted and weakened to be able to do good on its own—though of course, free will is not completely annulled.[113]

But how to reconcile this with the existence of human free will? For Augustine, free will was the more perfect, the more God had restored it to its original goodness. In this sense, grace does not extinguish free will, but rather strengthens and perfects it.[114] Left to their own devices, humans would always reject grace, because original sin inclines them too much towards evil.[115] There is, therefore, an Augustinian distinction between "free will" and "freedom." Free will is the capacity to choose, either good or evil. Free will may choose good if it relies on grace but can only choose evil when it relies on itself. In other words, without grace, human "freedom" is merely the

---

[111] Ibid., 152—153.
[112] Ogliari. *Gratia et Certamen*, 256.
[113] Ibid., 258.
[114] Ibid., 258.
[115] Ibid., 245.

freedom to sin. Man is said to be *liber* ("free") but not *liberatus* ("freed").[116] As Donato Ogliari, current abbot of St. Paul Outside the Walls, writes in his book on the subject *Gratia et Certamen* ("Grace and Struggle"):

> This, however, does not imply the annihilation of human freedom, and it is precisely with the aim of doing away with such an objection that Augustine eventually comes to the formulation of grace acting irresistibly (*indeclinabiliter et insuperabiliter*), through the will of man. The context of such a formulation is the presupposition that man's will is attracted by what gives pleasure and that it loves that which gives delight. The acting grace adapts itself to such spontaneous and natural movement of the will, and it does it gradually, taking as it were the will by the hand. . . The love for the good (*inspiratio caritatis*) is so deeply instilled by the Holy Spirit in the hearts of man, that the will lets itself be guided by him, and while it experiences delight, it is inclined steadily and infallibly towards God. Augustine tries to show that grace can cause the will to act irresistibly and infallibly without being constrained to do so.[117]

In other words, since the will chooses what gives delight, and since the unjustified Man delights on evil, then God's grace must possess a "conquering delight of the will." Through grace, Man ceases to delight on evil and starts delighting on good, so that Man

---

[116] Ibid., 248.
[117] Ibid., 245-6.

Chapter 6: Pelagianism and Self-Sufficiency

starts desiring and loving God's commandments. In this sense, free will is not constrained, since it still freely chooses according to its pleasure/delight, but God's initiative is also safeguarded, since His grace grounds the decision of the will by changing its innermost inclinations[118] (see also chapter 3 on following moral directives out of virtue versus out of a sense of duty).

To summarize, according to Augustine, God's grace acts through love/delight. "The law of love is the law of liberty."[119] This is the proper understanding of Augustine's famous maxim: "love and do what you will."[120] It is interesting how Pope Francis ends his *Gaudete et Exsultate* section on "Contemporary Pelagianism" by explaining how love is the summation of the law:

> To avoid this, we do well to keep reminding ourselves that there is a hierarchy of virtues that bids us seek what is essential. The primacy belongs to the theological virtues, which have God as their object and motive. *At the centre is charity.* Saint Paul says that what truly counts is "faith working through love" (Gal 5:6). We are called to make every effort to preserve charity: "The one who loves another has fulfilled the law... for love is the fulfilment of the law" (Rom 13:8.10). "For the whole law is summed up in a single commandment, 'You shall love your neighbour as yourself'" (Gal 5:14).
>
> In other words, amid the thicket of precepts and prescriptions, Jesus clears a way to seeing two faces, that of the

---

[118] Ibid., 246-7.
[119] Ibid.
[120] Augustine. "Homily 7."

Father and that of our brother. He does not give us two more formulas or two more commands. He gives us two faces, or better yet, one alone: the face of God reflected in so many other faces. For in every one of our brothers and sisters, especially the least, the most vulnerable, the defenceless and those in need, God's very image is found. Indeed, with the scraps of this frail humanity, the Lord will shape his final work of art. For "what endures, what has value in life, what riches do not disappear? Surely these two: the Lord and our neighbour. These two riches do not disappear!"[121]

Grace works through love, and love connects us both with God and with our neighbor, in whom we can meet God Himself. But this neighbor reflects, not only the face of God, but the frailty of humanity. Elsewhere, Pope Francis instructs us that God is a "patient and merciful artisan," by quoting St. Paul's famous passage about humankind carrying "this treasure in earthen vessels, that the excellence of the power may be of God and not of us" (2 Cor 4:7).[122]

But for God to show His artisanship and His power, we must allow ourselves to be moulded by Him. For this to happen, we must "detach ourselves from our comfortable habits, from the rigidity of our mindsets and the presumption that we have already arrived, and have the courage of placing ourselves in the Lord's presence, that He can resume His work on us, form us, and transform us."[123] Francis

---

[121] Francis. *Gaudete et Exsultate*, 60—61.

[122] Francis. "Address to Participants in the International Congress of the Congregation for the Clergy."

[123] Ibid.

invites us to convert, by reminding us of the etymology of the word "convert": "*metanoeín*" in Greek, from "*metá*" (meaning "beyond") and *noéin* ("to think"). In other words, to convert is to "think beyond": "to go beyond our usual ways of thinking, beyond our habitual worldview. All those ways of thinking that reduce everything to ourselves, to our belief in our own self-sufficiency. Or those self-centred ways of thinking marked by rigidity and paralyzing fear, by the temptation to say 'we have always done it this way, why change?'"[124]

Certainly, "there are commandments, and we must follow the commandments." But "attachment to the law ignores the Holy Spirit" because following the commandments must always be done from "the view of the grace of this great gift, which has been given to us by the Father. Only in this way can we truly understand the law, without reducing the Spirit and the Son to the Law."[125]

Pope Francis's theology here is profoundly Augustinian, and for a good reason. In the end, Augustinianism became *the* Catholic teaching on grace. For a century, both Augustinians and Massilians were allowed to confront themselves without any formal condemnation of any party.[126] But in 529 AD, the Second Synod of Orange (cited by Pope Francis in *Gaudete et Exsultate*)[127] condemned the three main Semipelagian tenets mentioned in the beginning of this section. This synod dogmatically defined the entire powerlessness of nature for good, the absolute necessity of prevenient grace for good acts (especially for the beginning of faith), and the absolute gratuity

---

[124] Francis. Homily of in the "Megaron Concert Hall."
[125] Francis, "Half a life."
[126] Ogliari. *Gratia et Certamen*, 432.
[127] Francis. *Gaudete et Exsultate*, 53.

of the first grace and of final perseverance.[128] These canons would be solemnly ratified by the pope, thereby enshrining Augustine's views of grace as Catholic teaching. The last "relics of Pelagius" had been banished from Catholic orthodoxy, though they would always remain as a temptation for faithful Catholics to this very day.

---

[128] Pohle. "Semipelagianism." See also Ogliari. *Gratia et Certamen*, 435-6.

Chapter 7

Medieval Heresies and Spiritual Worldliness

[T]he path of prayer, is open to all those who humbly open themselves to the action of the Spirit in their lives, and the sign that we are advancing on this path is to be ever more humble, more attentive to the needs of our brothers and sisters, better children of the holy People of God. Such a path is not open to those who consider themselves to be pure and perfect, the Cathars of all the centuries, but to those who, aware of their sins, discover the beauty of the mercy of God who welcomes and redeems everyone, and invites everyone to friendship.

—Francis, Video-message to the International Congress "Mujer Exceptional"

One of the greatest ills undermining the Church's credibility today is corruption. Whether it be financial or sexual, these scandals gravely besmirch the Church's name and therefore, its ability to convincingly evangelize the world at large. This is why Pope Francis has continuously stressed—echoing his predecessor Benedict XVI—how important it is that the Church grows "through attraction, not proselytism."[1] Preaching without giving an example will not convince anyone on this day and age.

---

[1] See, for example, Francis. "General Audience," January 11, 2023: "It is a vital dimension for the Church: the community of Jesus' disciples was

Pope Francis has dedicated a significant part of his pontificate to implementing policies geared towards curtailing corruption within the Church[2]—a corruption he calls "the Devil's dung."[3] Certainly, there is still much work to be done in that area, and concerns about corruption within the Church should not be downplayed or explained away. However, it is important to note a disturbing trend among some of the pope's critics: they weaponize a righteous disgust for corruption to achieve their own predetermined ends. For them, "corruption" is a fruit of worldliness within the Church, and they think they were tasked with doing away with worldliness, on their own terms.

Let us not mince words: corruption *is* a fruit of worldliness within the Church. The problem here is that, for these critics, the fight against worldliness and corruption cannot be disassociated from their *a priori* projects in the areas of liturgy and doctrine.[4] The answers to the scourge are already predefined: they are what these

---

in fact born apostolic, born missionary, not proselytizing. And from the start, we had to make this distinction: being missionary, being apostolic, evangelizing, is not the same as proselytizing. They have nothing to do with one another... or as Pope Benedict taught us, 'The Church does not engage in proselytism. Instead, she grows by attraction'. Do not forget this: when you see Christians proselytizing, making a list of people to come... these are not Christians; they are pagans disguised as Christians, but the heart is pagan. The Church grows not by proselytism, it grows by attraction."

[2] See, for example, Muhammad. "Pope Francis issues orders." See also Francis. *Vos Estis*.

[3] Ljubas. "Pope Francis: Corruption is an Ancient Evil, Devil's Dung."

[4] See, for example, Schaetzel. "How to Deal with Corruption in the Catholic Church." See also Reno. "Faith Amid Corruption."

Chapter 7: Medieval Heresies and Spiritual Worldliness

critics already wished to implement in the Church beforehand, whether there was corruption or not. So, there is a danger here of applying ineffective measures because the focus is not on the main anti-corruption goal, but on something else that must be done no matter what. This is also a kind of rigidity.

Once again employing one of his neologisms, Pope Francis calls this error "habriaqueísmo,"[5] from the Spanish "habria que" ("what should be done.") For the Holy Father, this is *also* a form of worldliness. In fact, Francis introduces this new word in his programmatic apostolic exhortation *Evangelii Gaudium*, in a section dealing with what he calls "spiritual worldliness."[6]

Spiritual worldliness "reduces spirituality to an appearance: it leads us to be 'traders of the spirit,' men clothed in sacred forms that in reality continue to think and act according to the fashions of the world. This happens when we allow ourselves to be fascinated by the seductions of the ephemeral, by mediocrity and habit, by the temptations of power and social influence... by vainglory and narcissism, by doctrinal intransigence and liturgical aestheticism."[7] Spiritual worldliness manifests itself in many ways: "an ostentatious preoccupation for the liturgy, for doctrine and for the Church's prestige... a fascination with social and political gain, or pride in their ability to manage practical affairs... a concern to be seen, into a social life full of appearances, meetings, dinners and receptions... a business mentality, caught up with management, statistics, plans and evaluations

---

[5] Francis, *Evangelii Gaudium*, 96.

[6] That section extends throughout paragraphs 93-7 of *Evangelii Gaudium*.

[7] Francis. "Letter to the Priests of the Diocese of Rome."

whose principal beneficiary is not God's people but the Church as an institution."[8] In summary, a worldly Church with superficial spiritual and pastoral trappings.[9]

Though it does not seek the Lord's glory, but rather human glory and personal well-being, spiritual worldliness hides behind the appearance of piety and even love for the Church. Since it is based on appearances, it is not always linked to outward sin: from without, everything appears just fine.[10] It is a "gentle temptation" by "elegant demons," hiding "behind good appearances, even within religious motivations."[11] For this reason, it is particularly insidious: if it were "to invade the Church and work to corrupt it by undermining its very principle, it would be infinitely more disastrous than any simply moral worldliness."[12] *"This is a tremendous corruption disguised as a good."*[13]

According to Pope Francis, rigidity and spiritual worldliness are "stepsisters," one inviting the other.[14] This is because spiritual worldliness can be fueled by two deeply interrelated errors, which (as we are seeing throughout this book) are also connected with rigidity. One is Neopelagianism, which we have explored in the last

---

[8] Francis, *Evangelii Gaudium*, 95.

[9] Ibid., 97.

[10] Ibid., 93. In this sense, Pope Francis compares this spiritual worldliness to the hypocrisy of the Pharisees. Looking for personal glory under the guise of searching for God's glory does indeed look like the "double life" we have explored in chapter 3.

[11] Francis. "Letter to the Priests of the Diocese of Rome."

[12] Ibid.

[13] Francis, *Evangelii Gaudium*, 97.

[14] Francis. Address to the Apostolic Union of the Clergy.

chapter. The other is Neognosticism, a "purely subjective faith whose only interest is a certain experience or a set of ideas and bits of information which are meant to console and enlighten, but which ultimately keep one imprisoned in his or her own thoughts and feelings."[15] In this sense, it is important to note how Pope Francis often reminds us to not turn the faith into an ideology.

"If forms and methods become ends in themselves, they become ideological, removed from reality which is constantly developing; closed to the newness of the Spirit, such rigid forms and methods will eventually stifle the very charism which gave them life."[16] Ideologies of any sort are always rigid.[17] They take God's gift, which is always free, and then "turn it into their property... caged in a doctrine of laws... [T]he covenant comes to be interpreted according to '*my*' opinion, becoming an ideology."[18]

Though the critics of the pope may not see themselves in these words—they would argue they believe in an objective, not subjective doctrine or morality—the truth is that theirs is still a subjective faith reducible to their opinion, since it breaks communion with the Church as a whole, which must be under the pope, the guarantor of unity.[19] The Holy Father reminds us how the "saints we

---

[15] Francis, *Evangelii Gaudium*, 93. See His Holiness's description of this Neognosticism in Francis. *Gaudete et Exsultate*, 36—46.

[16] Francis. "Address to the Third World Congress of Ecclesial Movements."

[17] Francis. "Disciples of the Lord and not of ideology."

[18] Francis. "Let us not forget the gratuitousness."

[19] John Paul II. *Ut Unum Sint*, 88.

commemorate today were pillars of communion."[20] We "are not soloists in search of an audience, but brothers arranged as a choir." Unfortunately, some Catholics have the pretense of "taking over the space of the Church"[21]: "content to have a modicum of power," they "would rather be generals of a defeated army than a mere private in a unit which continues to fight. How often we dream up vast apostolic projects, meticulously planned, just like defeated generals."[22]

But, as the Pope says, this is "not a new illness. The Apostle John speaks of Christians who lose their faith and prefer ideologies in his First Letter."[23] We can also find vestiges of this illness across Church history. In this chapter, I would like to focus on the Middle Ages and on the profusion of heresies at this time, thriving on spiritual worldliness and Church corruption.

The Cathars

Catharism was the most widespread heresy of the Middle Ages.[24] We have already seen the word "Cathar" pop up in this book: the Novatianists called themselves *Katharoi*—meaning the "Pure" (see chapter 5). The Greek word *Katharos* was also used for the Manichaeans, the spiritual predecessors of the medieval Cathars.[25]

---

[20] Francis. Homily on the 400th Anniversary of the Canonization of St. Ignatius of Loyola.

[21] Francis, *Evangelii Gaudium*, 95.

[22] Ibid., 96.

[23] Francis. "Disciples of the Lord and not of ideology."

[24] England. "The Reformers and the Heretics," 3.

[25] Weber. "Cathari." It is interesting to note that some authors believe that "Cathar" might not derive from the Greek "Katharos," but from the

However, when referring to heretics of the Middle Ages, the word "Cathar" seems to be an exonym. They never referred to themselves like that. Rather, they called themselves "the Church of Christ,"[26] "Friends of God," and "Good Christians,"[27] as they considered themselves to be the only true practitioners of Christianity,[28] the one true church that continued to imitate the practices, beliefs, and lifestyles of the apostles.[29]

Despite this belief, Cathar religious tenets bore little resemblance to apostolic tradition as we know it. The Cathars were dualists. They did not believe in one God, but in two: a good god and an evil god.[30] The good god had created the invisible, spiritual universe, while the bad god had created the material world.[31] Likewise, the former had created human souls, but the latter imprisoned these souls in material bodies after deceiving them into leaving the spiritual world. Therefore, earth is a place of punishment just like hell,[32] and all evil comes from matter.

During an initial phase, Cathars believed in a kind of mitigated or *partial dualism*, in which the evil god was identified with Satan, a fallen angel, a creature inferior to the good God. However, at a later

---

German "Katze," meaning "cat," since cats were associated with sin, perversion, and witchcraft in Medieval Europe. See England, "The Reformers and the Heretics," 3.

[26] Weber. "Albigenses."
[27] England, "The Reformers and the Heretics," 3.
[28] Myers. "Morality among Cathar Perfects," 4.
[29] England, "The Reformers and the Heretics," 16.
[30] Myers. "Morality among Cathar Perfects," 5.
[31] Weber. "Cathari."
[32] Weber. "Albigenses."

stage, they professed an *absolute dualism*, where both gods were co-eternal and equally powerful. Therefore, neither god could be all-powerful, since they limited each other's freedom. The bad god came to be identified with the Creator of the Old Testament, whereas the good god was the Father of the New Testament.[33] Obviously, the two kinds of dualists were not in communion with each other.[34]

Of course, these theological tenets translated into practical effects. If a human soul was imprisoned in an evil, material body dwelling in an evil, material world, then one's purpose in life would be to liberate the spirit from such prison. To achieve this, the person should renounce the evil god and all his (physical) works. If the person achieved this, he or she would become "perfect" and be free to return to the spiritual realm after death. Otherwise, the poor soul would undergo a cycle of reincarnations, being repeatedly imprisoned in human or animal bodies, until the day it would indeed achieve "perfection."[35]

Cathars were, therefore, divided into two classes: the *perfecti* (or "perfect") and the *credentes* (or "believers").[36] The *perfecti* were the leaders of the movement—they had attained purity and, consequently, the liberation of their spirit. They had achieved this by undergoing a ritual called *consolamentum*[37] (Latin for "consolation.")

---

[33] Myers. "Morality among Cathar Perfects," 6. See also Weber. "Cathari."

[34] See Weber. "Cathari": "Not only were the Albanenses and Concorrezenses opposed to each other to the extent of indulging in mutual condemnations, but there was division among the Albanenses themselves"

[35] Myers. "Morality among Cathar Perfects," 7.

[36] Weber. "Albigenses."

[37] Myers. "Morality among Cathar Perfects," 7.

Chapter 7: Medieval Heresies and Spiritual Worldliness 221

As for the *credentes*, the second tier, they could not be called Cathars in the proper sense of the word, since they had not yet become "perfect." They still believed in the doctrines of the Cathar Church, actively participated in the religion and its ceremonies, and yearned to receive the *consolamentum*, at least on their deathbeds.[38]

In order to reject the physical world, the *perfecti* needed to submit themselves to a strict life, eschewing any physical pleasures and comforts. Since procreation resulted in the imprisonment of another soul in an evil body, the *perfecti* would not engage in sexual activity, whether marital or extra-marital. They would not eat anything related to animal coitus, be it meat, eggs, or cheese.[39] They would also abstain from alcohol and live in voluntary poverty, moving from town to town preaching and practicing rituals.[40] Since the *perfecti* had become pure by undergoing the ritual of *consolamentum*, a *perfectus* who would thenceforth commit a sin of the flesh would destroy his purity and, consequently, his salvation, being thereafter condemned to an eternity of nothingness.[41]

As for the *credentes*, the mere believers, they could continue their pre-Cathar lifestyles,[42] though avoidance of the aforementioned physical activities was certainly advisable and would bring the believer closer to perfection. A believer who wanted to become a *perfectus* would have to undergo a very rigid probation period,

---

[38] Ibid., 44.
[39] Ibid., 8.
[40] England, "The Reformers and the Heretics," 19.
[41] Myers. "Morality among Cathar Perfects," 10.
[42] England, "The Reformers and the Heretics," 19.

where novices would have to prove they could withstand the harsh demands of Catharism, like undergoing three 40-day fasts.[43]

Despite these rigid moral norms, the Cathars were (and still are) often associated with deviant behaviors, like ritual suicide and sexual immorality. The ritual suicide, known as *endura*, would be needed since many who had remained as mere believers for years would receive the *consolamentum* on their deathbed. Given that relapsing into sin after the *consolamentum* could have dire consequences for the salvation of the soul, the Cathar would commit suicide through starvation or poisoning if the illness proved not being fatal, to prevent subsequent moral transgressions. Furthermore, since procreation was seen as evil, concubinage would be seen as preferrable to marriage.[44]

However, in the last half a decade, an increasing number of scholars has questioned the veracity of these accusations. Most of the accounts of these deviant Cathar behaviors come not from primary sources, but from heavily biased accounts, like Catholic clergy (who prosecuted them) and gossipers.[45] Sometimes the accusations do not distinguish between *credentes* or *perfecti* defendants (we must keep in mind that both had very different moral duties.)[46] Also, even if we do have undisputable proof of sexual immorality among some Cathars (even *perfecti*), there is no evidence that we can generalize

---

[43] Kaelber. "Weaver into Heretics?" 120—121.

[44] Weber. "Albigenses." See also Myers. "Morality among Cathar Perfects," 27—28.

[45] England, "The Reformers and the Heretics," 5. A very thorough examination of these sources can be found in Myers. "Morality among Cathar Perfects," 41—55.

[46] Myers. "Morality among Cathar Perfects," 41.

Chapter 7: Medieval Heresies and Spiritual Worldliness

from these individual cases to the overall Cathar population, just like we cannot do the same from individual accounts of depravity among Catholic clergy today.[47] Though we do not know how they fared in practice, we know that in theory the Cathars advocated for a very strict morality.[48]

There is an additional reason to remain skeptical of these accusations of licentiousness: if the Cathars were so immoral, this would detract from their popularity. If the Catholic clergy of their time was widely seen as unreliable due to corruption, why would the Cathars not be subject to the same kind of suspicion? Yet, Cathar influence grew through moral persuasion.[49] Many times, the believers did not have a good grasp of theology, but they considered the perfect to be faithful and reliable due to their moral example.[50]

It is instructive to study how Catharism spread so successfully, in spite of the Catholic Church's influence during the Middle Ages. It is very tempting to related Catharism to other dualistic heresies from the times of the early Church, like Gnosticism, Manichaeism, and Marcionism. However, the historical link between these heresies is tenuous at best.[51] I believe a much more convincing

---

[47] Ibid., 58, 62.

[48] Ibid., 52.

[49] Ibid., 59-60.

[50] See, for example, the testimony of Izarn of Castelsarraisn, as relayed in England, "The Reformers and the Heretics," 18.

[51] Even the *Catholic Encyclopedia* admits to this. See Weber. "Cathari": "However attractive it may be to trace the origin of the Cathari to the first centuries of Christianity, we must be cautious not to accept as a certain historical fact what, up to the present, is only a probable conclusion." See also Weber. "Albigenses": "The contact of Christianity with the Oriental

hypothesis is to be found in a thesis by Matthew England at the University of Alabama in Huntsville: the spread of Catharism was due to a reformist spirit arising from widespread immorality among the Catholic clergy. Interestingly, even the (conservative and pre-Vatican II) *Catholic Encyclopedia* acknowledges this, as it lists among the many reasons for the rise of the Cathars: "their contempt for the Catholic clergy, caused by the ignorance and the worldly, too frequently scandalous, lives of the latter."[52]

This clerical corruption led to an understandable desire to counteract it through reforms. Sometimes, this reformist spirit came from grassroots movements, both orthodox (like, for example, St. Francis of Assisi and the Franciscans) and heterodox (like Peter Waldo and the Waldensians).[53] But it could also come from above, from the heights of the hierarchy. In 1049, Pope St. Leo IX kickstarted a streak of reformist popes, which would see its greater extent in the Gregorian reforms by Pope St. Gregory VII in 1073.[54] These reforms would be further consolidated during the First and Second ecumenical Lateran Councils.[55]

The reforms aimed especially at curbing two great ills: simony (i.e., the purchase of ecclesiastical offices,) and sexual immorality.

---

mind and Oriental religions had produced several sects (Gnostics, Manichaeans, Paulicians, Bogomilae) whose doctrines were akin to the tenets of the Albigenses. But the historical connection between the new heretics and their predecessors cannot be clearly traced."

[52] See Weber. "Albigenses."

[53] Myers. "Morality among Cathar Perfects," 59.

[54] England, "The Reformers and the Heretics," 8—10. See also Gabriel. *Heresy disguised as Tradition*, 44—45.

[55] O'Malley. *What Happened at Vatican II*, 41.

Chapter 7: Medieval Heresies and Spiritual Worldliness

To address simony, Gregory prohibited the investiture of bishops and abbots, which until then could be done by lay rulers and kings—an obvious source of political corruption. Instead, Gregory insisted that these members of the clergy should be canonically elected.[56] As far as sexuality was concerned, the reformist popes felt like marriage was corrupting the clergy, leading them to disperse Church property through family ties. Also, it made it easier for priests to hold concubines. Therefore, popes and councils aimed at enforcing obligatory celibacy among the clergy.[57] In this way, priests were to live a lifestyle more akin to monks than socialites.

The papal and conciliary reforms were successful insofar as they codified a legal prohibition against simony and clerical marriage/concubinage in canon law.[58] There was also an increased interest in a different lifestyle altogether, both inside and outside the clergy: the *vita apostolica* or "apostolic life," a call to radical poverty and evangelical action, in imitation of the apostles and the early Church.[59] Finally, the reforms were able to firmly convince the European population that simony and sexual immorality were sinful and unpriestly.[60] But these two last successes also contained the seeds of a terrible side-effect.

The reforms were not completely successful in eradicating Church corruption. Many times, the Church was unable or

---

[56] Blumenthal. "Gregorian Reform". See also England, "The Reformers and the Heretics," 7.

[57] Mullin, *A Short World History of Christianity*, 98—99. See also England, "The Reformers and the Heretics," 8.

[58] England, "The Reformers and the Heretics," 10.

[59] Mullin, *A Short World History of Christianity*, 100.

[60] England, "The Reformers and the Heretics," 10.

unwilling to enforce the reforms she had ordained. Since the population was now sensitized to disdain clerical corruption, this led to a widespread perception of the Catholic Church as being corrupt.[61] Against the backdrop of this corrupt, worldly Church, people who lived "apostolic lives" were seen as a breath of fresh air.

The first wave of heresy in the wake of the clerical reforms came in the shape of the Radical Gregorians i.e., more Gregorian than Gregory VII. These were extremist preachers taking advantage of the people's alienation from the Church, calling for the utter extermination of corrupt clergy. So disgusted were they with clerical corruption, they resurrected the Donatist trend of invalidating the sacraments from sinful priests (see chapter 5). Practical rigidity soon gave way to doctrinal heresy. Some of these preachers urged the faithful to confess their sins, not to a priest, but to each other, dissolving Church unity. Eventually, other doctrinal errors ensued, as some Radical Gregorians began to privately interpret scripture: they discarded the Old Testament laws altogether and saw the New Testament and its apostolic life instructions as the only ones worthy of being pursued.[62]

To be sure, there is no known connection between the Radical Gregorians of the eleventh century and the Cathars of the twelfth century onwards. However, it is hard not to see the former as an intermediate step towards the latter, especially since both share the same foundation: a strong anticlericalism, suspicious of the institutional Church; and a certain fascination for the apostolic life, mixed

---

[61] Ibid., 11.
[62] Ibid., 13-4.

with some Marcionism (which could easily degenerate into dualism.)[63]

By the twelfth century, the Catholic clergy was still as weak on authority as it was weak on morality.[64] The general population was generally distrustful, if not suspicious, of the Church.[65] This created a spiritual vacuum, easily filled by those who would show themselves to be morally consistent with the ideals of a *vita apostolica*. The Cathar *perfecti* lived in poverty, practiced asceticism, and preached the gospel, seemingly as the apostles did. Therefore, they drew unto themselves the theologically unsophisticated common folk, more influenced by an apostolic life than by rational demonstrations of orthodoxy.[66] In short, the Cathars grew more by attraction than by doctrine.

The contrast was aggravated by the Cathars' frequent denunciation of Catholic clergy's laxity, often with very aggressive and hostile rhetoric. The Cathars believed that these corrupt men could not pose themselves as priests. Likewise, they censured the wealth displayed by the higher echelons of the hierarchy.[67] Moreover, the Cathars further eroded the Church's authority by claiming that the sacraments were mere tricks to deceive the faithful away from the one, true, Cathar faith. They replaced the Catholic sacraments with

---

[63] England, "The Reformers and the Heretics," 13—15. See also Myers. "Morality among Cathar Perfects," 60.

[64] England, "The Reformers and the Heretics," 20.

[65] Ibid., 4.

[66] Kaelber. "Weaver into Heretics?" 115.

[67] England, "The Reformers and the Heretics," 27—28.

the Cathar *consolamentum* and deemed the Catholic Church as a creation of the evil god.[68]

It was obvious the Catholic Church could not sit idly as the Cathars expanded through Europe. It is true, at the height of their influence, the Cathars never exceeded 100,000 (*perfecti* and *credentes* alike), a small number when compared with the 25 million French and Italian populations of the time.[69] Still, the Church perceived them as a threat that needed to be dealt with in a decisive way.

During a first stage, the Church responded peacefully, sending missionaries (namely Franciscans or Dominicans, who also lived according to the ideals of "apostolic life") to convince the Cathars away from their erroneous ways and bring them back into the fold.[70] However, these efforts failed, and Catharism kept increasing. In a second phase, the Church responded with a crusade, using the power of the state to conquer cities posing as focal points of Cathar activity.[71] But it would be only during the third stage, with the setting up of an inquisition, that Catharism was successfully ended.[72]

---

[68] Myers. "Morality among Cathar Perfects," 60. See also Weber. "Cathari."

[69] Kaelber. "Weaver into Heretics?" 112.

[70] Myers. "Morality among Cathar Perfects," 11-2.

[71] Ibid., 12-3. It is true that this violent response has blemished the Church's reputation for decades to come, as the crusade killed many common folks, Cathars and Catholics alike. But it is also important to note that the famous sentence "Slay all; God will know His own," allegedly uttered by the papal legate during the capture of Béziers was never pronounced. See Weber. "Albigenses."

[72] Ibid., 13.

Chapter 7: Medieval Heresies and Spiritual Worldliness

Was the Church justified in acting like this towards such a small minority? Nowadays, we disapprove of the Church's methods, and rightfully so. Regardless, it is hardly disputable that the Cathars posed a credible threat to the Church's authority. Even if we acknowledge that the evidence for ritual suicide and sexual immorality is flimsy at best, the fact that the Cathars viewed the world as inherently evil and proscribed everything related to reproduction was a menace to basic societal continuity and cohesiveness. Properly followed, Catharism would lead to the extinction of humanity.[73] Also, by disconnecting themselves from the Church's magisterial guidance, the Cathar's doctrinal errors multiplied. For them, the spiritual nature of Jesus could not have undergone the corruption of a material body, binding Him to the dominion of the evil god. Therefore, there had been no incarnation: Jesus had a celestial body, which had entered through the ear of the Virgin Mary (who, according to some Cathar sects, was also not human, but an angelic being like Jesus, sent beforehand to make it possible for Him to be born.) Likewise, the crucifixion and the resurrection had been illusory, not real events. Neither could there be resurrection of the bodies on the last day since that would merely prolong the evil god's yoke. This means that, just like the Pelagians (see chapter 6), the Cathars believed Jesus's redemption to have been instructive, not operative.[74] Finally, Cathar theology destroyed the very notion of sin itself. Surely, Cathars avoided immorality, sometimes in the same way and even more forcefully than Catholics. However, they did this not

---

[73] Weber. "Cathari."

[74] Weber. "Albigenses." See also Myers. "Morality among Cathar Perfects," 11.

because they wanted to avoid sin, in the proper sense of the word. For them, sins of the flesh were the byproduct of the evil god—they had no relation to the good god, since the latter did not have any intercourse with matter. In other words, no sin of the flesh could offend or turn people away from the good god. The reason why Cathars wanted to avoid acts of the flesh was not moral, but practical. Only by doing so could the faithful free themselves from the evil god and liberate their souls.[75]

Consequently, it is not strange to see why the Church acted so decisively against the Cathars. Pope Innocent III, who did condemn some of the excesses committed by the nobles during the Albigensian crusade, is still on record as saying that the Cathars were "worse than the Saracens" (i.e., Muslims).[76] And the *Catholic Encyclopedia* cites the scholar Henry Charles Lea, who cannot be suspected of partiality towards the Catholic Church, of writing:

> However much we may deprecate the means used for its (Catharism) suppression and commiserate those who suffered for conscience' sake, we cannot but admit that the cause of orthodoxy was in this case the cause of progress and civilization. Had Catharism become dominant, or even had it been allowed to exist on equal terms, its influence could not have failed to prove disastrous.[77]

---

[75] Myers. "Morality among Cathar Perfects," 9.
[76] Weber. "Albigenses."
[77] Weber. "Cathari."

Some scholars argue that the fall of Catharism has, unfortunately, precipitated a decline in moral and dogmatic coherence.[78] But, as we shall see, true reform would spring from within the Church, and in obedience to her.

The Fraticelli

It would seem God also understood the Church's urgent need for reform during those dire times of widespread ecclesial corruption, since He raised many saints to achieve this very goal. Chief amongst them was a certain Francis, born of a merchant couple in the Italian town of Assisi during the twelfth century. Though he grew up as a knight from a wealthy household, God had other plans for him: a fame unsurpassed by any feats of chivalry he could ever attain.

One day, as Francis passed by the abandoned church of San Damiano, he felt a strange urge to go inside and pray before the Orthodox-styled crucifix there. While kneeling in prayer, Francis heard a voice: "Go and rebuild my Church." The youth looked to the ruins around him and logically understood this command as meaning the restoration of the crumbling church of San Damiano. Immediately, he started rebuilding the church with his bare hands, brick by brick.[79] But God had meant something else, something more extraordinary: the restoration of the whole universal Church, for which Francis would provide an undeniable contribution.

---

[78] Kaelber. "Weaver into Heretics?" 129.
[79] Finnis. "Rebuild my Church."

Francis of Assisi would eventually abandon his wealth, giving away all his possessions except a humble brown habit. He also founded the Order of Friars Minors (a.k.a. the Franciscans), and later on, also the Order of the Poor Clare sisters (the Franciscan's feminine branch, also founded by St. Clare of Assisi) and the Brothers and Sisters of Penance (a lay third-order, with the same charism of poverty).[80]

Eventually, as his order grew, Francis found the need to write down a Rule explaining their charism and what bound the friars together. The original Rule consisted mostly of passages of the gospel, to which very few things were added[81]: the three customary vows of obedience, chastity, and poverty, as well as some other practical rules allowing them to pursue the so-much desired *apostolic life*.[82] In 1209, Francis presented this Rule in oral form to Pope Innocent III, who approved it. Later, he would put it in written form in 1221 and 1223 (the latter with some juridical components not present in the original.)[83]

The Franciscan Order spread through Christendom and thoroughly reinvigorated the Church, providing her with a missionary and apostolic drive that for centuries had remained dormant under layers of corruption and clericalism. However, it was not just the Franciscan Order that changed the Church. As it disseminated

---

[80] Ibid.

[81] Perez. "Franciscanos, tras Ideales Utópicos," 68.

[82] Oliger. "Rule of Saint Francis."

[83] Perez. "Franciscanos, tras Ideales Utópicos," 68. See also Oliger. "Rule of Saint Francis."

around the world, the Order also had to adapt to new circumstances and demands.

Whereas the friars had been itinerants at an earlier stage, they eventually settled in fixed places. These would, in due course, be converted into cloistered convents. Previously the means of sustenance was obtained mainly through manual labor, with alms playing a secondary role. In time, though, the friars became more and more dependent on outside contributions. In short, the Franciscans adopted a monastical and mendicant asceticism. But as the Order became more clericalized, inequality rose inside it: the lower "laity" performed the menial chores (sometimes even employing secular servants,) whereas the higher "clerical" stratum assumed the acts of governance within the Order and received privileged treatment.[84]

Even during St. Francis's lifetime, these changes produced two hermeneutics battling for the soul of the Order: some, holding superior offices, wished the strictness of the primitive Rule to be lessened, while others, closer friends with Francis, wished to adhere to the original Rule as strictly as possible.[85]

After St. Francis's death, the Rule underwent successive papal (re)interpretations, aggravating its clericalization.[86] Of course, St. Francis did not wish his Rule to be altered after his death, to maintain the Franciscan charism as closer as possible to its radically reforming origin. However, the popes disregarded his death wish, building up a veritable "superstructure over the original Rule."[87]

---

[84] Perez. "Franciscanos, tras Ideales Utópicos," 69.
[85] Douie. *The Nature and Effect of the Heresy of the Fraticelli*, 2.
[86] Perez. "Franciscanos, tras Ideales Utópicos," 69.
[87] Douie. *The Nature and Effect of the Heresy of the Fraticelli*, 2.

These changes were not something imposed merely by the popes' whims. They were necessary to enhance the Order's great services to the Church and the community. The strictness of the original Rule had to be eased for practical reasons. For example, the original Rule said that friars should not receive money, either directly (in person) or indirectly (through intermediaries.) But Pope Gregory IX allowed alms to be given indirectly to the friars through a nuncio or spiritual friend, who would keep the money until the time when the friars would need it.[88] At a later date, Pope Nicholas III solved this problem by decreeing that all property left to the Franciscans should belong to the Church, not the Order: the friars could make use of those assets for their livelihood and daily needs, but in the end, the papacy held those possessions.[89]

But these reinterpretations of the original Rule came at a cost. It could be argued that "much of the freshness and spontaneity of the first days of the movement was inevitably lost."[90] Furthermore, corruption once again started rearing its ugly head: money poured into the collection plate, leading to spending on an unnecessarily large number of habits, or on lavish liturgical vestments, as well as pictures and stained glass to adorn the churches. Usurers benefitting the Order would be absolved, even before making restitution.[91]

Again, there would be two different reactions to the new situation, picking up on the hermeneutical tensions already present during St. Francis's lifetime. These two diametrically opposed responses

---

[88] Ibid., 3.
[89] Ibid., 9—10.
[90] Ibid., 3.
[91] Ibid., 10.

Chapter 7: Medieval Heresies and Spiritual Worldliness

would crystallize into two parties: on one side the Conventuals, also called Moderates[92] or *Relaxati* (Italian for "Relaxed,")[93] embracing the new monastical paradigm; on the other side, the stricter Spirituals, also called *Zelanti* (Italian for "Zealous") and Rigorists,[94] who wanted a return to the narrower interpretation of St. Francis's Rule.

The Spirituals were also profoundly influenced by the writings of a certain Joachim of Fiore, contemporary with St. Francis. This Cistercian monk tried to predict the future by looking into patterns in the past. To do so, he divided history into three age periods: in the age of the Father (before the birth of Christ,) people lived under servile obedience; in the age of the Son (between the coming of Jesus and the time of Joachim), they lived under filial obedience; in the upcoming age of the Spirit, people would live out of love. This meant a change from a hierarchical Church to a more *spiritual* Church (hence the name "Spirituals" to those who adhered to Joachim's writings,) a Church where the faithful would own nothing, but have everything in common,[95] just like in the time of the apostles.

There were other important aspects of Joachim's writings pertaining to the Friars Minor. The first age had been the age of the married, the second was the age of the celibate priests, the third would be the age of the contemplative monk.[96] The ushering in of the third age would be resisted by an antichrist, but in the end, it

---

[92] Perez. "Franciscanos, tras Ideales Utópicos," 70.

[93] Bihl. "Fraticelli."

[94] Perez. "Franciscanos, tras Ideales Utópicos," 70.

[95] Ibid. See also Douie. *The Nature and Effect of the Heresy of the Fraticelli*, 6. See also Nagy and Biron-Ouellet. "A Collective Emotion in Medieval Italy," 5.

[96] Douie. *The Nature and Effect of the Heresy of the Fraticelli*, 24.

would triumph, brought about by barefooted monks. Of course, the Franciscan Spirituals saw themselves in these predictions. They absorbed Joachinite theology into their own mysticism, though wisely avoiding its excesses.[97] Yet, they believed that these predictions foretold the triumph of their party and the return of the Order to its original state.

It is important to note that Joachim of Fiore never wrote anything against the papacy, or the pope for that matter.[98] In fact, the beginning of the third age would be guided, not only by the monks, but also by a *"pontifex angelicus,"* a saintly pope.[99] However, Joachinite theology also contained the seeds of rebellion, though unwittingly. For example, the third age would also be preceded by an "angel of the sixth seal" who would bear stigma and bring about the "eternal gospel": the Spirituals interpreted this angel as meaning St. Francis and the "eternal gospel" as the Rule.[100] Also, the third age would crush the corruption within the Church, namely simony and pride, so prevalent in the clergy at the time.[101] Finally, Joachim contrasted the hierarchical Church of the second age, signified by St. Peter, with the spiritual Church of the third age, foreshadowed by St. John, the beloved disciple, preferred to St. Peter himself.[102] The dice were cast.

---

[97] Ibid., 6, 27. See also Perez. "Franciscanos, tras Ideales Utópicos," 71.

[98] Douie. *The Nature and Effect of the Heresy of the Fraticelli*, 25. See also Perez. "Franciscanos, tras Ideales Utópicos," 71.

[99] Ibid.

[100] Ibid.

[101] Ibid., 70.

[102] Douie. *The Nature and Effect of the Heresy of the Fraticelli*, 24.

Chapter 7: Medieval Heresies and Spiritual Worldliness

In 1278, a certain Spiritual friar named Angelo da Clareno was raising troubles for the Franciscan leaders at the March of Ancona. Fra Angelo was extremely cultured and widely praised for his austerity, boosting the Spirituals' influence in the region. The Provincial Minister, from the Conventual party, threw Angelo and other Spiritual friars into prison for heresy and schism. For more than ten years, Fra Angelo and his companions lingered in their dungeon, fettered to the walls of their cells, deprived of books and sacraments. This torment the Spiritual friar did endure exemplarily—so much so that his jailers were forbidden from speaking to him, lest they grow indignant of such a cruel and unjust punishment. In 1289, the new General of the Order found out that the sole charge against these friars was the excessive strictness of their observance of their vow of poverty. Enraged to know this, the General shouted: "Would that we ourselves and the whole Order were guilty of such a crime!" Angelo was released from prison but exiled to Armenia for an additional decade.[103]

Fra Angelo would find a temporary respite in 1294, when a certain hermit was elected Pope Celestine V. This pontiff, just like St. Francis and Fra Angelo, was renowned for his asceticism and moral purity. Angelo had made his acquaintance during his earlier years, while Celestine was still an eremite chased by many who wanted to follow his example.[104] Furthermore, the Spirituals interpreted Celestine's election as fulfilling the Joachinite prophecy of the *pontifex angelicus*. This was a "poor pope," who was certainly the

---

[103] Ibid., 53-4.
[104] Ibid., 51.

embodiment of the "evangelical pope" guiding the Church into the third age.[105]

Obviously, Celestine reciprocated the Spirituals' sympathy: he was also an ascetic, after all. Under his pontificate, the Spirituals were released from their vows of obedience to their Franciscan superiors and allowed to live in accordance with the Rule of St. Francis, in its stricter sense.[106]

But this was not to last. Celestine's pontificate would be very short. Scarce six months after his election, he abdicated, being the last pope to voluntarily do so until Benedict XVI.[107] The following popes, certainly more mundane, would not allow the Celestinian concessions to stand. For Celestine's successors, the Church possessed the "power of two swords, the spiritual and the temporal."[108] This was incompatible with the Spiritual Franciscans' conception of the Church of the third age. They started to denounce the "carnal" Church, identifying Rome with the "harlot of Babylon" from the Book of Revelation,[109] an adulteress that, while wed to Christ, had engaged in extra-marital intercourse with the Antichrist.

The clashes between the Conventual and the Spiritual factions were at a boiling point. The Church attempted some compromises to resolve the conflict. A new constitution interpreting the Rule of St. Francis in a stricter sense was approved at the ecumenical

---

[105] Perez. "Franciscanos, tras Ideales Utópicos," 73.

[106] Bihl. "Fraticelli." See also Douie. *The Nature and Effect of the Heresy of the Fraticelli*, 55.

[107] Allen. "Next Sunday, remember that popes can admire resignation."

[108] Perez. "Franciscanos, tras Ideales Utópicos," 74.

[109] Rev 17:5—6.

Council of Vienne, held in 1311—1312.¹¹⁰ In return for this concession, the Spirituals were ordered to return to their convents and reconcile with their superiors. Yet, they refused to comply. It is true, they did not want to separate from their Order, but they did not wish to be obedient either.¹¹¹ By the end of 1312, a Spiritual rebellion in Tuscany forcibly occupied several monasteries, expelling the Conventuals from their grounds. The pope answered by excommunicating the insurrectionists.¹¹²

In the meantime, Angelo da Clareno became the leader of the Spiritual Franciscans and moved to the Curia to help with the negotiations regarding the status of the radical friars. According to Fra Angelo's own writing, his time at the Curia was more painful to him than any of his fasts and sacrifices. He could not endure the luxury, noise, and intrigue of a courtly environment, harsher as they were for his ascetic sensibilities than the strictness, silence, and isolation of a hermitage.¹¹³ But his worst scourge was yet to come.

In 1316, a certain Jacques d'Euse was elected pope, taking the name John XXII. Some readers may have already recognized his name. He is one of the allegedly heretical popes, used by papal critics today as proof that sometimes it is fitting to resist and correct the Roman Pontiff.¹¹⁴ I have written elsewhere why this accusation does

---

[110] Bihl. "Fraticelli."

[111] Douie. *The Nature and Effect of the Heresy of the Fraticelli*, 15—17.

[112] Bihl. "Fraticelli."

[113] Douie. *The Nature and Effect of the Heresy of the Fraticelli*, 61.

[114] See, for example, Kwasniewski. "How to Properly Understand the Role of the Papacy": "But what happened when John XXII preached that? Did everybody just bow their heads and fold their hands and say, 'We have to accept that. We better start rewriting the catechism'? Did they say, 'Well,

not hold.[115] However, let me summarize my defense very briefly here:

After becoming pope, John XXII preached a few homilies where he said that the souls of the blessed departed would not experience the beatific vision *immediately*. Rather, they would remain under the altar of God and enjoy only a vision of the human nature of Christ before the general judgment, when they would be elevated to the beatific vision.[116] John's immediate successor Benedict XII, on his end, would infallibly define the immediate beatific vision as a dogma of the faith. Also, John's sermons caused quite a ruckus even during his lifetime, with several theologians correcting his claims. However, it is important to note that John XXII explicitly said, in his controversial homilies, that he was merely exposing his own personal opinion on the matter, and that if anyone found that he was mistaken, that they should come forward and correct him.[117] This is what the theologians did, taking advantage of the space of discussion voluntarily opened by John on this question.[118] When the discussion showed that the doctrine of the immediate beatific vision was correct, the pontiff changed his mind and adhered to it. In his deathbed, John solemnly confessed the immediate beatific vision before his cardinals, clarifying that, in his sermons, he had never intended to teach

---

that's wrong, but out of respect, out of religious submission of intellect and will, we have to go along with what the Pope was saying'? No, they opposed him. His theologians, Dominicans, Franciscan, they objected to him. They said, 'This is false. You have to recant this.'"

[115] Gabriel. *Heresy disguised as Tradition*, 341—348.
[116] Le Bachelet. "Benoit XII," 659-60.
[117] Ibid., 662.
[118] Ibid., 666.

delayed beatific vision in a magisterial way, but only as his personal opinion.[119]

Interestingly, John XXII's quarrels with the Spirituals might have played a role in these polemics, both as a cause and as an effect. On the one hand, John possibly addressed the topic of beatific vision to counter some of the mystical views presented by some Spiritual leaders.[120] On the other hand, the revolting Franciscan friars would weaponize the beatific vision controversy to undermine the authority of an inconvenient pope. More than the theologians who discussed the matter, it was the Spirituals who went about calling the pope a heretic. They went as far as asking for the convocation of an ecumenical council to condemn the Holy Father—a call which did not come to fruition.[121]

John XXII knew his shortcomings: he did not have a solid theological training. His area of expertise was the law, namely canon law. But for this very reason, he was even more diligent in tackling the sensitive issue of the Franciscan Spirituals, which he knew—even with his crude theological formation—were heretical and damaging to Church unity. Pope John scrutinized the Rule of St. Francis very thoroughly, analyzing it through his perspective as a jurist.[122] But he did not stop there. He established inquisitorial procedures and commissioned several experts to investigate the matter of the Spirituals' theological claims. Furthermore, he was not easily satisfied: after the first rounds of conclusions came in, he formulated new questions

---

[119] Ibid., 668.
[120] Lambert. "The Franciscan Crisis," 138.
[121] Kirsch. "Pope John XXII."
[122] Lambert. "The Franciscan Crisis," 125-6.

and requested deeper deliberations.[123] How ironic that a so-called "heretical pope" would be so industrious in the defense of orthodoxy, and that this scrupulous care for doctrinal integrity would contribute to his bad fame, bolstered by the scandalmongering of his enemies (the true heretics)!

The pope's task was not easy. It required a great deal of nuance. John wished to condemn the heresies of the Franciscan Spirituals without hindering the ideals of poverty of their brethren, the Conventuals. Both sets of Franciscans believed the same ideals of radical poverty, though they might differ on the best way to practice it. Furthermore, John had to avoid the impression that previous popes had erred when they had repeatedly approved and praised Franciscan poverty in general.[124]

In the end, John XXII identified five heresies prevalent among the Franciscan Spirituals: 1) that the Roman Church was carnal and corrupt whereas they were the spiritual ones; 2) that the Roman See did not have all power and jurisdiction; 3) that taking oaths was forbidden; 4) that priests in a state of sin could not administer the sacraments (a Donatist claim, see chapter 5); and 5) that they were the sole true observers of the gospel.[125]

Though many scholars and thinkers, both at the time and today, may have a biased view against John XXII's treatment of the Spirituals,[126] his insistence on this matter was justified and based on a sound realism. The pope's conclusions on this matter—decided after

---

[123] Ibid., 132-3.
[124] Ibid., 134.
[125] Bihl. "Fraticelli."
[126] Lambert. "The Franciscan Crisis," 125, 145.

Chapter 7: Medieval Heresies and Spiritual Worldliness 243

careful examination—make a lot of sense and accurately show the faults of the Spirituals.[127] Though one cannot deny some level of pettiness in John's motivations, the reality is that his concerns were sensible and reasonable: the Spirituals had ossified into a reactionary opposition to any reform,[128] which could not be sustained in the long run.

For example, the rebellious friars had asserted the Rule of St. Francis—namely in what pertained to the poverty of Christ—to be definitive and unchangeable, even by papal *fiat*.[129] John XXII pointed out that the Rule had indeed changed before, and that these changes had been sanctioned by previous pontiffs. The pope also pointed out how the Rule also included a vow of obedience besides the vow of poverty, and that the former was more important than the latter.[130] By showing the faults of their hardened resistance to reform, John was providing them, as it were, with "a blueprint for a fresh start."[131]

In fact, John asserted his authority in a very clever and practical way: if the Spirituals believed that the Franciscans could not hold any property, either in direct or indirect ways, then the papacy would no longer hold the Franciscan Order's property. John cancelled this arrangement and transferred these possessions back to

---

[127] Ibid., 138.
[128] Ibid., 137.
[129] Ibid., 135.
[130] Ibid., 137-8.
[131] Ibid., 138.

the Franciscans,[132] leaving a hot potato on their hands. This he did to show how they could not fiddle with the pope's authority.

Unfortunately, the Spirituals turned a deaf ear to all of the pope's magisterial acts. Truly, they hardened their resistance even more.[133] They declared John XXII's election invalid and denounced him (and eventually, his successors) as heretics with no right to the papacy, thus showing the dangerous mindset of their sect.[134]

Some scholars argue that Fra Angelo adopted a moderate stance, condemning the excesses on his side,[135] and showing himself always "obedient and enemy of all rupture."[136] I do not believe these points stand. Angelo was still a sedevacantist, believing that John XXII had been uncanonically elected. Moreso, he believed Pope John to be the illegitimate pastor preaching heresy against the poverty of Christ, foretold in an alleged prophecy by St. Francis. Angelo's "obedience" was more pragmatic than faithful: he thought that prayer and patience were a more Christian form of resistance than violence,[137] but his was still a form of resistance.

Fra Angelo would end up founding a new order, in the image and likeness of what he thought the Franciscan Order should be: the "*fraticelli della povera vita*" (Italian for "little brothers of the poor life").[138] Though the expressions "Spirituals" and "Fraticelli" are sometimes used interchangeably, they cannot be fully equated.

---

[132] Ibid., 136. See also Bihl. "Fraticelli."

[133] Douie. *The Nature and Effect of the Heresy of the Fraticelli*, 13.

[134] Bihl. "Fraticelli."

[135] Douie. *The Nature and Effect of the Heresy of the Fraticelli*, 65.

[136] Perez. "Franciscanos, tras Ideales Utópicos," 73.

[137] Douie. *The Nature and Effect of the Heresy of the Fraticelli*, 65.

[138] Perez. "Franciscanos, tras Ideales Utópicos," 75.

Chapter 7: Medieval Heresies and Spiritual Worldliness

Spirituals were religious people influenced by the writings of abbot Joachim of Fiore. The Fraticelli were a radical faction of the Franciscan Order. Not all Spirituals were Fraticelli—in fact, not all Spirituals were even Franciscans. Also, not all Spirituals had trouble with Church hierarchy: some were indeed rupturists, but others were continuists, advocating for a reform preserving unity. However, all Fraticelli were a particularly extreme kind of Spirituals, veering into heresy.[139]

Though the Fraticelli were indeed concerned with Church purity, they would end up developing heterodox views, since they were cut off from the magisterium. At first, their heterodoxy was mainly concerned with Church authority. They thought that the pope had no power to change the Rule of St. Francis. But from then on, their ideas became more extravagant. For them, property, dominion, money, and civil law in temporal things were not instituted by divine or natural law but introduced because of sin and iniquity. Christ, as the perfect reformer, did not want evangelical men to have any ownership, whether of property or money. People were to *use* property, not *own* it. For this reason, Christ and the apostles had given us their example, by being perfect poor.[140] John XXII would condemn as heretical the proposition that Christ and the apostles did not possess property, either separately or collectively, in his bull *Cum inter nonnullos*.[141]

This heterodoxy eventually extended also to the way they perceived their founder. At the beginning, Fra Angelo's depictions of

---

[139] Ibid., 76-7.
[140] Lambert. "The Franciscan Crisis," 139.
[141] Bihl. "Fraticelli."

St. Francis of Assisi did not contain any of the innocence or child-likeness of the saint: rather, he was shown as somber and austere, always ready to cast dark prophecies on those who would corrupt his Order.[142] In short, Fra Angelo was writing a St. Francis more akin to his own mirror image than the real person. But the Fraticelli would go on even further, making Francis almost another Christ, writing his Rule under divine inspiration—making it set in stone, even against the authoritative judgment of the Rock itself.[143]

Additionally, the Fraticelli had created division within the Church by casting shade on John XXII's legitimacy as pope. They were—so they thought—the sole true observers of the gospel against a Church become apostate. To sustain this extraordinary claim, the Fraticelli completely reworked the Joachinite eschatology in ways never intended by the orthodox and obedient abbot of Fiore. Through this eschatology, the Fraticelli thought of John's papacy as a period of suffering they would have to endure before their final vindication in an indeterminate future.[144]

In 1337, Fra Angelo da Clareno died. Multitudes of people surrounded his deathbed, seeking the help of that holy man with such an exemplary life. Accounts of miracles associated with his intercession spread like wildfire among the populace.[145] Despite this, Angelo never rose to the honor of the altars, unlike St. Francis of Assisi or

---

[142] Douie. *The Nature and Effect of the Heresy of the Fraticelli*, 71.

[143] Lambert. "The Franciscan Crisis," 141.

[144] Douie. *The Nature and Effect of the Heresy of the Fraticelli*, 68. See also Lambert. "The Franciscan Crisis," 139.

[145] Douie. *The Nature and Effect of the Heresy of the Fraticelli*, 68. See also Bihl. "Fraticelli."

even Pope St. Celestine V, the hermit pontiff. Thus, St. Cyprian's maxim (see chapter 5) was once again fulfilled: all of Angelo's asceticism and poverty could not erase the sin of wilful and obstinate schism, so he could never be venerated as a saint.

After Angelo's death—and predictably—the Fraticelli split into several groups, each holding its own doctrine. There would be other waves of Fraticelli, led by other rigorist friars, but all of them amounted to naught, quashed as they were by John XXII and his successors.[146] Still, the Fraticelli had spread throughout Christendom, from Portugal to Armenia, from Germany to Sicily.[147] Some went as far as, without any authority to do so, electing their own generals, bishops, and popes.[148] But in the end, they fizzled away, buried by the overwhelming numbers of Franciscans who remained faithful to the true Order and the Church.[149]

Eventually, in 1473, the remnants of the Fraticelli would, at their own request, be reincorporated into the true Franciscans, under the obedience of the General of the Order.[150] The *Relaxati* had, by remaining united with the Church, triumphed over the *Rigorists*.

The Flagellants

One of the most prevalent caricatures of medieval Europe in popular media features public processions of religious zealots

---

[146] Bihl. "Fraticelli."
[147] Ibid.
[148] Ibid.
[149] Ibid.
[150] Perez. "Franciscanos, tras Ideales Utópicos," 75.

whipping themselves in the back. These depictions portray a real phenomenon, which began to emerge almost at the same time as the Fraticelli—and probably triggered by the same causes. Those were the *Flagelatti* or Flagellants.

Though our modern sensibilities may have a hard time understanding this trend, it made a lot of sense for people at the time. The world was a harsher place. In Italy, in particular, war and violence were widespread. Cities often took up arms against each other, sometimes driven by feuds or vendettas between ruling families. Politics was a risky business, in which political adversaries were often killed or banished if they fell out of grace with the higher nobility, raising conflicts among those who supported and those who opposed them.

Society was divided between the *popolo*, or common folk, and the *milites*, or soldiers. The latter were the most usual prevaricators, but the former were the ones caught up in the middle of the wars, suffering the brunt of violence.[151] The *popolo* felt that they should resist this bellicose *status quo*, but they had no means to do so—at least not directly. If the common folk wanted to stop all the bloodshed, they could achieve it only by undermining the very societal fabric allowing such ills.[152] It was to fulfill this psychological need that the Flagellants appeared.

In 1260, a hermit from the Italian town of Perugia, named Raniero Fasari, claimed to have received several apparitions from Our Lady, the archangels, and local saints. In one of the apparitions, the

---

[151] Nagy and Biron-Ouellet. "A Collective Emotion in Medieval Italy," 2.

[152] Ibid.

Virgin revealed to Raniero that God was going to destroy the world, unless everyone did penance to atone for humankind's sins.[153] As the message reached the population, Raniero began self-flagellating: a practice he, as an ascetic, already observed often. But soon, more and more people joined him, stripping themselves from the waist up and whipping themselves in the back, seeking to ward off the impending doom. It was Good Thursday, and the accounts of the Lord's Passion were at a peak, kindling the fire of devotion within their hearts, impressed as they were by the sufferings undergone by Christ for the salvation of sinners. A long procession of Flagellants formed and traversed the streets of Perugia.[154]

Self-flagellation was not a new practice. Raniero Fasari was not a stranger to it. But until then, it had been confined to monasteries and hermitages, to be practiced solely by trained ascetics or penitents of grave sins. What had made this procession unique was that, for the first time, this self-flagellation had been done in public and involving almost the entire population of a town.[155] The effect of the procession was so intense, that on Easter Monday the city government issued ordinances regulating violence and arms-bearing by the *milites*.[156] The *popolo*'s unconscious calls for peace had worked.

---

[153] Lowe-Martin. "Comparing Penitential Acts," 97. See also Nagy and Biron-Ouellet. "A Collective Emotion in Medieval Italy," 2-3.

[154] Nagy and Biron-Ouellet. "A Collective Emotion in Medieval Italy," 3.

[155] Vincent, "Discipline du corps," 600-1. See also Nagy and Biron-Ouellet. "A Collective Emotion in Medieval Italy," 6.

[156] Nagy and Biron-Ouellet. "A Collective Emotion in Medieval Italy," 3.

Soon, the Flagellants went from town to town, all throughout Italy, spreading the news—and their ritual. As they processed through the streets of a new community, more people were enticed to join in. The processions, sometimes reaching 10,000, would consist in a multitude of people, bare from the waist up, scourging themselves till blood drew up, while singing chants to the Passion of Christ.[157] Everyone was affected by this social contagion: clerics and laypeople, nobles and peasants, men and women (though the latter would participate in the privacy of their homes), adults and even children,[158] all would whip their own bodies to call the world to repentance. The participants were to endure penance for thirty-three and a half days (as many as the years of Jesus's earthly lifetime), through heat and cold, sun, rain, or snow.[159]

But it is true, wherever they passed, good fruits seemed to spring forth. Where before there had been war and dissension, now peace and concord seem to abound. People would prostrate themselves before their longstanding enemies in a public act of self-humiliation and reconciliation. It is not possible to overestimate the efficacy of these acts in bringing about harmony to the otherwise quarrelsome Italian peninsula.[160] Besides the reconciliation of enemies, the Flagellants also brought with them the payment of debts, the restoration of ill-gotten gains, and the release of prisoners.

---

[157] Toke. "Flagellants."

[158] Nagy and Biron-Ouellet. "A Collective Emotion in Medieval Italy," 1, 6. See also Toke. "Flagellants."

[159] Toke. "Flagellants."

[160] Nagy and Biron-Ouellet. "A Collective Emotion in Medieval Italy," 1.

Chapter 7: Medieval Heresies and Spiritual Worldliness 251

However, the search for peace in violent times was not the only root cause of the Flagellant phenomenon. Other factors also contributed, many of which were already mentioned earlier in this chapter. The predictions of Joachim of Fiore had created "an eschatological atmosphere with a sense of existential urgency," prompting the populace to be more receptive to apocalyptic warnings.[161] Also, the idea of an apostolic life had been promoted by the precursors of the Cathars, and the "imitation of Christ" incentivized by St. Francis of Assisi. In fact, Assisi and Perugia were in close geographical proximity,[162] so it is not hard to see how one could influence the other.

Though ecclesiastical authorities were initially lukewarm, or even favorable to this epiphenomenon, soon they found this tendency to be potentially dangerous and withheld their support. One year later, the pope disowned the Flagellant processions. Without ecclesiastical sanction, popular adherence fell, and the trend naturally waned away, ceasing almost as suddenly as it had appeared.[163]

But the story of the Flagellants was not through yet. In 1348, a new wave emerged. At the time, the Black Plague was ravaging Europe. The death toll was tremendous: it would eventually kill around 50 million people (60% of the continent's total population).[164] Of

---

[161] Ibid., 5-6. See also Douie. *The Nature and Effect of the Heresy of the Fraticelli*, 31, and Toke. "Flagellants."

[162] Nagy and Biron-Ouellet. "A Collective Emotion in Medieval Italy," 6.

[163] Toke. "Flagellants." However, some scholars believe that this first wave of Flagellants were not condemned by the Church, and even received religious legitimacy. See Lowe-Martin. "Comparing Penitential Acts," 96.

[164] Benedictow. "The Black Death"

course, such a catastrophe was bound to elicit the same kind of apocalyptic and eschatological mindset on which the Flagellants thrived.

This was not the sole reason, however. The Black Death was merely a trigger, the spark igniting the flammable feelings and emotions simmering beneath the surface. The scandals and corruption affecting the world, and most especially the Church, made many people believe humankind to be irredeemably lost and that, therefore, the end was near.[165] Once again, we see a rigorist movement emerging as a legitimate reaction to ecclesiastical corruption, but ultimately spiraling out of control.

This second wave of Flagellants spread throughout Italy, almost as sudden as the first wave had. But it did not stop there—rather it kept spreading northward reaching Germany, the Netherlands, Poland, even Denmark.[166] It also crystallized into a more organized fashion. Whereas they were originally itinerants, going from town to town, this second kind eventually condensed into confraternities: the confreries of the so-called Penitents or *Disciplinati* (the "Disciplined.")[167]

Within these confraternities, the rituals and practices became more structured. The self-flagellation should now adhere to very rigid norms and be conducted by a "master."[168] They would wear a white mantle and habit with a red cross and process to the public squares twice a day. Once at the plazas, they would remove their shoes, strip themselves from the waist up and prostrate themselves

---

[165] Toke. "Flagellants."
[166] Ibid.
[167] Vincent, "Discipline du corps," 597, 599.
[168] Ibid., 603.

in a circle. Each particular sin would correspond to a specific posture: for example, the murderer would lie on his back and an adulterer on his face. First, each sinner would be stricken by the master, and only afterwards would they self-flagellate, while crying that their penance was forestalling the apocalypse. At the end, the master would read a letter supposedly conveyed by an angel to the church of St. Peter of Rome, saying that God's wrath would destroy the world, but that the Virgin Mary had promised that all those who joined the confraternity would be saved.[169] They would also hold regular private meetings wherein they would repeat the scourging.[170]

Most importantly, new members were required to undergo penance for thirty-three and a half days. During this period, the novice would swear complete obedience to the master, and also pay four pennies for each day of penance. Furthermore, the confraternities received sponsorships from nobles and city leaders. Of course, this became a source of corruption—an ironic twist for a movement formed from the reaction to ecclesial corruption. The Penitent congregations became wealthier and would display their richness with the fine garments and flags displayed in the processions. With wealth came power and influence: there are reports of priests who joined so they would not lose access to food.[171]

These kinds of manipulations alone would be enough to warrant a strong response from the Church. However, the Penitents also claimed for themselves undue independence from ecclesial authorities. For them, what was central was the imitation of Christ, without

---

[169] Toke. "Flagellants."
[170] Vincent, "Discipline du corps," 603.
[171] Lowe-Martin. "Comparing Penitential Acts," 100.

any need for ecclesiastical intermediaries.[172] Therefore, there was no need for sacraments: they could confess to their master, who would apply penance in the form of self-flagellation. This was aggravated by the fact that priests could not become masters or join the secret council. The Flagellants eschewed any kind of Church oversight, claiming that ordinary ecclesiastical jurisdiction was suspended for thirty-three and a half years (the amount of time their pilgrimages would continue.)[173]

Other heterodox practices, of a more rigorous bent, were also prevalent among them. They would assert the sinfulness of any contact with a woman, even if accidental. They imposed more rigid fasts on Fridays than the ones prescribed by the Church.[174] They treated the blood spilled during the rituals as if they were relics of saints.[175] Certain sinners would not be accepted on their midst: usurers, prostitutes, homosexuals, or tavern owners.[176]

Understanding the dangers posed by these new Flagellants, the Church took action once again. But whereas the reaction against the 1260 version had been relatively tame, the reaction against the 1349 form was decisive. The former had been much more in line with Church teaching and practice,[177] the latter was completely irreconcilable with a proper understanding of Christianity. After careful examination, Pope Clement VI condemned the movement and

---

[172] Vincent, "Discipline du corps," 599, 605-6.

[173] Lowe-Martin. "Comparing Penitential Acts," 101. See also Toke. "Flagellants."

[174] Toke. "Flagellants."

[175] Lowe-Martin. "Comparing Penitential Acts," 101.

[176] Vincent, "Discipline du corps," 612.

[177] Lowe-Martin. "Comparing Penitential Acts," 96, 101.

Chapter 7: Medieval Heresies and Spiritual Worldliness

forbade all processions, sending letters to that effect to many bishops of Northern Europe.[178]

Though the Flagellants had received a fatal wound, spontaneous recurrences would pop up in the next couple of centuries. For example, in 1360, a certain Konrad Schmid, calling himself Enoch (which, according to pious legend, was one of the two witnesses in Rev:11), would claim to have transferred all ecclesiastical authority away from the Church and unto himself. For nine years, Konrad was able to deceive thousands of men, until the Inquisition quashed his movement.[179]

Other movements would appear, also inspired by Flagellant practices. However, these would thrive, as they kept themselves under the wing of the magisterium. The *Bianchi* (Italian for "the Whites",) for example, were started by orthodox preachers, who never went against Church authority. Also, not all participants would self-flagellate. Pilgrims would join the procession, but not scourge themselves.[180] Other ecclesiastically sanctioned processions of Flagellants would happen throughout the centuries and across the world—though not commonly—right until the pontificate of Leo XIII, in the nineteenth century.[181]

In the end, though the 1349 Flagellants were raised as a legitimate reaction against widespread ecclesiastical corruption, and though they produced very good fruits at the beginning, they would turn heterodox as they moved away from obedience to the Church.

---

[178] Toke. "Flagellants."
[179] Ibid.
[180] Vincent, "Discipline du corps," 596-7.
[181] Toke. "Flagellants."

Thus, as the *Catholic Encyclopedia* so aptly puts it, the Flagellants "exemplified the fatal tendency of emotional pietism to degenerate into heresy."[182] A flagrant example of spiritual worldliness indeed.

---

[182] Ibid.

Chapter 8

Jansenism and Rigorism

The worst of these [sins] is pride, which can even infect people who live a profound religious life. There was once a well-known convent of nuns, in the 1600-1700s, at the time of Jansenism. They were utterly perfect, and it was said of them that they were really pure like angels, but also proud like demons.

—Francis, General Audience
April 10, 2019

In chapter 1, we have already made mention to Pope Francis' first big controversy: the provisions allowing communion for divorced and remarried people who are not in a state of mortal sin, due to mitigating circumstances hindering full knowledge or full consent. I have written extensively on how this is permitted by Catholic doctrine: the only condition infallibly defined as forbidding one from properly receiving the Eucharist is being in a state of mortal sin. All other restrictions are based on the Church's prudential judgment and can, therefore, be adjusted or even reversed if the Church discerns it as fitting to the circumstances and demands of the time.[1]

---

[1] Council of Trent, "13th Session, Chapter VII": "If it is unbecoming for any one to approach to any of the sacred functions, unless he approach in a spirit of piety; assuredly, the more the holiness and divinity of this heavenly sacrament are understood by a Christian, the more diligently ought he to give heed that he approach not to receive it but with great reverence

Some critics have attacked the prudence of this measure. For a sin to be a mortal sin, three conditions must be present: grave matter, full knowledge, and full consent.[2] In the cases of non-continent divorced and remarried couples, grave matter is always present, but whether the sin is committed with full knowledge or full consent must be discerned on a case-by-case basis. Since grave matter can be objectively determined, whereas the other factors cannot be verified with certainty, the Eucharistic discipline should focus on the former, lest a sinner risks taking a sacrilegious communion.[3]

---

and holiness, especially as we read in the Apostle those words full of terror; He that eateth and drinketh unworthily, eateth and drinketh judgment to himself. Wherefore, he who would communicate, ought to recall to mind the precept of the Apostle; Let a man prove himself. *Now ecclesiastical usage declares that necessary proof to be, that no one, conscious to himself of mortal sin, how contrite soever he may seem to himself, ought to approach to the sacred Eucharist without previous sacramental confession.* This the holy Synod hath decreed is to be invariably observed by all Christians." See also my comment at Gabriel. *The Orthodoxy of Amoris Laetitia*, 87—88.

[2] CCC, 1857.

[3] See, for example, Hickson, "Interview: Joseph Seifert on *Amoris Laetitia*": "It is impossible for a priest in 5 minutes' conversation in the confessional to determine that an unrepentant sinner is invincibly ignorant and in the state of grace, even though he intends to keep committing what are, objectively speaking, grave sins. From this practical impossibility of applying discernment which can hardly fail to end in a general opening of Confession and the Eucharist to unrepentant adulterous and homosexual couples, the imprudence of the decision of admitting the 'irregular couples' to the sacraments immediately follows. . . And as soon as we find a new pastoral decision of the Pope inapplicable in good conscience, such as giving the sacraments to unrepentant sinners on the basis of an (impossible for us) 'discernment' of whether their sin is compatible with their being in the state of grace for subjective reasons. . . In praxis, the failing attempt

Chapter 8: Jansenism and Rigorism

However, this discernment happens daily with a myriad of other objective sins. As Victor Fernandez, current Prefect of the Dicastery for the Doctrine of the Faith and alleged ghostwriter for *Amoris Laetitia*, wrote in an article on the matter, one is never "certain" of being in a state of grace, "even if one does not have conscience of having violated a commandment." Therefore, we are talking about a certain "moral security" that the person is not in mortal sin. This "moral security can be attained through a personal and pastoral discernment, which cannot base itself only in general norms."[4] In *Amoris Laetitia*, Pope Francis himself says that, though he understands "those who prefer a more rigorous pastoral care which leaves no room for confusion," he still believes that the Church should always do "what good she can, even if, in the process, her shoes get soiled by the mud in the streets."[5]

A more recent Eucharistic controversy emerged during the recent World Youth Day in Lisbon. During the final Papal Mass, the Eucharist was distributed to a massive gathering of 1.5 million people. But on the eve of this event, the Blessed Sacrament was stored in ciboria, which were placed in plastic boxes at the campsite.[6] Though cries for a more respectful handling and storage of the Blessed Sacrament during these crowded occasions is a good thing, many on social media fell on the diametrically opposite mistake,

---

to separate these 'good' and 'bad' grave sinners will inevitably lead to admitting every adulterer and homosexual to the sacraments, and many sacrileges will be committed."

[4] Fernández, "El capítulo VIII de *Amoris Laetitia*," 459—460.
[5] Francis. Amoris Laetitia, 308.
[6] Domingues, Claire and Pedro Gabriel. "World Youth Day and plastic containers."

postulating that the Eucharist should be withheld altogether from these events.[7] This would mean, in practice, that 1.5 million people—a staggering number! —would be deprived of the sanctifying grace of the sacrament, so as to keep it locked in a more proper container.

For both of these controversies, it would be instructive to read what Pope St. Pius X taught in his decree *Sacra Tridentina Synodus*:

> Moreover, the desire of Jesus Christ and of the Church that all the faithful should daily approach the sacred banquet is *directed chiefly to this end,* that the faithful, being united to God by means of the Sacrament, may thence derive strength to resist their sensual passions, to cleanse themselves from the stains of daily faults, and to avoid these graver sins to which human frailty is liable; *so that its primary purpose is not that the honor and reverence due to our Lord may be safeguarded,* or that it may serve as a reward or recompense of virtue bestowed on the recipients.[8]

Some readers may be surprised to know that Pius X, often hailed by conservatives today as a rigid pope cracking down on the liberal

---

[7] See, as an illustrative example of this social media reaction, the comment by JohnFoxFlash on the r/Catholicism Reddit thread "A look behind the WYD Eucharist controversy": "You have to attend mass on a Sunday, you do not have to receive communion every time you attend mass. I don't think communion ahould be given out at such large scale events, since it becomes really hard for it not to become irrevarant due to the logistics of it all."

[8] Pius X. *Sacra Tridentina*.

Chapter 8: Jansenism and Rigorism

and laxist heresy of Modernism, may have written something like this. But the truth is, Pius did not merely fight against the modernist laxists: he also had his own confrontations with the Jansenist rigorists of his day. But in order to better understand Pius's position on the Eucharist, we must contextualize what Jansenism is and how it came into being.

The eve of Jansenism: Calvin and Baius

As the name implies, the Reformation was triggered by a desire to curb widespread corruption and abuse in the Church through *reform*. On October 31, 1517, a monk named Martin Luther nailed ninety-five theses to the door of the cathedral of Wittenberg. Besides being a monk, Luther was also a successful moral theology professor and suffered from scrupulosity (see chapter 2). Among his theses was a condemnation of the practice of selling indulgences, which allowed a person to, in effect, pay money to lessen time in Purgatory. Luther also complained that the Church had grown too corrupt and luxuriant, namely at the higher echelons of the hierarchy. Though a need for reform would be acknowledged during the Council of Trent, Luther also made a series of doctrinal claims setting him at odds with the Church.[9] In this sense, he fell into the exact same pattern outlined in the previous chapter.

After releasing the genie from the bottle, Luther was not able to put it back in. Other reformers piggybacked on the momentum created by Luther while holding on to extravagant theologies never

---

[9] Morris, "Martin Luther as Priest." See also Mullin, *A Short World History of Christianity*, 122-3.

anticipated by him. One of such reformers was John Calvin, a French theologian. His followers would naturally be called Calvinists, but also "the Reformed."[10]

The Protestants wanted to nip Roman Catholic abuses in their theological bud, by asserting that good works (like buying indulgences) do not merit salvation. As an alternative, they proposed the doctrine of *sola fide* ("faith alone"), meaning that God's forgiveness of sins is granted through and received only through faith, excluding good deeds. It is no wonder then, that Protestants in general, and Calvin in particular, would take recourse to the profoundly anti-Pelagian writings of St. Augustine (see chapter 6).[11] Not only did Augustine give primacy to grace over works, but he was also a respected Church Father, from whom Calvin could squeeze authority.

There were, however, substantial differences between Calvinism and Augustinianism, though Calvin was probably unaware of it. For Calvin, original sin was not a privation of original righteousness (as Augustine thought), but total depravity and corruption. Whereas the Church Father saw Original Sin as a kind of illness or wound, Calvin thought of it as utter ruin.[12] Of course, this prevented Calvin from viewing grace as a healing medicine working *in* sinners. On the

---

[10] Mullin, *A Short World History of Christianity*, 123, 127—128.

[11] Sharp. "The Doctrine of Grace in Calvin," 84—85. As an example of Protestant anti-Pelagian rhetoric against Catholicism, see Bavinck. "The Influence of the Protestant Reformation", 76: "Opposing the so-called abuses of the Romish system, the Reformers discovered that these 'abuses' were but the natural fruit of the tree of Pelagianism, on which they grew."

[12] Sharp. "The Doctrine of Grace in Calvin," 85.

Chapter 8: Jansenism and Rigorism

contrary, grace would be God working through Jesus Christ to save the sinners.[13]

This had a profound impact on how Calvinism viewed good works and free will. For Augustine, salvation is a gift from God indeed, but God saves by bestowing on His elect the gifts of faith, works, and merits.[14] God takes what good is left in us and increases it, while healing us from our sinful inclinations (though no one achieves perfection on this side of eternity, *contra* the Pelagians.) Yet, for Calvin, the only goodness that exists is the one Jesus imputes in us. Righteousness is not infused *in* us, but something working completely *outside* us and accomplished by Christ. This means that, for Calvin, our will is not truly free, but is enslaved by sin. As we have seen in chapter 6, Augustine was indeed fighting against an absolutization of free will to the detriment of grace. But Augustine never sought to deny free will, whereas Calvin thought that the very term "free will" should be abolished, lest any free human action robbed God of His honor.[15]

One can ask: how can a theology that deemphasizes free will and good works so much end up as morally rigoristic? True, if an individual does good, then that person must ascribe the merit to God. On the other hand, if the same individual commits a sin, then he or she is to blame, not God. As a corollary, the individual assumes full responsibility for all errors and failures. The person is asked to obey a set of laws of which he or she will always fall short. This humbles the person before God, so he or she will accept His plan of salvation,

---

[13] Sharp. "The Doctrine of Grace in Calvin," 85.
[14] Ibid., 87.
[15] Ibid., 90-1.

patiently enduring any misfortune as just and good. Even if the Calvinist does not find salvation in good works, he or she still works hard for the glory of that God Who saves.[16]

It is interesting to note how, once again, one does not flee error by taking refuge on the diametrically opposite extreme. Both Pelagianism and Calvinism stand at polar opposites as regards free will and good works, yet they both fall into moral rigidity. Just like Pelagianism, Calvinism resurrected a certain Stoicism in terms of discipline (see chapter 6).[17] The Reformed condemned theater and viewed art as idolatry.[18] For them, displays like Michelangelo's

---

[16] Ross. "The Ethical Basis of Calvinism," 440—441. See also what is written in the proceedings of a Reformed council held in Toronto in 1892: "And yet, we must not forget that Calvinism, even in its strictest form, differs on principle from the Romish asceticism and from the Anabaptist 'avoidance.' These originate in despisal of the world; in the thought that the natural life, as being of a lower order, cannot be sanctified. But the Calvinistic rigorism was born from the desire to consecrate the whole life to God... And now that it may be true that Calvinism, by its strict preaching of God's justice and law, awakens a deep feeling of guilt and un-worthiness in man, and that it prostrates him deeply in the dust before God's sovereign majesty; but equally true it is, that afterwards, it elevates him to a singular height of blessedness, and that it causes him to rest in the free, eternal, and unchangeable good pleasure of the Father. This system is certainly not adapted to the making of 'soft and dear' people, and it is averse to all sickly sentimentality. But it creates men of marble, with a character of steel, with a will of iron, with an insuperable power, with an extraordinary energy" (Bavinck, "The Influence of the Protestant Reformation", 78, 80).

[17] Ross. "The Ethical Basis of Calvinism," 449.

[18] Ibid., 444-5.

Chapter 8: Jansenism and Rigorism

nudes in "The Last Judgment" at the Sistine Chapel were signs of the moral laxity and worldliness of the Catholic Church.[19]

In fact, one of the branches that would spring from the Calvinist tree would be the famous Puritans, who sought to "purify" a corrupt world the same way they themselves had been purified by God's grace. The Puritans knew that nature was corrupt (and would always remain so in this life), so they would always distrust every impulse.[20] They also sought to "purify" the Anglican Church of the theological remnants of what they perceived as "Roman Catholic popery."[21] As we have seen in chapters 5 and 7, they were not the first moral rigorists to avail the name of "Pure."

Though, as we shall see, Jansenism would be influenced by Calvinism, this would not be its only root. As the Council of Trent was convened to address both the Protestants' theological errors and the need for moral reform of the Church, another theologian participated in those proceedings. His name was Michel Baius, a theologian at the University of Louvain, sent as a delegate of the king of Spain

---

[19] Kedmey. "How the Sistine Chapel spawned a public relations nightmare": "The unveiling took place against the backdrop of the Reformation, when Protestant reformers were lambasting the Vatican as a 'den of iniquity.' Within the Papal Court, there was a group of austere clergymen known as the Theatines, who were quite sensitive to Protestant critiques. To them, Michelangelo's nudes had the makings of a PR disaster. 'They just see a wall of naked bodies,'" See also Frazier. "Major Influences Contributing to Michelangelo's Last Judgment": "Despite Michelangelo's efforts, the Protestant Reformers and the Catholic Church attacked The Last Judgment. For the Protestants, Michelangelo's images were forms of idolatry, and examples of the worldliness that had invaded the church."

[20] Ross. "The Ethical Basis of Calvinism," 443.

[21] Editors of the Encyclopaedia Britannica. "Puritanism."

to Trent. Baius's orthodoxy, however, was suspect and his ideas did not curry favor with the Council Fathers.[22]

Baius wanted to help the Church counter the Reformation.[23] He believed that developing a proper Catholic understanding of grace would bring the Protestants back into the Church's fold.[24] For this reason, he created a theological system, later creatively named "Baianism." In this system, the original state of Man before the Fall (the "state of innocent nature") was not supernatural, but was the normal condition of humanity, including destination to heaven, immunity from ignorance, and the inherent power of meriting. These could not, therefore, be called gratuitous gifts of grace, properly understood. After the Fall came the state of fallen nature, in which Original Sin was not the forfeiture of supernatural, gratuitous gifts, but an actual evil taking hold of human nature. Original Sin was—as Augustine thought—transmitted through the laws of heredity, but more than that, Baius thought that it was a sin in itself, so that even babies were sinners, even before attaining the age of reason or will. For Baius, to be a moral agent, one need not be free from

---

[22] Sollier. "Michel Baius."

[23] See Sollier. "Michel Baius": "A partial explanation of, if not excuse for, that monomania is, however, found in the fact that at the very outset of his theological career Baius came under the influence of men who, like the Dominican Peter de Soto, believed the Catholic reaction against the Reformers had gone somewhat too far, and suggested that more stress be laid on Scripture and Patrology and less on Thomism. That, in his intention at least, Baius only wanted to take the most advantageous position in order the better to defend the Faith against heretics, we know from a letter he wrote."

[24] O'Connor. "Jansenism," 320.

internal determinism, but only from external compulsion. Finally, after Jesus's sacrifice on the cross, there was the state of redeemed nature, in which primitive innocence was restored by Christ, so that the redeemed sinner could perform good deeds and merit heaven. In this sense, even the Eucharist had no other power besides being a good action aiding the sinner get closer to God.[25]

This Baianist system was not, however, compatible with Catholic orthodoxy. Regarding the "state of innocent nature" it was unduly influenced by Pelagianism, whereas its "state of fallen nature" was too Calvinist. At the Council of Trent, it was infallibly defined that original innocence was a supernatural gift, that Original Sin was a forfeiture of purely gratuitous privileges, and that justification is an interior renovation of the soul by grace.[26]

In 1567, Pope St. Pius V published his bull *Ex omnibus afflictionibus*, condemning a series of Baianist propositions—without, however, singling out Baius. Many followers of the Baianist system (and, eventually and briefly, Baius himself) tried to evade these condemnations by arguing that they did not address any of Baius's claims, but merely imaginary propositions attributed to Baius. It would be under the pontiff's purview to condemn those hypothetical theories, but they had missed the mark. They did not, therefore, truly condemn Baius or Baianism, as they *really* were in practice. We will see similar evasion tactics later in this chapter, when dealing with Jansenism. Still, Baius recanted his errors, in the same way as Pius had formulated them. Though the professor came very close to infringing on Church teaching, he would die in communion with the

---

[25] Sollier. "Michel Baius."
[26] Ibid.

Church.²⁷ The seeds planted by his system, however, would still wreak havoc in the following centuries.

Facts that were not right

There were other attempts at countering the Protestant Reformation besides Baius's failed system. One of the most successful was the foundation of the Society of Jesus (a.k.a. the Jesuit Order) by St. Ignatius of Loyola in 1545. In addition to the classical vows of poverty, chastity, and obedience, the Jesuits added a special vow of obedience to the pope. At first, this vow had mostly to do with missionary work, but it eventually ended up partially offsetting the widespread disobedience to the papacy, so prevalent at the time.²⁸

In this context, one Jesuit tried to do something very similar to Baius: to develop a Catholic theology of grace aimed at answering

---

²⁷ Ibid.

²⁸ Cameron, "The Counter-Reformation," 89: "Despite increasingly focused guidance from the centre, the Counter-Reformation witnessed many spontaneous initiatives in Catholic Christianity from the body of the Church. Most conspicuous was the rise of a multiplicity of new religious orders... The largest and most influential was the Society of Jesus, incorporated in 1540 though active informally before that date. An important recent insight into the Society of Jesus suggests that its members, at least in the first generation, were largely detached from the waves of 'Counter-Reformation' thought, with its focus on doctrinal definition, administrative control, and militant re-conquest of lost regions of Europe. The first Jesuits sought 'the good of souls' through pastoral preaching and teaching, including missions abroad, and were not especially concerned either with theology or government. However, circumstances soon conspired to deflect the Jesuits somewhat from their original intent."

Chapter 8: Jansenism and Rigorism

Protestant concerns. This Jesuit, however, went about it in the opposite direction of Baius: by strongly reasserting the Catholic understanding of free will. This Jesuit's name was Luis de Molina.

Molina accepted the Augustinian tenet of prevenient grace: God's grace is necessary even for the person to "start" the process of conversion. It is God Who takes the initiative (see chapter 6). However, God also has foreknowledge of that person's free choices, so He knows whether the person is going to freely accept or reject grace. In His omniscience, God can bestow the necessary amount of grace, sufficient for the sinner to turn away from sin, but only efficacious insofar as the person responds positively to that grace.[29] Any other interpretation, according to Molina, would be mere determinism from an arbitrary God.[30] This way, free will was preserved, thus providing an appropriate alternative to Calvinism.

This Molinist theology did not sit well with those who followed a more classical Thomistic understanding of grace, leading to fierce debates in Catholic theological circles. For this reason, the Inquisition forbade publications on the topic of grace without explicit papal permission in 1611.[31] But Thomists were not the only ones to dislike Molina's ideas. Cornelius Jansen, the Bishop of Ypres (current-day Belgium), would become one of Molinism's most formidable adversaries.

Jansen was a renowned theologian and professor of exegesis at the University of Louvain. During the course of his studies, Jansen would be influenced by teachers who were fond of Baianism. Still,

---

[29] Pohle. "Molinism."
[30] Blanchard. "Are Jansenists among us?"
[31] O'Connor. "Jansenism," 322.

Jansen's doctorate thesis was a superb defense of papal infallibility. As he would write: "The Roman Pontiff is the supreme judge of all religious controversies; when he defines a thing and imposes it on the whole Church, under penalty of anathema, his decision is just, true, and infallible."[32]

But this Jansen also had a profound distaste for Molina's theories. While Molina thought he was safeguarding human free will, Jansen thought he was actually sacrificing the total gratuity of grace by making humans the authors of their own salvation. For Jansen, God predestined mortals for salvation, but not because of any foreseen faith or good works.[33] Influenced by Baius, Jansen contrasted the fallen and unfallen Man, so that humans could only reach their true nature by means of divine grace. Man deprived of God's grace inevitably chooses evil, but God's grace is *also* irresistible. In other words, just like Man's will, corrupted by sin, cannot but choose evil, Man cannot also reject the gift of God's grace: humans are effectively and irresistibly determined by this gift.[34]

This was inspired on the principle of the "victorious delectation of grace," which we have already explored in chapter 6. A soul delights in evil when deprived of God's grace, but delights in good when given this grace, which then triumphs over concupiscence. Both delights—the earthly and the heavenly—are therefore like two plates of a scale (with the heavenly one being preponderant), inevitably determining a person's choices. Man inevitably obeys what gives delight, being either dominated by concupiscence or grace: he

---

[32] Forget. "Jansenius and Jansenism."
[33] Blanchard. "Are Jansenists among us?"
[34] Palmer. *Jansenism and England*, 139—140.

Chapter 8: Jansenism and Rigorism

cannot resist either, according to his state.[35] Grace is not merely sufficient, but efficacious.

Jansen's anthropological pessimism could not be reconciled with the typical Jesuitical optimism of Molina and his followers.[36] Molinism was a "pagan argument,"—so Jansen argued—since God would be a mere dispenser of grace to autonomous individuals, turning the universe into a *de facto* godless world. Jansen also tried to highlight the parallels between the Molinists and the "Semipelagians" (see chapter 6), effectively equating the former with the latter.[37] It is unsurprising then, that Jansen took recourse to St. Augustine, that great champion against Pelagianism, to fight his own war. He wrote a book (later named *Augustinus de gratia*), where he set out to revive an Augustinian view of grace with the intent of displacing the Semipelagian threat of Molinism.

Jansen would never see his book published. In 1638, Ypres was swept over by a deadly epidemic which also took Jansen's life. The good bishop died, still within the bosom of the Catholic Church. Whether he would be subservient to the Church's judgment had he lived is a matter of speculation. On the one hand, he requested his book to be published with the condition that if "the Holy See wishes

---

[35] Forget. "Jansenius and Jansenism."

[36] O'Connor. "Jansenism," 320.

[37] Radner. "Early Modern Jansenism," 438. Please remember what I wrote in chapter 6: "However, most scholars nowadays dislike this term [Semipelagian], since it was produced in connection with later debates on grace in the 16th century." See also Blanchard. "Are Jansenists among us?": "The Augustinians who came to be known as Jansenists thought that this new system was basically semi-Pelagian." See also Palmer. *Jansenism and England*, 139.

any change, I am an obedient son, and I submit to that Church in which I have lived to my dying hour. This is my last wish." On the other hand, some of Jansen's correspondence in the years before showed a different disposition, predicting upcoming disputes for which there was need to prepare, "lest like so many others I be tripped up by Rome before everything is ripe and seasonable" (possibly referring here to Baius's precedent.)[38] In the end, it would have been up to Jansen's free will, meaning his reaction would be unpredictable.

Still, Jansen's followers tried to fulfill the dying bishop's testament by posthumously publishing the *Augustinus*. The book would be a smashing success, especially in France. At its peak, it would claim some of most brilliant minds of French Catholicism, like the great apologist and mathematician Blaise Pascal. Of course, the Jesuits correctly saw this as an attack against their theology and derisively dubbed the disciples of the new movement "Jansenists."[39]

Unfortunately, despite its success, Jansenism was fraught with error. It is true, as we have seen in chapter 6, that St. Augustine did indeed speak of grace as causing the will to act "irresistibly and infallibly." However, as we also saw, he never said this in a way meant to contradict human free will. Grace leads Man "infallibly and invincibly" to beatitude, not by suppressing freedom. Rather, it is implied that this happens with human consent. The delectation of grace is "deliberate," not a "necessity" (*voluptas, non necessitas*). Or rather, Man *necessarily* wills what gives most pleasure, but he only wills it by embracing it with *consenting* pleasure. It is with this caveat

---

[38] Forget. "Jansenius and Jansenism."
[39] O'Connor. "Jansenism," 318.

Chapter 8: Jansenism and Rigorism   273

in mind that we should read Augustine's dictum that "in acting we necessarily follow what gives us most pleasure." Also, when Augustine talked about the "victorious delight of grace," he mentioned it as grace triumphing not over human will, but over concupiscence, so that, free from the constraints of sinful inclinations, Man may better choose the good. In this sense, grace does not crush free will, but strengthens it.[40] Finally, Jansen's theology also presupposed that, if Man cannot resist neither sin nor grace, then some are gratuitously elected to attain salvation, while others are arbitrarily condemned to eternal damnation. This double predestination bore a terrible resemblance with Calvinism (see above). Since not all would be saved, it could not be said that Christ died for all.[41]

These theological errors did not escape the eyes of the Church, especially since the *Augustinus*'s book on grace had, contrary to the explicit instructions of the Holy Office, been published without papal approval. Also, the book had too many similarities with the condemned propositions of Baius. In 1641, the Inquisition forbade the reading of *Augustinus*, and the next year Pope Urban VIII renewed the condemnation and interdiction in his bull *In eminenti*.[42]

Augustinus, however, was already too popular, taking hold of many reputed minds. The emerging Jansenist movement found a leader in Jean Duvergier de Hauranne, the abbé of Saint-Cyran.[43] Though an elderly man, he was rather active, influential, and well-connected. He strove to keep the book in circulation and to promote

---

[40] Forget. "Jansenius and Jansenism."
[41] Palmer. *Jansenism and England*, 132.
[42] Forget. "Jansenius and Jansenism."
[43] Radner. "Early Modern Jansenism," 436.

its principles of moral rigorism and discipline. Later on, his *protegé* Antoine Arnauld succeeded him at the helm of the Jansenist movement.[44] Antoine's sister, Angelique, became abbess of the convent of Port-Royal des Champs, outside Paris, where she instituted overhauling reforms to oppose the convent's excessive laxism. From a laxist establishment, Port-Royal would evolve to become a major hub of Jansenism.[45] At a certain moment during the 18th century, half of the Parisian clergy had been "jansenized."[46]

This could not be allowed to stand. After a papal commission examined *Augustinus*, Innocent X issued the bull *Cum occasione*, condemning five propositions from Jansen's book:

1. Some of God's commandments are impossible to just men who wish and strive (to keep them) considering the powers they actually have, the grace by which these precepts may become possible is also wanting;
2. In the state of fallen nature no one ever resists interior grace;
3. To merit, or demerit, in the state of fallen nature we must be free from all external constraint, but not from interior necessity,
4. The Semipelagians (i.e., Molinists) admitted the necessity of interior preventing grace for all acts, even for the beginning of faith; but they fell into heresy in pretending that this grace is such that man may either follow or resist it;

---

[44] O'Connor. "Jansenism," 323. See also Forget. "Jansenius and Jansenism."

[45] Blanchard. "Are Jansenists among us?"

[46] O'Connor. "Jansenism," 327.

5. To say that Christ died or shed His blood for all men, is Semipelagianism.[47]

The first four propositions were condemned absolutely, and the fifth only if understood in the sense that Jesus died only for the predestined. But of all the five, the second one was the axis of error from whence all other errors sprung.[48]

The Jansenists, however, refused to accept the pope's correction. To achieve this while at the same time maintaining their orthodoxy, they devised a clever argument, already attempted a century before by the Baianists (see above). Antoine Arnauld argued that the pope had indeed the God-given authority to condemn the five propositions, and he rejected these propositions in the way the pope had expressed them. However, Arnauld lawyered himself out of that mess by affirming that none of the five propositions was present in the *Augustinus*—or if they were, they were there in a different sense than the one the pope had condemned.[49] In other words, even if the pope had the *right* ("*droit*") to condemn those propositions, he could not make an authoritative pronouncement on the *fact* ("*fait*") of whether or not these propositions were in the *Augustinus*.[50] Matters of fact were outside of divine revelation and were, therefore, not covered by the Church's infallibility. In matters pertaining to *right*—so was argued—Catholics should conform unreservedly, whereas in matters of *fact*, the proper Catholic response would be a respectful

---

[47] Forget. "Jansenius and Jansenism."
[48] Ibid.
[49] Ibid.
[50] O'Connor. "Jansenism," 325.

silence, but internal assent could be safely withheld.[51] Through this subterfuge, Arnauld convinced many that the book could still be read by Catholics in good standing with the Church.

Of course, the Church correctly interpreted this as an affront to her authority. If the Church was only able to condemn heretics in an abstract way, without being able to affirm whether a certain heretic held those heresies or not, then the gates were wide open to relativism. Innocent's successor, Alexander VII, issued another bull, titled *Ad sanctam*, wherein he stated that the five propositions were indeed contained in the *Augustinus*, and that they were condemned in the sense intended by Jansen. In a later bull, *Regiminis apostolici*, Alexander condemned Arnauld's false dichotomy between *right* and *fact*.[52]

Unfortunately, this did not end the controversy. The pope drew up a formulary to be signed by those assenting to his teaching. The nuns of Port-Royal refused to sign it. Alongside them, some French bishops also refused to sign the formulary. And the more the Inquisition cracked down, the more this was seen as a Roman abuse of power on French episcopal prerogatives by an increasing Gallican public opinion. Alexander's successor, Clement IX sought to avoid a schism by extending an olive branch: the wayward bishops would not need to retract or face any penalties, only sign the formulary.[53] This the bishops did, but while muddying the waters: even if they signed the formulary in written, they said orally (both in person or through intermediaries) that they maintained a respectful silence on

---

[51] Forget. "Jansenius and Jansenism."
[52] O'Connor. "Jansenism," 326.
[53] Ibid.

Chapter 8: Jansenism and Rigorism 277

matters of fact. The pope, deceived and wishing for a quick end for the controversy, did not press too much on this, and the *status quo* was allowed to be maintained[54]: the pope honestly thought that the bishops had submitted to his authority and the Jansenists had, through cunning, safeguarded their conscience.

This would be called the "Clement IX's peace." As we shall see later, it was a rotten peace. Here, we can see a nasty side effect sprouting from religious rigidity: those who place an undue emphasis on the law tend to, as we have seen in chapter 3, stick too avidly to the "letter of the law" and not its "spirit." By doing so, rigid people tend to find loopholes in the law to justify their own disobedience, for they cannot bear to admit their rebellion to themselves and others. The Jansenists' false dichotomy between right and fact was an excuse they repeated to themselves to assuage their consciences when disobeying the pope's manifest mind and will, while maintaining that they were perfectly within the bounds allowed by the Catholic faith, no matter what the pope said or thought. Thus, the *Catholic Encyclopedia* rightfully says:

> It is evident that, besides [Jansenism's] attachment to the *Augustinus* and its rigorism in morals, it is distinguished among heresies for crafty proceedings, chicane and lack of frankness on the part of its adherents, especially their pretence of remaining Catholics without renouncing their errors, of staying in the Church despite the Church itself, by

---

[54] Forget. "Jansenius and Jansenism."

skillfully eluding or braving with impunity the decisions of the supreme authority.[55]

Rigorism, Laxism, and Probabilism

There were other reasons for this "Clement IX's peace," besides an accurate fear of schism. Other errors, namely of a laxist bent, were seen at the time as being more urgent to tackle—and the Jansenists were seen as natural allies in the fight against laxism. Innocent XI used Antoine Arnauld's literary output to underpin his condemnations of certain laxist opinions defended by some moral theologians of his time.[56]

Blaise Pascal was particularly vocal against the alleged moral laxity of Jesuit casuistry and theology.[57] Furthermore, Arnauld was scandalized by Jesuit missionary attempts at inculturation, like the "Chinese rites," which tried to incorporate Chinese cultural elements into the liturgy to better evangelize the culture. The Jesuits justified themselves by appealing to "pagan virtues," known by natural reason, inscribed in the hearts of men.[58] These pagan virtues could be used as a springboard to achieve missionary goals. The concept of pagan virtue was actually quite traditional, based as it was on Aristotle's four cardinal virtues which Aquinas incorporated into his

---

[55] Ibid.

[56] O'Connor. "Jansenism," 327. See also Forget. "Jansenius and Jansenism."

[57] O'Connor. "Jansenism," 326. See also Forget. "Jansenius and Jansenism." See also Radner. "Early Modern Jansenism," 440.

[58] Rom 2:14—15.

Chapter 8: Jansenism and Rigorism

theology. But Arnauld went so far as denying the existence of pagan virtues, since *no one* is virtuous. If Christians were incapable of virtue, what more non-Christians! All attempts at inculturation were, therefore, folly.[59] Furthermore, Jansenists were also distrustful of what they perceived as abuses from popular piety and devotions.[60]

Jansenism led to moral rigidity, due to its pessimistic anthropology and predestinarian theology, in a similar way as the Puritans. In fact, the parallels between Jansenism and Puritanism are striking in certain respects. Just like the Puritans, Jansenists were wary of activities they tended to see as hedonistic, like music and theater. Both movements believed they could reform the Church through their moral purity.[61] Finally, they were both Augustinian—or so they thought.

Yet, for all their similarities, Jansenists abhorred Calvinism. For them, Calvin failed in the same way as their natural enemy Molina did: both Calvinism and Molinism seemed to underestimate the transformation exerted by God's grace on human sinfulness during the process of redemption. Both Calvinism and Molinism seemed to find assurances of salvation where none existed: the former in a "once saved always saved" principle wherein one is saved by faith alone once and for all; the latter because of a "work-based salvation,"[62] typical of a Catholic caricature so prevalent in those times. Nevertheless, it can be argued that the reason why Jansenism was so hostile to Calvinism was not so much theological as attitudinal: for

---

[59] Radner. "Early Modern Jansenism," 440.
[60] Forget. "Jansenius and Jansenism."
[61] Palmer. *Jansenism and England*, 133.
[62] Ibid., 212-3.

the Jansenist, one should suffer for the truth from *within* the Church; moral purity was not a justification to break communion with the Church, even if she was corrupt.[63] One could actually say, while Luther and Calvin "waged an open war, Jansenism was a secret plot."[64]

Interestingly enough, a parallel debate had been going on in the field of moral theology between rigorism and laxism. These are not moral labels coined by modernist theologians, but rather well-defined and acknowledged movements within moral theology. "Rigorism" was a word coined at around 1670 in the Spanish Netherlands as a derogatory term against those who believed in a delayed absolution to penitents, so as to excite a deeper contrition before absolution. As for "laxism," it is a more recent slur (from the 18th century), but denoting concepts already discussed in the previous century under the name "*relâchement*" (meaning "relaxation.")[65]

Rigorism and laxism came to be known as the two polar opposites of a moral question: regarding a moral choice, is it licit or not to follow the less safe moral venue? For us to fully appreciate what this means, some background is in order. If a law forbids a certain action, the subjects should abstain from said action, unless they have any kind of special exemption. On the other hand, if a law does not forbid an action, then the subject may practice that action if he or she sees fit. Until now, there is nothing controversial. But not everything is so clear cut. Sometimes, there can be doubts about whether

---

[63] Radner. "Early Modern Jansenism," 440.

[64] Dalgairns. *The Devotion to the Heart of Jesus*, 6.

[65] Van Hove. "Brief Notices: Quantin, Jean-Louis. *Le Rigorisme chrétien*," 171-2.

Chapter 8: Jansenism and Rigorism

a law really forbids a certain action. If that is the case, what should the subject do? Should he always err on the side of the law, or on the side of liberty?[66]

Erring on the side of the law is what is called the "safe opinion." But this does not mean that it is the more "probable opinion." Usually, in ascertaining what opinion is more probable, one would take recourse to a consensus of "prudent men" (theologians notable for their prudence and learning,) who would be convinced to hold that opinion by intrinsic or extrinsic arguments. But how many of these "prudent men" would be needed to form a consensus? Therein lied the crux of the problem.[67]

Laxism held that the less safe opinion could be followed with a safe conscience, even if it were only slightly probable. Rigorism, on the other hand, maintained that one could only follow the less safe opinion if the contrary opinion was very probable, almost certain.[68] To put it simply, one should always err on the side of the law, except in matters where one would be almost sure that erring on the side of liberty was allowed. For this reason, Rigorism was also sometimes dubbed Tutiorism, from the Latin *tutior*," meaning "safer."[69]

Someone unfamiliar with these debates might think that Catholic doctrine would be tutiorist, but they would be wrong. Neither Laxism nor Rigorism have ever gained general recognition among Catholic moral theologians. Truly, both have been condemned by the Church's magisterium, as we shall see later. On the contrary,

---

[66] Harty. "Probabilism."
[67] Ibid.
[68] Ibid.
[69] Redmond. "Conscience as a Moral Judgment," 401–402.

Catholic doctrine has tended to prefer moderate positions between the Laxist and Rigorist extremes.[70] Among these moderate positions, one can list, in general terms:

- Probabilism: One may follow the less safe opinion (i.e., the side of freedom as opposed to the law) if this opinion *is solidly probable* (which would mean, in practice, the opinion of five or six "prudent men");
- Equiprobabilism: One may follow the less safe opinion if it is *as probable as* (i.e., has the same probability as) the safe opinion;
- Probabiliorism: One may follow the less safe opinion only when it is *more probable than* the safe opinion;
- Compensationism: One must take into consideration, not only the *probability*, but also the *importance* of the law; The more important the law, and the less the probability, the greater the *compensation utility* of following the less safe opinion must be.[71]

It is not surprising to know that the Jansenists adopted the Rigorist / Tutiorist position. The greatest defender of Rigorism at the University of Louvain, the Irish theologian Sinnichius, was also a Jansenist. Pascal, in his *Lettres Provinciales*, severely criticized Probabilism.

---

[70] Harty. "Probabilism".
[71] Ibid. See also Redmond. "Conscience as a Moral Judgment," 402—403.

But this Jansenist support did not further the cause of Rigorism. Quite the contrary, it hindered it. Pope Alexander VII who, as we have seen above, issued two bulls condemning Jansenism, also censured Pascal's *Lettres Provinciales* in 1657. A few decades later, the main Rigorist propositions from Sinnichius would also be condemned by the pope.[72] Slowly, the resistance to Jansenism led the Church to adopt Probabilism or Equiprobabilism.

Obviously, Jansenists did not like Probabilism at all. Just like Calvinism and Molinism (see above), Probabilism seemed to be looking for certainty of salvation where none existed. By resting on a doctrine of merely probable opinions, Probabilism created a formalist casuistry that was over-eager to accommodate human frailty by sacrificing the necessary moral transformation the sinner must undergo.[73] Probabilism, according to the Jansenists, was detrimental to the spiritual life of the faithful, since it permitted actions which ought to be forbidden. They claimed that Probabilism would lead to Laxism, because people are often inclined to regard opinions as more probable than what they really are, basing themselves on flimsy arguments. Also, it would not be difficult to find five or six serious authors approving of lax opinions. The only sure way to avoid falling into Laxism would be to adopt a foolproof system like Rigorism / Tutiorism.[74]

However, Probabilism is not such an easy slippery slope towards Laxism. The arguments in favor of the probability of an opinion must be solid enough to gain the acceptance of five or six prudent

---

[72] Harty. "Probabilism".

[73] Palmer. *Jansenism and England*, 212—213.

[74] Harty. "Probabilism".

men. Also, those prudent men must have been given solid proof of their prudence and learning before their opinion is considered.[75] Furthermore, how foolproof could Rigorism be, if it was held by manifest heretics as the Jansenists?

It would be the weighty opinion of a certain prudent man that would definitely tip the Church's scales against Rigorism. He was one of the greatest moral theologians of all times: St. Alphonsus Liguori (see chapter 2). No one can argue that he is a laxist. In fact, St. Alphonsus is held in high esteem even among those who would proudly consider themselves rigid against Pope Francis's warnings.

Alphonsus certainly struggled with the rigorist leanings imputed to him by his theological upbringing. However, his contact with the concrete experiences of the people seeking his help in the sacrament of Reconciliation helped Alphonsus temper his rigid inclinations. As Pope Francis recounts:

> The Holy Doctor, formed according to a rigourist moral mentality, converted to "benignity" through listening to reality... The missionary experience in the existential peripheries of his time, the search for those far away and listening to confessions, the founding and guidance of the nascent Congregation of the Most Holy Redeemer, and in addition the responsibilities as bishop of a particular Church, led him to become a father and master of mercy...
>
> The gradual conversion towards a decidedly missionary pastoral ministry, capable of closeness to the people, of being

---

[75] Ibid.

able to accompany their steps, to share in their real life even in the midst of great limits and challenges, drove Alphonsus to review, not without effort, even the theological and juridical grounding he had received in the years of his formation; initially marked by a certain rigour, it then turned into a merciful, dynamic approach, an evangelising dynamism able to act by attraction...

Saint Alphonsus, then, was neither lax nor strict. He was a realist in the true Christian sense, because he understood clearly that "at the very heart of the Gospel is life in community and engagement with others."[76]

St. Alphonsus's pipeline went from Rigorist, to Probabiliorist, to Probabilist, to Equiprobabilist. The latter system was the one adopted at the time of the later editions of his seminal work: "Moral Theology."[77] Since this work became one of the most influential volumes of Catholic moral theology, it became increasingly more difficult for the Church to condemn Probabilism or Equiprobabilism without standing condemned herself.

As the Church slowly moved towards Probabilism during the 18th century, "Clement IX's peace" was bound to break. After all, it had been grounded on false pretences and Jansenist deceit. In 1701, an academic discussion began around the so-called "case of conscience": could absolution be granted to a cleric holding certain Jansenist sentiments, like that of respectful silence on matters of fact?

---

[76] Francis. "Message to mark the 150th Anniversary of the Proclamation of St. Alphonsus Maria de Liguori."

[77] Harty. "Probabilism".

Though many respected scholars thought this could be done, it exposed the Jansenist ruse. Pope Clement XI was quick to side with those voting "nay" on this question. A couple of years later, he condemned the "case of conscience."

Clement XI issued a papal bull stating that respectful silence was not sufficient to obey the peace established by his namesake predecessor. When the pope asked the clergy and religious to accept this new bull, many said they would only do so "without derogating from what had taken place in regard to them at the time of the peace of the Church of Clement IX."[78] In other words, their obedience had been a sham all along. They complied with their mouths, but not with their hearts (see chapter 3).

The convent of Port-Royal was ordered to be literally razed to the ground, and its nuns scattered by other monasteries.[79] Clement XI wrote another bull, titled "*Unigenitus*," firmly condemning additional 101 propositions associated with a new Jansenist book, imaginatively titled *Augustinus*.[80] With *Unigenitus*, Jansenism had received its magisterial coup de grâce.

Jansenism did not die immediately, though. It lingered in France through one pretext or another, until the French Revolution's anti-clerical streak tried to eradicate all traces of religion (and thus, Jansenism) from the midst of France's collective conscience.[81] Still, as

---

[78] Forget. "Jansenius and Jansenism." See also Radner. "Early Modern Jansenism," 436—437.

[79] Blanchard. "Are Jansenists among us?"

[80] Forget. "Jansenius and Jansenism." See also Radner. "Early Modern Jansenism," 436—437.

[81] O'Connor. "Jansenism," 332.

we shall soon see, residues of Jansenist thought kept contaminating the Catholic milieu during the next couple of centuries, "especially in the rigorism which for a long time dominated the practice of the administration of the sacraments and the teaching of moral theology."[82]

Eucharist: not a reward for virtue

Another point of contention between Jansenists and Protestants was the Eucharist. Protestants rejected the traditional Catholic teaching of transubstantiation, wherein the bread and wine become the true Body and Blood of Christ during the consecration at Mass. The Council of Trent, called in response to the Reformation, had reaffirmed the dogma of transubstantiation. The Jansenists, who saw themselves as fulfilling Catholic doctrine, naturally sided with Trent on this question.

In 1659, the notable Jansenist leader Antoine Arnauld wrote a preface to the eucharistic liturgy used by the nuns of Port-Royal. In this preface, Arnauld came strongly in favor of transubstantiation, drawing solid arguments from tradition to prove the dogma.[83] By embroiling himself in this controversy, Arnauld also sought to cement his credentials as an orthodox thinker. Here, he was not merely writing against the Jesuits or the papacy but defending undeniable Catholic principles. The Church would have to recognize his

---

[82] Forget. "Jansenius and Jansenism."
[83] Hamilton. "From East to West," 83.

arguments as legitimate,[84] and this could help Jansenist theology to slowly creep into the Catholic intellectual and spiritual spheres.

Unfortunately for him, his plan backfired, for unbeknownst to Arnauld, he was set on a collision course with the Jesuits and the papacy. Scandalized protests echoed in Port-Royal against the frequent communion of a certain Marquise de Sablé, a philosopher, writer, and salon hostess. The Marquise defended herself with the instructions of her Jesuit spiritual director, who in turn based himself on Molinist theology.[85]

This would not do. Arnauld immediately set out to write a lengthy tome titled *De la fréquente Communion* ("On frequent Communion"), though a more appropriate title would be "On *in*frequent Communion"[86] or "*Against* frequent Communion."[87] This book would lay the foundation for Jansenist sacramental theology. The main purpose of the work was to refute the idea that immoral people could atone for continued sin through frequent communion without repentance.[88] The Eucharist should be held with the highest venerations, so the communicant should undertake a rigorous preparation before partaking of the sacrament.[89] One could not risk the smallest chance of the Eucharist being profaned by a sacrilegious communion.[90]

---

[84] Ibid., 84.

[85] Dougherty. *From Altar-Throne to Table*, 12.

[86] Ibid.

[87] Forget. "Jansenius and Jansenism."

[88] Orcibal. "*Les Provinciales.*"

[89] Hamilton. "From East to West," 84.

[90] Dougherty. *From Altar-Throne to Table*, 13.

Of course, this would also impact how Jansenists viewed the sacrament of Reconciliation. They would remind Catholics of their day that, in the early centuries of Church history, certain sinners would only be readmitted to communion after years of public penance (see chapter 5). Emboldened by this venerable tradition, Arnauld argued that the confessor had the duty to delay absolution until he was certain of the authenticity of the penitent's contrition.[91] Doing otherwise would be to manipulate the law, by acquitting people of sins they had never abandoned, bypassing the necessary moral transformation of the sinner by God's grace.[92] Absolution did not remit sin, it merely declared the sin to be forgiven, but it would be only valid if the penitent had achieved a perfect contrition.[93] In fact, it would be salutary for some souls if, even after absolution, they would withhold from communion for a time, in a kind of "supernatural fast" to atone for their previous sins.[94]

Arnauld's mistake was that he was making the highest ideals for receiving the Eucharist as the bare minimum requirements.[95] The Jansenists would not allow lesser expectations for sinners than for saints.[96] As Fr. Ronald Know, a notable 20th century Catholic priest said: the rigorists did not understand the maxim "*sacramenta propter homines*" ("sacraments are for the sake of men.") They would rather have most people wither away in a spiritual desert, while an elite

---

[91] Ibid.
[92] Palmer. *Jansenism and England*, 212.
[93] Dougherty. *From Altar-Throne to Table*, 15.
[94] Ibid., 13.
[95] Ibid.
[96] Palmer. *Jansenism and England*, 212.

would become the Eucharistic police, "pure as angels, proud as Lucifer."[97] A 19th century priest and disciple of St. Cardinal Newman, Fr. John Dalgairns, would also criticize the Jansenist movement in these terms:

> [Jansenism] takes away from God all the long-suffering and compassion with which His grace pleads with a sinner to the very last; it converts our most loving Creator into an arbitrary tyrant, imposing upon man laws too severe for his weak nature, without giving him supernatural power to fulfill them. It takes away from the very tenderness of Jesus on the cross, and destroys the gracefulness of His Passion, since it holds that He, by a distinct act, marred the all-sufficiency of His sufferings, by refusing to offer them up for more than a chosen few.[98]

Despite its glaring errors, its unmerciful outlook, and its 700 pages, *On frequent communion* became a smashing bestseller. It sold out in a couple of days and had four editions during its first semester.[99] Predictably, as the sales were going up, communion was going down. The situation was so bad, some Catholics were even abandoning their Easter duties.[100] A Parisian deacon is on the record as not communing for two years.[101] From that point onward, "Jansenism"

---

[97] Dougherty. *From Altar-Throne to Table*, 13.
[98] Dalgairns. *The Devotion to the Heart of Jesus*, 5.
[99] Dougherty. *From Altar-Throne to Table*, 13.
[100] Ibid.
[101] Forget. "Jansenius and Jansenism."

Chapter 8: Jansenism and Rigorism

would become *the* word to blame for any decrease in Eucharistic attendance, long after Jansenism as a movement was gone.[102] Among those who were horrified by the lowering numbers at the communion lines were St. Vincent de Paul[103]... and the Jesuits.[104]

The Society of Jesus had become the greatest proponent of frequent communion. They were upholding a revered tradition of theirs, since their own founder St. Ignatius of Loyola had advocated for it. Here, Ignatius was fulfilling the will of the Council of Trent.[105] This ecumenical council had not limited itself to defining the dogma of transubstantiation; it had asked for frequent communion as well:

> The holy council wishes indeed that *at each mass* the faithful who are present should communicate, not only in spiritual desire but also by the sacramental partaking of the Eucharist, that thereby they may derive from this most holy sacrifice a more abundant fruit.[106]

The Council of Trent was not innovating but retrieving the oldest and most venerable practice from the ash heap of history. During the early Church, the faithful communicated—or were expected to communicate—as often as Mass was celebrated. Sometimes, the sacred species were even brought to the houses of the communicants, namely if they were sick or lived far from the place where Mass took

---

[102] Dougherty. *From Altar-Throne to Table*, 15.
[103] Ibid., 13.
[104] Hamilton. "From East to West," 84.
[105] Dougherty. *From Altar-Throne to Table*, 6.
[106] Trent. "22nd Session, Chapter VI."

place. There are even accounts of saints lamenting infrequent communion or rebuking the faithful for not communicating more often. It had been during the Middle Ages that this traditional and pious practice had fallen into disuse.[107] An increased popularity of Eucharistic adoration had led to a shift of the devotion "away from the chalice and towards the monstrance,"[108] making the faithful more hesitant to consume the Eucharist.[109]

But this quote from Trent would become a "banner" for the campaigns favoring frequent communion during the following centuries.[110] From the 16th—17th century Jesuits, the movement for frequent communion went on to include St. Alphonsus Liguori in the 18th century,[111] and then expanded to the 19th century Eucharistic congresses. During the same century, popes Pius IX and Leo XIII also recommended daily communion as a healthy practice.[112]

But one of the greatest champions for frequent communion would be a certain Giuseppe Sarto, the Cardinal-Patriarch of Venice. Informed by his pastoral practice as a priest,[113] the patriarch became an enthusiastic proponent of frequent communion. Under Cardinal Sarto's direction, Venice would host the Italian Eucharistic Congress in 1897. One year later, he would have the patriarchal synod adopt frequent communion.[114] Obviously, Cardinal Sarto

---

[107] Scannell. "Frequent Communion."
[108] Wedig. "Reception of the Eucharist."
[109] See Gabriel. *Heresy Disguised as Tradition*, 158.
[110] Dougherty. *From Altar-Throne to Table*, 6.
[111] Scannell. "Frequent Communion."
[112] Ibid.
[113] Dougherty. *From Altar-Throne to Table*, 86.
[114] Ibid., 83.

Chapter 8: Jansenism and Rigorism

maintained his ideas and devotion to frequent communion when he was elected... Pope Pius X in 1903.

A couple of years after his election, he tried to promote the Eucharistic movement by inviting the International Eucharistic Congress to meet at Rome, under the auspices of the pontiff himself, with some of his most distinguished cardinals serving as legates. During the congress' closing address, Pius asked priests to recommend frequent communion. At the same time, Pius divulged a prayer to encourage daily reception.[115]

Also in 1905, Pius charged the Sacred Congregation for the Propagation of the Faith to study and decide on the matter of frequent communion. The Congregation produced a decree, which would be ratified, confirmed, and ordered for publication by Pius X, under the name *Sacra Tridentina Synodus*.

In this decree, the Congregation and Pius X cited Jesus Himself, Who taught us to pray for "our *daily* bread,"[116] and Who contrasted the Eucharist with the manna of the Old Testament[117] (manna having been a daily bread as well.)[118] They also enumerated many of the precedents already mentioned in this chapter as traditional underpinnings of their decision. First, they used the famous quote from the Council of Trent that had become a staple of the movement for daily communion. Afterwards, they brought forth two papal precedents: 1) a decree from Innocent XI (the pope who had condemned laxism using the writings of Arnauld) declaring "that all the faithful

---

[115] Ibid., 80.
[116] Mt 6:11.
[117] John 6:48-50.
[118] Exod 16:4.

of whatsoever class. . . could be admitted to frequent communion"; and 2) a decree from Alexander VIII condemning a proposition from Baius, "requiring a most pure love of God, without any admixture of defect, on the part of those who wished to approach the Holy Table."[119]

Pius and his Congregation also reiterated Church history, explaining how the first Christians "daily hastened to this Table of life," and how the "holy Fathers and writers of the Church testify that this practice was continued into later ages and not without great increase of holiness and perfection."[120] Pius, like many since the 17th century, blamed the decline of this practice on the emergence of Jansenism:

> Piety, however, grew cold, and especially afterward because of the widespread plague of Jansenism, disputes began to arise concerning the dispositions with which one ought to receive frequent and daily Communion. . .
>
> The poison of Jansenism, however, which, under the pretext of showing due honor and reverence to the Eucharist, had infected the minds even of good men, was by no means a thing of the past. The question as to the dispositions for the proper and licit reception of Holy Communion survived the declarations of the Holy See, and it was a fact that certain theologians of good repute were of the opinion that

---

[119] Pius X. *Sacra Tridentina*.
[120] Ibid.

daily Communion could be permitted to the faithful only rarely and subject to many conditions.[121]

It is interesting how Pius X, so often championed by those critical of Francis as a paragon of tradition and morality, literally condemned the word "rigorism" in this decree:

> [W]riters vied with one another in demanding *more and more stringent conditions as necessary to be fulfilled*. The result of such disputes was that *very few were considered worthy to receive the Holy Eucharist daily*, and to derive from this most health-giving Sacrament its more abundant fruits; the others were content to partake of it once a year, or once a month, or at most once a week. To such a degree, indeed, was *rigorism* carried that whole classes of persons were excluded from a frequent approach to the Holy Table, for instance, merchants or those who were married.[122]

To counter this rigorism, Pius X proposed a healthy perspective on the Eucharist. It is uncanny how many of his statements mirror the much-maligned *Amoris Laetitia* of Pope Francis. For example, while *Amoris Laetitia* points out that the Eucharist "is not a prize for the perfect, but a powerful medicine and nourishment for the weak,"[123] *Sacra Tridentina* says that the Eucharist does not "serve as a reward or recompense of virtue bestowed on the recipients," but

---

[121] Pius X. *Sacra Tridentina*.
[122] Ibid.
[123] Francis. *Amoris Laetitia*, n351.

as an "antidote whereby we may be freed from daily faults and be preserved from mortal sin."[124]

Another example: as *Amoris Laetitia* makes use of the "law of gradualness" (already previously expounded by St. John Paul II), whereby a human being "knows, loves, and accomplishes moral good by different stages of growth,"[125] *Sacra Tridentina* explains how, thanks to frequent communion, "daily communicants should *gradually* free themselves even from venial sins, and from all affection thereto."[126]

Also, just like *Amoris Laetitia* grounds its sacramental discipline on the distinction between mortal and venial sin (taking into account mitigating circumstances),[127] *Sacra Tridentina* teaches:

> Although it is especially fitting that those who receive Communion frequently or daily should be free from venial sins, at least from such as are fully deliberate, and from any affection thereto, nevertheless, *it is sufficient that they be free from mortal sin*, with the purpose of never sinning in the future...
>
> Confessors, however, must take care not to dissuade anyone from frequent or daily Communion, provided *he is*

---

[124] Pius X. *Sacra Tridentina*.
[125] Francis. *Amoris Laetitia*, 295.
[126] Pius X. *Sacra Tridentina*.
[127] Francis. *Amoris Laetitia*, 301-3. Note especially #301: "Hence it can no longer simply be said that all those in any 'irregular' situation are living in a state of mortal sin and are deprived of sanctifying grace."

found to be in a state of grace and approaches with a right intention.[128]

In the end, Pius X settled the matter by defining:

Frequent and daily Communion, as a practice most earnestly desired by Christ our Lord and by the Catholic Church, should be open to all the faithful, of whatever rank and condition of life; so that *no one who is in the state of grace*, and who approaches the Holy Table with a right and devout intention (*recta piaque mente*) *can be prohibited therefrom*...

[A]fter the publication of this Decree, all ecclesiastical writers are to cease from contentious controversy concerning the dispositions requisite for frequent and daily Communion.[129]

---

[128] Pius X. *Sacra Tridentina*. Some may object that *Amoris Laetitia* allows communion for people without the "right intention," since they would not have a "purpose of never sinning in the future." But this resolution to not sin again must be read in light of what Prof. Rocco Buttiglione wrote on this matter: the sinner must have "the desire of leaving his irregular situation and strive to perform acts that will allow him to effectively leave such a situation. It is possible, however, that the sinner will not be in a stage where he can realize this detachment and reconquer his own sovereignty in an immediate way.... *He must strive, so as to keep the resolution, to leave the situation of sin.*" See Buttiglione, *Risposte amichevoli*, 172.

[129] Pius X. *Sacra Tridentina*.

Some scholars argue that Jansenism, as a movement, was already long gone by the beginning of the 20th century, so it could not be faulted for the lack of Eucharistic attendance during Pius X's pontificate. They mention as potential culprits, for example, the increased secularization and industrialization of society, with its spiritual apathy and severe labor practices. Therefore, "Jansenism" as mentioned in the decree would not have any ties to the real movement but be merely a slur to denote a repugnant avoidance of the Eucharist.[130]

However, ecclesiastical authors during the 19th and 20th centuries were indeed concerned with the "remnants" of Jansenistic "doctrine and theology." As one of them said: "Habits are more tenacious than doctrines," in that the practices acquired during the Jansenistic disputes lived on, even if only because of the natural inertia of the Church. Yet, one could trace an undeniable pedigree for those ideas regarding the sacraments: they went back to Jansen.[131] Also, Pius X lamented: "in our own day the controversy has been continued with increased warmth, and not without bitterness, so that the minds of confessors and the consciences of the faithful have been disturbed, to the no small detriment of Christian piety and fervor."[132]

Be that as it may, Pius X's decree seems to have been well-received. If there was resistance to the decree, it was not in printed form, so evidence of it has not survived to our days. Maybe that resistance was not willful, but merely the overcoming of the aforementioned ecclesial inertia.[133] However, frequent daily communion is

---

[130] Dougherty. *From Altar-Throne to Table*, 15—16.
[131] Ibid.
[132] Pius X. *Sacra Tridentina*.
[133] Dougherty. *From Altar-Throne to Table*, xxiv.

relatively uncontroversial nowadays. In this sense, I believe that Pius's petitions were answered, when he prayed: "May He [the Holy Spirit] bend whatever is rigid, inflame whatever has grown cold, and bring back whatever has gone astray."[134]

Nevertheless, I believe that those "remnants" of Jansenistic "doctrine and theology" live to this very day. Pope Francis experienced them in his own lifetime, as he recalls:

> [W]hen Pope Pius XII freed us from that very heavy cross of the Eucharistic fast. You couldn't even drink a drop of water—not even while brushing your teeth... as a child, I went to confess that I had taken Communion, because I believed that a drop of water had gone inside. Therefore, when Pope Pacelli changed the discipline —"Ah, heresy! He touched the discipline of the Church!" —so many Pharisees were scandalized. Because Pius XII did what Jesus had done: he saw the needs of the people: "The poor people, with such zeal!". These priests who were saying three Masses, the last one at one o'clock, after midday, fasting. And these Pharisees were like this —"our discipline" —rigid in the flesh, but as Jesus says, "decayed in the heart", weak until decayed. Darkness in the heart.[135]

But I would go even farther and dare say that nowadays, these Jansenist residues manifest themselves whenever Catholics—especially those most resistant to the magisterium—seem to police the

---

[134] Pius X. *Il Fermo Proposito*, 27.
[135] Francis. "Darkness of the Heart."

Eucharistic lines, placing a misguided safeguarding of the dignity of the sacrament above its primary purpose: conferring grace to sinners, so that it is not a reward for the perfect, but a medicine for the weak.

In this sense, it is ironic how Jansenism, trying as it did to combat the "Semipelagianism" of Molina, ended up adopting a rigid approach, making it so similar to that which it detested:

> Jansenism, intertwined with Pelagianism, taught a false perfectionistic state attainable by human effort alone that allowed for no mistakes; it also stressed a rigorous spirit of penance for sins and inevitable mistakes as well as a constant fear of divine wrath.[136]

---

[136] Schmidt. *Everything is Grace: The Life and Way of Thérèse of Lisieux*, as quoted in Dougherty. *From Altar-Throne to Table*, 16.

Conclusion

We have now completed a tour around Church history, from the first to the twenty-first century. We have found out that, unlike what many of his critics assert, Pope Francis did not make up his constant rebukes against rigidity out of thin air. Since the beginning, the Church has had to deal with several kinds of rigid heterodoxy, threatening to thwart God's project of mercy for all humankind. Then, as now, the Church had to overcome rigidity for this project to advance and fructify. Through the guidance of the living magisterium, orthodoxy inevitably prevailed—an orthodoxy less strict than the more rigorous position available at the time.

To be clear, I am not trying to argue that the rigid Catholics of today profess any of these past heresies. I have no authority to deem anyone a heretic. But I think it is important for us to learn from them, so we may recognize remnants of these heresies in our own mindset, so we can correct our course accordingly. More importantly, I hope to have shown that choosing the most rigorous course does not necessarily protect one from falling into error. Rigidity does not automatically entail faithfulness to Catholic doctrine.

Neither do I want this book to be a justification for laxism. As I have explained in chapter 1, rigidity is not an antidote to laxism, but a different poison altogether. The true antidote for laxism is a proper understanding of Catholic truths and praxis, not rigidity. Where does this proper understanding lie? How do we find the balance? As mere mortals, our understanding is too clouded by our sinful nature for us to be trustworthy judges of where the equilibrium sits, especially when we are evaluating our own souls. In this case, a third party may grant the necessary objectivity of what our errors are. Not just any third party, though: rather, a third party with God-given authority to make such determinations. As we have seen throughout the historical precedents in this book, this third party is either Jesus Christ, the very incarnation of God. . . or the magisterium He instituted to be the Church's visible guide on earth.

Knowing this, if the Vicar of Christ himself, who enjoys "divine assistance in the integral exercise of its mission,"[1] is making ceaseless appeals against rigidity, our response should not be to derisively dismiss him, but to pay heed. It may very well be that there are severe errors in our perception of the Catholic faith we must correct. And, as we have seen in chapter 1, this is the more urgent, the more inclined we are towards rigidity. Otherwise, we may end up rationalizing our own errors under the guise of "faithfulness."

Nor can we do as all rigid heresies of the past did, and chide the pope for his guidance against rigidity, under the pretext that laxity is more widespread, so it is more expedient to deal with it first. Faithful Catholics are the ones going into the world to evangelize and spread the Good News. How can they fulfill this noble mission, if they have failed to grasp such a central aspect of our faith (arguably, one of the most important to be presented to sinners in the clutches of laxity) as God's unfathomable mercy (see chapter 5)?[2] How can they ask sinners to renounce their own prejudices in favor of a higher truth, if the faithful themselves act as self-sufficient, relying

---

[1] CDF, *Donum Veritatis*, 24.

[2] In this sense, I advise the reading of my article: Gabriel. "The Remnant: it is not what you've been told."

Conclusion

on the perfection of their own works (see chapter 6)? How can the faithful ask sinners to accept correction if they eschew correction themselves? A laxist, sinful world awaits eagerly for the Christian message, and the faithful fall short of it because of their rigidity: they are no longer salt of the earth, for they have lost their flavor.[3]

Pope Francis has granted us a wealth of resources to deal with this. I have tried to gather as many interventions of his on this matter as I could possibly pack in this book. He is not ambiguous or unclear about it. He is merely talking about aspects of our faith that many Catholics—reliant on their knowledge of other parts of doctrine—have not fully exercised and find, therefore, strange. If we stop combing Francis's words for faults, and instead sit down to filially listen to our Holy Father (as Catholics are supposed to do), we will notice the patterns emerging, as I have tried to show throughout this book. I am particularly reminded of a papal address to catechists, where Pope Francis brings up a very ancient precedent, the one of Prophet Jonah:

> Here I think of the story of Jonah, a really interesting figure, especially for these times of great change and uncertainty. Jonah is a devout man, with a tranquil and ordered life, which causes him to have a clear-cut way of seeing things and to judge everything and everyone accordingly. He has it all figured out: this is the truth! He is rigid! So, when the Lord called him and told him to go and preach to Nineveh, the great pagan city, Jonah doesn't like it. "Go there? But I

---

[3] Mt 5:13.

have the whole truth here!" He doesn't like it. Nineveh is outside his comfort zone; it is on the outskirts of his world. So he escapes, he sets off for Spain; he runs away and boards a ship that will take him there. Go and re-read the Book of Jonah! It is short, but it is a very instructive parable, especially for those of us in the Church.[4]

As Francis explains us, rigidity "basically means taking a whip in hand with the People of God: 'you cannot do this, you cannot do that.' And thus, many people approach, seeking a bit of consolation, a little understanding, but instead they are distanced by this rigidity."[5] This attitude renders them "a closed people, a people whose ministers are rigid."[6] But this is not what we are called to do, as a Church:

> We cannot run the risk that a penitent not perceive the maternal presence of the Church, which welcomes and loves each one. Should this perception fail, due to our rigidity, it would do serious harm in the first place to the faith itself, because it would impede the penitent from feeling included in the Body of Christ. Moreover, it would greatly limit the penitent's sense of belonging to a community. Instead, we are called to be the living expression of the Church which as mother welcomes whomsoever approaches her.[7]

---

[4] Francis. "Address to Participants in the Pilgrimage of Catechists."
[5] Francis. "Mediators or intermediaries."
[6] Francis. "Salvation is drawn from rejection."
[7] Francis. "Address at the Meeting with the Missionaries of Mercy."

This is the way forward if we want, as a Church, to be able to effectively evangelize a thoroughly secularized, laxist world, thirsty for God's love and mercy (even if unconsciously), but tired and wounded by the totalitarian regimes of the recent past and the misbehavior of so many individual Catholics. As Pope Benedict XVI so aptly puts it: "Being Christian is not the result of an ethical choice or a lofty idea, but the encounter with an event, a person, which gives life a new horizon and a decisive direction."[8]

Our faith is not mainly a faith of rules or laws, but a faith of love and freedom. As we have seen in chapter 2, we are not slaves to the law, but children of God. Does this mean we can just break the commandments? Not at all. But, as we have seen in chapter 3, the commandments are to be lived as an expression of that very same love and freedom, not as a burden (especially when that burden is imposed on others and not oneself.) Everything depriving the commandments of this perspective, turning them into mere rules to be followed (even when paying lip-service to love and freedom), empties them of their spiritual significance and regenerative power. This is the great danger of rigidity.

As St. John Paul II wrote in his seminal encyclical *Veritatis Splendor*, we must recognize the "pedagogic function of the law."[9] "To imitate and live out the love of Christ is not possible for man by his own strength alone"[10] (see chapter 6). The law, then, enables the "sinful man to take stock of his own powerlessness and by stripping him of the presumption of his self-sufficiency, leads him to ask for

---

[8] Benedict XVI. *Deus Caritas Est*, 1.
[9] John Paul II. *Veritatis Splendor*, 23.
[10] Ibid., 22.

and to receive life in the Spirit" (see chapter 6).[11] With this in mind, it is obvious how using the law as "dead stones to be hurled at others"[12] will always backfire, for no one can perfectly fulfill the law but Jesus Christ.

We must, therefore, "transcend a legalistic interpretation of the commandments"[13] "Love and life according to the gospel cannot be thought of first and foremost as a kind of precept, because what they demand is beyond man's abilities. They are possible only as the result of a gift of God who heals restores, and transforms the human heart by his grace."[14] These words, contained in an encyclical so revered by papal critics today, are the core of Pope Francis's message when he deals with the topics of mercy and rigidity. And this is what we need to put in practice if we really want to be faithful Catholics.

Let us pray, then, that God may heal our rigidity, so that, docile to the guidance of the magisterium, we may fulfill His law as best we can, while being agents of His mercy in the world, bringing the gospel to sinners and aiding in their conversion through our benignity and love. Amen.

---

[11] Ibid., 23.
[12] Francis. *Amoris Laetitia*, 49.
[13] John Paul II. *Veritatis Splendor*, 16.
[14] Ibid., 23.

Bibliography

Allen, John. "Next Sunday, remember that popes can admire resignation without dropping hints." *Crux*, August 21, 2022. https://cruxnow.com/news-analysis/2022/08/next-sunday-remember-that-popes-can-admire-resignation-without-dropping-hints/.

Alt, Henry. "Newman, St. Catherine, and Pius X: Three Papalolators." *To Give a Defense*, June 30, 2016. https://www.patheos.com/blogs/scottericalt/newman-st-catherine-and-pius-x-three-papalolators/.

Altieri, Christopher. "'Synodality' means whatever Pope Francis wants it to mean." *Catholic World Report*, June 16, 2022. https://www.catholicworldreport.com/2022/06/16/synodality-means-whatever-pope-francis-wants-it-to-mean/.

Aquinas, Thomas. *Summa Theologiae*. Translated by Fathers of the English Dominican Province. Second and Revised Edition, 1920. https://www.newadvent.org/summa/.

Aristotle. *The Nicomachean Ethics*. Translated by W.D. Ross. Kitchener: Batoche Books, 1999.

Augustine of Hippo. "Homily 7 on the First Epistle of John." Translated by H. Browne. From *Nicene and Post-Nicene Fathers*, First Series, Vol. 7. Edited by Philip Schaff. Buffalo, NY: Christian Literature Publishing Co., 1888. Revised and edited for *New Advent* by Kevin Knight. http://www.newadvent.org/fathers/170207.htm.

Bavinck, Herman. "The Influence of the Protestant Reformation on the Moral and Religious Conditions of Communities and Nations." *Mid-America Journal of Theology* (2014) 25, 75-81.

"Being 'Rigid' Is a Badge of Honor, Your Holiness." *One Peter Five*, September 26, 2019. https://onepeterfive.com/rigid-badge-honor/.

Benedict XVI. *Deus Caritas Est*. Libreria Editrice Vaticana, 2005. Vatican.va.

———. *Jesus of Nazareth: from the Baptism in the Jordan to the Transfiguration*. New York: Doubleday Broadway Publishing Group, 2007.

Benedictow, Ole. "The Black Death: The Greatest Catastrophe Ever." *History Today*, Vol 55, Issue 3 (March 2005). https://tinyurl.com/bdhnpwsx.

Bergoglio, Jorge. *Reflexiones en Esperanza*. Avelladena: Ediciones Universidad del Salvador, 1992.

Bihl, Michael. "Fraticelli," *The Catholic Encyclopedia*. Vol. 6. New York: Robert Appleton Company, 1909. http://www.newadvent.org/cathen/06244b.htm.

Blanchard, Shaun. "Are Jansenists among us?" *Church Life Journal*, October 4, 2019. https://churchlifejournal.nd.edu/articles/are-jansenists-among-us/.

Blumenthal, Uta-Renate. "Gregorian Reform". *Encyclopedia Britannica*, September 23, 2011. https://www.britannica.com/event/Gregorian-Reform.

Bray, Gerald. "Augustine and the Pelagian Controversy." *Tabletalk Magazine*, September 2020. https://tabletalkmagazine.com/article/2020/09/augustine-and-the-pelagian-controversy/.

Browne, Christian. "*Misericordiae Vultus*: Mercy Without Repentance?" *Crisis Magazine*, April 16, 2015. https://crisismagazine.com/opinion/misericordiae-vultus-mercy-without-repentance.

Brugger, Christian. "Five Serious Problems with Chapter 8 of Amoris Laetitia." *Catholic World Report*, April 22, 2016.

https://www.catholicworldreport.com/2016/04/22/five-serious-problems-with-chapter-8-of-amoris-laetitia/.

Bryant, Joseph. "Decius & Valerian, Novatian & Cyprian: Persecution and Schism in the Making of a Catholic Christianity - Part I" *Athens Journal of History*. April 2023, Vol 9, Issue 2, 125-58.

———. "Decius & Valerian, Novatian & Cyprian: Persecution and Schism in the Making of a Catholic Christianity - Part II" *Athens Journal of History*. April 2023, Vol 9, Issue 2, 159-84.

Buccholz, Jennifer, Jonathan Abramowitz, Bradley Riemann, Lillian Reuman, Shannon Blakey, Rachel Leonard, Katherine Thompson. "Scrupulosity, Religious Affiliation and Symptom Presentation in Obsessive Compulsive Disorder." *Behavioral and Cognitive Psychotherapy*. 2019 Jul;47(4):478-92.

Buttiglione, Rocco. *Risposte Amichevoli Ai Critici Di Amoris Laetitia*. Ragione & Fede. Milano: Edizioni Ares, 2017.

Cameron, Euan. "Chapter 6: The Counter-Reformation" In *The Blackwell Companion to the Bible and Culture*, edited by John Sawyer. Malden: The Blackwell Publishing Ltd, 2006.

Catholic Church, ed. *Catechism of the Catholic Church*. Libreria Editrice Vaticana, 1993. Vatican.va.

Chapman, John. "Donatists." *The Catholic Encyclopedia*. Vol. 5. New York: Robert Appleton Company, 1909. https://www.newadvent.org/cathen/05121a.htm.

———. "Novatian and Novatianism." *The Catholic Encyclopedia*. Vol. 11. New York: Robert Appleton Company, 1911. http://www.newadvent.org/cathen/11138a.htm.

———. "Pope Cornelius." *The Catholic Encyclopedia*. Vol. 4. New York: Robert Appleton Company, 1908. https://www.newadvent.org/cathen/04375c.htm.

Charlier, Michael. "What is 'indietrism' (backwardness) anyway?" *Rorate Caeli*, May 15, 2023. https://rorate-caeli.blogspot.com/2023/05/what-is-indietrism-backwardness.html.

Chesterton, Gilbert. *The Everlasting Man*. San Francisco: Ignatius Press, 1993.

Chretien, Claire. "Pope Francis on the young who like Latin Mass: 'Why so much rigidity?'" *LifeSiteNews*, November 11, 2016. https://www.lifesitenews.com/news/pope-francis-blasts-rigid-young-catholics-who-like-the-latin-mass/.

Congregation for the Doctrine of the Faith. "Instruction *Donum Veritatis* on the Ecclesial Vocation of the Theologian," December 29, 1975. Vatican.va.

Cook, Donald. "A Gospel Portrait of the Pharisees." *Review & Expositor* (Spring 1987), 84.2: 221-33.

Dalgairns, John. *The Devotion to the Heart of Jesus; with an Introduction on the History of Jansenism*. London: Thomas Richardson and Son, 1853.

Delany, Joseph. "Scruple." *The Catholic Encyclopedia*. Vol. 13. New York: Robert Appleton Company, 1912. http://www.newadvent.org/cathen/13640a.htm.

DeVille, Adam. "Rigidity in defense of the liturgy is no vice." *Catholic World Report*, November 16, 2016. https://www.catholicworldreport.com/2016/11/16/rigidity-in-defense-of-the-liturgy-is-no-vice/.

Devine, Arthur. "Passions." *The Catholic Encyclopedia*. Vol. 11. New York: Robert Appleton Company, 1911. http://www.newadvent.org/cathen/11534a.htm.

Dicastery for Communication. "The Coat of Arms of Pope Francis." Libreria Editrice Vaticana, 2019. Vatican.va.

Domingues, Claire and Pedro Gabriel. "World Youth Day and plastic containers: What really happened." *The City and the World*. August 13, 2023. https://thecityandtheworld.com/world-youth-day-and-plastic-containers-what-really-happened/.

Dougherty, Joseph. *From Altar-Throne to Table: The Campaign for Frequent Holy Communion in the Catholic Church*. ATLA Monograph Series, No. 50 (Lanham: Scarecrow Press Inc, 2010.)

Douie, Decima. *The Nature and the Effect of the Heresy of the Fraticelli*. Manchester: Manchester University Press, 1932.

Douthat, Ross. "Jesus and the Pharisees: an extract from Ross Douthat's 'To Change the Church.'" *Catholic Herald*, April 6, 2018. https://catholicherald.co.uk/jesus-and-the-pharisees-an-extract-from-ross-douthats-to-change-the-church/.

Duffield, Ian. "Difficult texts: Matthew 23." *Theology*, 2020, Vol. 123(I), 16-9.

Editors of the Encyclopaedia Britannica. "Novatian." *Encyclopedia Britannica*, September 2, 2022. https://www.britannica.com/biography/Novatian/.

——. "Pelagianism." *Encyclopedia Britannica*, May 30, 2022. https://www.britannica.com/topic/Pelagianism.

——. "Puritanism." *Encyclopedia Britannica*, June 21, 2023. https://www.britannica.com/topic/Puritanism.

England, Matthew. "The Reformers and the Heretics: The Reforms of the Mid-Eleventh Century Catholic Church and the Rise of Catharism." Honors Capstone Projects and Theses, 2017, 326. https://louis.uah.edu/honors-capstones/326.

Fernández, Victor. "El capítulo VIII de *Amoris Laetitia*: lo que queda después de la tormenta." *Medellín* (May–August 2017), XLIII, no. 168, 449-68.

Finnis, Elizabeth. "Rebuild my Church." *Franciscan Seculars* (website). August 13, 2018. http://franciscanseculars.com/rebuild-the-church/.

Forget, Jacques. "Jansenius and Jansenism." *The Catholic Encyclopedia*. Vol. 8. New York: Robert Appleton Company, 1910. http://www.newadvent.org/cathen/08285a.htm.

Francis. "A daily struggle." November 20, 2015. Vatican.va.

———. "A grandmother's lesson." December 14, 2015. Vatican.va.
———. "A house not for rent." June 5, 2014. Vatican.va.
———. "Address of His Holiness Pope Francis at the Ceremony commemorating the 50th Anniversary of the Institution of the Synod of Bishops." October 17, 2015. Vatican.va.
———. "Address of His Holiness Pope Francis at the Opening of the Pastoral Congress of the Diocese of Rome." June 16, 2016. Vatican.va.
———. "Address of His Holiness Pope Francis in the Meeting with Bishops, Priests, Deacons, Consecrated Persons, Seminarians and Pastoral Workers during the Apostolic Journey to Kazakhstan." September 15, 2022. Vatican.va.
———. "Address of His Holiness Pope Francis in the Meeting with Priests, Consecrated Persons, Deacons, Catechists, Ecclesial Associations and Movements of Cyprus." December 2, 2021. Vatican.va.
———. "Address of His Holiness Pope Francis on the Occasion of the Concluding Holy Mass of the 52nd International Eucharistic Congress." September 13, 2021. Vatican.va.
———. "Address of His Holiness Pope Francis to Management and Staff of the Newspaper 'Avvenire' with their Families." May 1, 2018. Vatican.va.
———. "Address of His Holiness Pope Francis to Members of the Global Researchers Advancing Catholic Education Project." April 20, 2022. Vatican.va.
———. "Address of His Holiness Pope Francis at the Meeting with the Missionaries of Mercy." February 9, 2016. Vatican.va.
———. "Address of His Holiness Pope Francis to Participants in a Course of Formation of the Cursillos de Cristiandad movement." April 30, 2015. Vatican.va.

———. "Address of His Holiness Pope Francis to Participants in the General Chapter of the Little Missionary Sisters of Charity." May 26, 2017. Vatican.va.

———. "Address of His Holiness Pope Francis to Participants in a Course on the Internal Forum Organized by the Apostolic Penitentiary." March 12, 2015. Vatican.va.

———. "Address of His Holiness Pope Francis to Participants in the International Assembly of the Apostolic Union of the Clergy." November 16, 2017. Vatican.va.

———. "Address of His Holiness Pope Francis to Participants in the International Congress organized by the Congregation for the Clergy." October 7, 2017. Vatican.va.

———. "Address of His Holiness Pope Francis to Participants in the Meeting promoted by the Pontifical Council for Promoting the New Evangelization." October 11, 2017. Vatican.va.

———. "Address of His Holiness Pope Francis to Participants in the Plenary Session of the Congregation for the Clergy." June 1, 2017. Vatican.va.

———. "Address of His Holiness Pope Francis to Participants in the Third World Congress of Ecclesial Movements and New Communities" November 22, 2014. Vatican.va.

———. "Address of His Holiness Pope Francis to Participants of the 3rd World Meeting of Popular Movements." November 5, 2016. Vatican.va.

———. "Address of His Holiness Pope Francis to Pilgrims from Slovakia, on the Occasion of the 200th Anniversary of the Erection of the Eparchy of Presov." July 14, 2022. Vatican.va.

———. "Address of His Holiness Pope Francis to the Bishops ordained over the past year." September 14, 2017. Vatican.va.

———. "Address of His Holiness Pope Francis to the Community of the Pontifical Seminary of the Campania Region." May 6, 2017. Vatican.va.

———. "Address of His Holiness Pope Francis to the Faithful of the Diocese of Rome." September 18, 2021. Vatican.va.

———. "Address of His Holiness Pope Francis to the Members of Communion and Liberation." October 15, 2022. Vatican.va.

———. "Address of His Holiness Pope Francis to the Participants in the General Chapters of the Basilian Order of Saint Josaphat, the Order of the Mother of God, and the Congregation of the Mission." July 14, 2022. Vatican.va.

———. "Address of His Holiness Pope Francis to the Participants in the International Thomistic Congress organized by the Pontifical Academy of Saint Thomas Aquinas." September 22, 2022. Vatican.va.

———. "Address of His Holiness Pope Francis to the Pontifical Biblical Institute." May 9, 2019. Vatican.va.

———. "Address of His Holiness Pope Francis to the Roman Curia." December 23, 2021. Vatican.va.

———. "Address of Holy Father Francis to Participants in the Pilgrimage of Catechists on the Occasion of the Year of Faith and of the International Congress on Catechesis." September 27, 2023. Vatican.va.

———. "Address of Pope Francis in a Meeting with the Clergy, Consecrated People and Members of Diocesan Pastoral Councils." October 4, 2013. Vatican.va.

———. "Address of Pope Francis to the Parish Priests of the Diocese of Rome." March 6, 2014. Vatican.va.

———. "Address of Pope Francis to Young Consecrated Persons." September 17, 2015. Vatican.va.

———. *Amoris Laetitia*. Libreria Editrice Vaticana, 2016. Vatican.va.

———. "Angelus." March 24, 2019. Vatican.va.

———. "Angelus." March 27, 2022. Vatican.va.

———. "Angelus." November 1, 2021. Vatican.va.

———. "Angelus." November 13, 2022. Vatican.va.

———. "Angelus." September 15, 2019. Vatican.va.

———. "Attitudes that prevent us from knowing Christ." November 13, 2022. Vatican.va.

———. "Christians of action and truth." June 27, 2013. Vatican.va.

———. "Darkness of the Heart." December 14, 2014. Vatican.va.

———. "Disciples of the Lord and not of ideology." October 17, 2013. Vatican.va.

———. *Evangelii Gaudium*. Libreria Editrice Vaticana, 2013. Vatican.va.

———. "Faith is not sold." April 6, 2013. Vatican.va.

———. "Flour and yeast." October 25, 2016. Vatican.va.

———. *Gaudete et Exsultate*. Libreria Editrice Vaticana, 2018. Vatican.va.

———. "General Audience." April 14, 2021. Vatican.va.

———. "General Audience." January 11, 2023. Vatican.va.

———. "God of surprises." May 8, 2017. Vatican.va.

———. "Half a life." October 6, 2016. Vatican.va.

———. "Homily," January 23, 2022. Vatican.va.

———. Homily at Blessing of the Sacred Pallium for the New Metropolitan Archbishops on the Solemnity of Saints Peter and Paul Apostles, June 29, 2021. Vatican.va.

———. Homily at Enrique Olaya Herrera airport (Medellín), September 9, 2017. Vatican.va.

———. Homily of His Holiness Pope Francis at the Celebration of Vespers with Priests, Men and Women Religious and Seminarians, September 20, 2015. Vatican.va.

———. Homily of His Holiness Pope Francis at the Eucharistic Celebration on the Occasion of the Feast of Our Lady of Guadalupe, December 12, 2015. Vatican.va.

———. Homily of His Holiness Pope Francis at the Holy Mass and Opening of the Holy Door – Basilica of St. John Lateran, December 13, 2015. Vatican.va.

———. Homily of His Holiness Pope Francis at the Holy Mass on the 400th Anniversary of the Canonization of St. Ignatius of Loyola, March 12, 2022. Vatican.va.

———. Homily of His Holiness Pope Francis at the Holy Mass on the Opening of the XIV Ordinary General Assembly of the Synod of Bishops, October 4, 2015. Vatican.va.

———. Homily of His Holiness Pope Francis at the Holy Mass on the Solemnity of Pentecost, May 24, 2015. Vatican.va.

———. Homily of His Holiness Pope Francis at the Morning Mass in the Capel of the *Domus Sanctae Marthae*, May 15, 2020. Vatican.va.

———. Homily of His Holiness Pope Francis at the Sunday of the Word of God, January 23, 2022. Vatican.va.

———. Homily of the Holy Father in the "Megaron Concert Hall" in Athens, December 5, 2021. Vatican.va.

———. "In-Flight Press Conference from Lesbos to Rome," April 16, 2016. Vatican.va.

———. "Let us not forget the gratuitousness of revelation," March 13, 2020. Vatican.va.

———. "Letter of His Holiness Pope Francis to Priests on the 160th Anniversary of the Death of the Holy Curé of Ars, St. John Vianney." August 4, 2019. Dicastero per la Comunicazione - Libreria Editrice Vaticana, 2013. Vatican.va.

———. "Letter of the Holy Father to the Priests of the Diocese of Rome." August 7, 2023. Dicastero per la Comunicazione - Libreria Editrice Vaticana, 2013. Vatican.va.

———. "Never slaves of the law," October 24, 2016. Vatican.va.

———. "Mercy first and foremost," October 6, 2015. Vatican.va.

———. "Mediators or intermediaries," December 9, 2016. Vatican.va.

———. "Message of His Holiness Pope Francis to mark the 150th Anniversary of the Proclamation of St. Alphonsus Maria de Liguori *Doctor Ecclesiae*." March 23, 2021. Vatican.va.

———. *Misericordia et Misera*, Libreria Editrice Vaticana, 2016. Vatican.va.

———. "Our relationship with God is gratuitous, it is friendship," May 15, 2020. Vatican.va.

———. "Press Conference during the flight of return to Rome from Cyprus and Greece," December 6, 2021. Vatican.va.

———. "Press Conference during the flight of return to Rome from Romania," June 2, 2019. Vatican.va.

———. "Press Conference on the return flight to Rome." July 29, 2022. Vatican.va.

———. "Resistance vs. docility," May 9, 2017. Vatican.va.

———. "Rigid but honest," May 5, 2017. Vatican.va.

———. "Salvation is drawn from rejection," June 1, 2015. Vatican.va.

———. "The holiness of negotiation," June 9, 2016. Vatican.va.

———. "Three judges and three women," March 23, 2015. Vatican.va.

———. "Two wonders," February 6, 2017. Vatican.va.

———. *Vos Estis Lux Mundi*. Libreria Editrice Vaticana, 2019. Vatican.va.

———. "What happens when Jesus passes," March 22, 2020. Vatican.va.

———. "Witnesses to obedience," April 27, 2017. Vatican.va.

Francis de Sales. *Selected letters*. Translated by Elisabeth Stopp. New York: Harper & Brothers Publishers, 1960.

Frazier, Robin. "Major Influences Contributing to Michelangelo's Last Judgment, 1536-1541: The Commission, The Subject, The Sack Of Rome, and The Counter-Reformation." Master Thesis on Art History (California State University, Los Angeles, 2015).

Ferrara, Christopher. "Pope Pelagius?" *The Remnant*, May 30, 2017. https://remnantnewspaper.com/web/index.php/articles/item/3219-pope-pelagius/.

Gabriel, Pedro. *Heresy Disguised as Tradition*. St. Louis: En Route Books and Media, 2023.

———. "Silence: the shield against Suspicious Man." *Where Peter Is*, December 10, 2018. https://wherepeteris.com/silence-the-shield-against-suspicious-man/.

———. *The Orthodoxy of Amoris Laetitia*. Eugene: Wipf and Stock, 2022.

———. "The Remnant: it is not what you've been told." *Where Peter Is*, April 8, 2019. https://wherepeteris.com/the-remnant-it-is-not-what-youve-been-told/.

Gleason, Maud. "Review of Stoicism and Emotion." *Common Knowledge*, 2009, Vol. 15, No. 2, 214-5. Project MUSE: muse.jhu.edu/article/262211/.

Grech, Mario. "Synodality at the core of Pope Francis' ministry," *Vatican News*, March 11, 2023. https://www.vaticannews.va/en/vatican-city/news/2023-03/cardinal-grech-synod-bishops-pope-10th-anniversary-synodality.html.

Grondin, Charles. "Why Did Jesus Condemn the Practice of Corban?" *Catholic Answers*, July 14, 2022. https://www.catholic.com/qa/why-did-jesus-condemn-the-practice-of-corban/.

Hamilton, Alastair. "From East to West: Jansenists, Orientalists, and the Eucharistic Controversy," In Willemien Otten et al. *How the West was Won: Essays on Literary Imagination, the Canon, and the Christian Middle Ages for Burcht Pranger*. Leiden: Brill, 2010, 83-100.

Harrison, Brian. "*Amoris Laetitia* Laxity Trickles Down to Parish Level." *One Peter Five*, June 13, 2016. https://onepeterfive.com/amoris-laetitia-laxity-trickles-parish-level/.

Harty, John. "Probabilism." *The Catholic Encyclopedia*. Vol. 12. New York: Robert Appleton Company, 1911. http://www.newadvent.org/cathen/12441a.htm.

Hickson, Maike. "Interview: Josef Seifert on the *Amoris Laetitia* Debate with Rocco Buttiglione." *One Peter Five*, November 7, 2017.

https://onepeterfive.com/interview-josef-seifert-amoris-laetitia-debate-rocco-buttiglione/.

Hirsch, Emil, Kaufmann Kohler, Joseph Jacobs, Aaron Friedenwald, Isaac Broydé. "Circumcision." *The Jewish Encyclopedia*, New York: Funk & Wagnalls, 1901—1906. https://www.jewishencyclopedia.com/articles/4391-circumcision/.

Hitchens, Dan. "An Ambiguous Exhortation." *First Things*, April 12, 2018. https://www.firstthings.com/web-exclusives/2018/04/an-ambiguous-exhortation/.

Huckabee, Tyler. "Christians, Stop Using 'Pharisee' as an Insult." *Relevant Magazine*, August 11, 2021. https://relevantmagazine.com/faith/christians-stop-using-pharisee-as-an-insult/.

Hunwicke, John. "Indietrism again." *Fr Hunwicke's Mutual Enrichment*, December 1, 2022. http://liturgicalnotes.blogspot.com/2022/12/indietrism-again.html.

"Hypocrite." *Merriam-Webster.com*. 2023. https://www.merriam-webster.com.

Ignatius of Loyola. *Ignatius of Loyola: The Spiritual Exercises and Selected Works*. Edited by Georg Ganss. New York: Paulist Press, 1991.

Ivereigh, Austen. *The Great Reformer: Francis and the Making of a Radical Pope*. New York: Henry Holt and Company, 2014.

John Paul II. *Familiaris Consortio*. Libreria Editrice Vaticana, 1981. Vatican.va.

———. *Ut Unum Sint*. Libreria Editrice Vaticana, 1995. Vatican.va.

———. *Veritatis Splendor*. Libreria Editrice Vaticana, 1993. Vatican.va.

Kaelber, Lutz. "Weaver into Heretics? The Social Organization of Early-Thirteenth Century Catharism in Comparative Perspective." *Social Science History*, Spring 1997, Vol. 21, No. 1, 111-37.

Kaufman, Peter. "Donatism Revisited: Moderates and Militants in Late Antique North Africa," *Journal of Late Antiquity*, 2009, Vol 2, No. 1, 131-42.

Kedmey, Dan. "How the Sistine Chapel spawned a public relations nightmare." *Ideas TED*, January 26, 2016. https://ideas.ted.com/how-the-sistine-chapel-spawned-a-public-relations-nightmare/.

Kraus, Kelly. "Queer Theology: Reclaiming Christianity for the LGBT Community." *e-Research: A Journal of Undergraduate Work*, 2011, Vol 2, No 3, 99-110.

Kirsch, Johann. "Pope John XXII." *The Catholic Encyclopedia*. Vol. 8. New York: Robert Appleton Company, 1910. http://www.newadvent.org/cathen/08431a.htm.

——. "Lapsi." *The Catholic Encyclopedia*. Vol. 9. New York: Robert Appleton Company, 1910. http://www.newadvent.org/cathen/09001b.htm.

Kwasniewski, Peter. "How to Properly Understand the Role of the Papacy (Guest: Dr. Peter Kwasniewski)" by Eric Sammons. *Crisis Magazine*, August 19, 2022. https://www.crisismagazine.com/podcast/how-to-properly-understand-the-role-of-the-papacy-guest-dr-peter-kwasniewski/.

——. "Pope Francis's Hermeneutic of Anti-Continuity." *The Remnant*, December 22, 2019. https://remnantnewspaper.com/web/index.php/articles/item/4708-pope-francis-s-hermeneutic-of-anti-continuity/.

——. "True Obedience: A Key Consideration for Our Time." *One Peter Five*, December 17, 2021. https://onepeterfive.com/true-obedience-a-key-consideration-for-our-time/.

Lamberigts, Mathijs. "Recent Research into Pelagianism with Particular Emphasis on the Role of Julian of Aeclanum." *Augustiniana*, 2002, Vol. 52, No. 2/4, 175-98.

Lambert, Malcolm. "The Franciscan Crisis under John XXII." *Franciscan Studies*, 1972, Vol. 32, 123-43.

Lambert, Mark. "What Does the Pope Mean By 'Rigid'?" *De Omnibus Dubitandum Est*, February 15, 2022. http://marklambert.blogspot.com/2022/02/what-does-pope-mean-by-rigid.html.

Lawler, Phil. "Pope Francis Has Become a Source of Division." *Catholic Culture*, January 27, 2017. https://www.catholicculture.org/commentary/pope-francis-has-become-source-division/.

Le Bachelet. "Benoit XII." *Dictionnaire de Théologie Catholique. Tome Deuxième*. 13th Edition. Paris: Letouzey et Ané Editeurs, 1910, 653-69.

Leo XIII. *Aeterni Patris*, Libreria Editrice Vaticana, 1879. Vatican.va.

Leone, Pietro. "The Church and Asmodeus - Part 5, conclusion." Translated by Francesca Romana. *Rorate Caeli*, April 6, 2017. https://rorate-caeli.blogspot.com/2017/04/the-church-and-asmodeus-part-5.html.

Lewis, Clive. *The Four Loves*. New York: Harcourt Inc., 1960.

Lewis, Mike. "Pope Francis, neologisms, and doctrinal development." *Where Peter Is*, August 2, 2022. https://wherepeteris.com/pope-francis-neologisms-and-doctrinal-development/.

———. "Why does Pope Francis pick on 'rigid Christians'?" *Where Peter Is*, October 19, 2018. https://wherepeteris.com/why-does-pope-francis-pick-on-rigid-christians/.

Liguori, Alphonsus. *Conscience: Writings from Moral Theology by Saint Alphonsus*. Translated by Raphael Gallagher. Liguori: Liguori Publications, 2019.

———. *The Sermons of St. Alphonsus Liguori for All the Sundays of the Year*. Fourth Edition. Charlotte: TAN Books, 1982.

LiMandri, Charles, "Faithful Catholics are condemned for being too rigid. They should wear the label proudly." *LifeSiteNews*, February 18, 2020. https://www.lifesitenews.com/opinion/faithful-catholics-are-condemned-for-being-too-rigid-they-should-wear-the-label-proudly/.

Ljubas, Zdravko. "Pope Francis: Corruption is an Ancient Evil, Devil's Dung." *OOCRP*, November 4, 2020. https://www.occrp.org/en/daily/13354-pope-francis-corruption-is-an-ancient-evil-devil-s-dung/.

Loader, William. *Jesus' Attitude Towards the Law: A Study of the Gospels*. Michigan: William B. Eerdman's Publishing Company, 2002.

Longley, Clifford. "*Amoris Laetitia*: Pope Francis Has Created Confusion Where We Needed Clarity." *The Tablet*, April 18, 2016. https://www.thetablet.co.uk/blogs/1/919/amoris-laetitia-pope-francis-has-created-confusion-where-we-needed-clarity.

Lowe-Martin, Aimee. "Comparing Penitential Acts: Why the Flagellants of 1349 were Condemned while those in 1260 were not." *The General*, 2022, Vol. 7, 96-102.

Luño, Angel. "Características y Temas Fundamentales de la Ética de la Virtud." (lecture, Pontificia Università della Santa Croce, March 9th, 2023).

———. "La Novedad de la Fe como Criterio de Interpretación y Actuación para la Existencia Moral" in *La Verdad os hará libres. Congreso Internacional sobre la Encíclica Veritatis Splendor*, ed. Carlos Scarponi, (Buenos Aires, Pontificia Universidad Católica Argentina –Ed. Paulinas, 2005), 235-54.

Mathews, Shailer. "The Council at Jerusalem." *The Biblical World*, Vol. 33, No. 5 (May 1909): 337-42.

McCusker, Matthew. "Key Doctrinal Errors and Ambiguities of *Amoris Laetitia*." *LifeSiteNews*, May 9, 2016.

https://www.lifesitenews.com/opinion/key-doctrinal-errors-and-ambiguities-of-amoris-laetitia/.

Ming, John. "Human Acts." *The Catholic Encyclopedia.* Vol. 1. New York: Robert Appleton Company, 1907. http://www.newadvent.org/cathen/01115a.htm.

Morris, David. "Martin Luther as Priest, Heretic, and Outlaw: The Reformation at 500." *The Library of Congress*, January 2, 2019. https://www.loc.gov/rr/european/luther.html.

Muhammad, Jeanette. "Pope Francis Issues Orders Aimed At Cracking Down On Vatican Corruption." *NPR*, May 1, 2021. https://www.npr.org/2021/05/01/992710917/pope-francis-issues-orders-aimed-at-cracking-down-on-vatican-corruption.

Mullin, Robert. *A Short World History of Christianity.* Louisville: Westminster John Knox Press, 2008.

Myers, James. "Morality among Cathar Perfects and Believers in France and Italy, 1100-1300." *Master's Theses*, 1976, 2385. https://scholarworks.wmich.edu/masters_theses/2385/.

Nagy, Piroska, and Xavier Biron-Ouellet. "A Collective Emotion in Medieval Italy: The Flagellant Movement of 1260." *Emotion Review*, 2020, Vol 12, Issue 3, 135-45.

Newman, John Henry. *An Essay on the Development of Christian Doctrine.* 6th Edition. Notre Dame: University of Notre Dame Press, 1989.

Novak, Michael. "The Holy Spirit did preside." *First Things*, August 2012. https://www.firstthings.com/article/2012/08/the-holy-spirit-did-preside/.

O'Connor, Thomas. "Jansenism" In *The Oxford Handbook of the Ancien Régime*, edited by William Doyle, New York: Oxford University Press, 2012.

O'Malley, John. *What Happened at Vatican II.* Cambridge: Belknap Press, An Imprint of Harvard University Press, 2010.

Ogliari, Donato. *Gratia et certamen: The Relationship between Grace and Free Will in the Discussion of Augustine with the So-called Semipelagians (Bibliotheca Ephemeridum Theologicarum Lovaniensium)*. Paris: Leuven University Press, 2003.

Oliger, Livarius. "Rule of Saint Francis," *The Catholic Encyclopedia*, Vol. 6. New York: Robert Appleton Company, 1909. http://www.newadvent.org/cathen/06208a.htm.

Olson, Carl. "Digging into Pope Francis' remarks about the 'old Latin Mass', 'rigidity' and 'insecurity.'" *Catholic World Report*, November 14, 2016. https://www.catholicworldreport.com/2016/11/14/digging-into-pope-francis-remarks-about-the-old-latin-mass-rigidity-and-insecurity/.

Orcibal, Jean "*Les Provinciales* of Blaise Pascal." *Encyclopedia Britannica*, October 19, 2020. https://www.britannica.com/biography/Blaise-Pascal/Les-Provinciales.

Ó Riada, Geoffrey. "Pelagius to Demetrias." *Sullivan County* (blog), December 3, 2003. https://sullivan-county.com/z/pelagius2.htm#3.

Palmer, Thomas. *Jansenism and England: Moral Rigorism across the Confessions*. New York: Oxford University Press, 2018.

Park, Jae-Eun. "Lacking Love or Conveying Love? The Fundamental Roots of the Donatists and Augustine's Nuanced Treatment of Them." *Reformed Theological Review*, Aug 2013, Vol. 72, No. 2, 103-21.

Perez, Echeverry. "Franciscanos, tras Ideals Utópicos," *Historia y Espacio*, 2007, Vol. 3, No. 28, 65—91.

Pelagius. "A letter from Pelagius." 413 AD, https://epistolae.ctl.columbia.edu/letter/1296.html.

Pickup, Martin. "Mathew's and Mark's Pharisees," In *In Quest of the Historical Pharisees*, edited by Neuser, Jacob, and Bruce Chilton, p. 67-113. Waco: Baylor University Press, 2007.

Pius X. *Il Fermo Proposito*. Libreria Editrice Vaticana, 1905. Vatican.va.

———. *Sacra Tridentina Synodus*, as published by *EWTN*. https://www.ewtn.com/catholicism/library/decree-on-frequent--daily-reception-of-holy-communion-2174.

Pius XII. *Humani Generis*. Libreria Editrice Vaticana, 1950. Vatican.va.

Pocetto, Alexander. "Freedom to Love: A Close Reading of Francis de Sales' Letter of 14 October 1604 to Jane de Chantal." *Studies in Salesian Spirituality*, 2004. http://hosted.desales.edu/files/salesian/PDF/PocettoFreetoLove.pdf.

Pohle, Joseph. "Molinism." *The Catholic Encyclopedia*. Vol. 10. New York: Robert Appleton Company, 1911. http://www.newadvent.org/cathen/10437a.htm.

———. "Pelagius and Pelagianism." *The Catholic Encyclopedia*. Vol. 11. New York: Robert Appleton Company, 1911. http://www.newadvent.org/cathen/11604a.htm.

———. "Semipelagianism." *The Catholic Encyclopedia*. Vol. 13. New York: Robert Appleton Company, 1912. http://www.newadvent.org/cathen/13703a.htm.

Pokorsky, Jerry. "Rigidity Dog Whistle." *The Catholic Thing*, November 16, 2016. https://www.thecatholicthing.org/2016/11/16/rigidity-dog-whistle/.

"Pope Spits At Faithful Catholics Again," *Catholicism Pure & Simple*, May 6, 2017, https://catholicismpure.wordpress.com/2017/05/06/pope-spits-at-faithful-catholics-again/.

Radner, Ephraim. "Chapter 28: Early Modern Jansenism" In *The Oxford Handbook of Early Modern Theology, 1600—1800*, edited by Ulrich Lehner, Richard Muller, and A.G. Roeber, New York: Oxford University Press, 2016, 436-50.

Rackett, Michael. "What's Wrong with Pelagianism? Augustine and Jerome on the Dangers of Pelagius and his Followers" *Augustinian Studies*, 2002, 33:2, 223-37.

Redmond, Walter. "Conscience as a Moral Judgment": The Probabilist Blending of the Logics of Knowledge and Responsibility." *The Journal of Religious Ethics* (Fall, 1998), Vol. 26, No. 2, 389-405.

Reno, Russell. "Faith Amid Corruption." *First Things*, May 8, 2019. https://www.firstthings.com/article/2019/05/faith-amid-corruption/.

——. "A Stubborn Givenness." *First Things*, April 11, 2016. https://www.firstthings.com/web-exclusives/2016/04/a-stubborn-givenness/.

Scalnell, Thomas. "Frequent Communion." *The Catholic Encyclopedia*. Vol. 6. New York: Robert Appleton Company, 1909. http://www.newadvent.org/cathen/06278a.htm.

Schaetzel, Shane. "How to Deal with Corruption in the Catholic Church." *Real Clear Catholic*, July 10, 2022. https://realclearcatholic.com/2022/07/10/how-to-deal-with-corruption-in-the-catholic-church/.

Schneider, Athanasius. "Catholics are not called to blind obedience to the Pope." *LifeSiteNews*, February 20, 2017. https://www.lifesitenews.com/news/bishop-schneider-catholics-are-not-called-to-blind-obedience-to-the-pope/.

Schneider, Matthew. "Aquinas: Some Sins Worse Than Sexual Sins (Updated)." *Fr. Matthew P. Schneider, LC* (blog), December 10, 2021. https://frmatthewlc.com/2021/12/aquinas-some-sins-worse-than-sexual-sins/.

Schönborn, Christoph. "A Conversation with Cardinal Schönborn on '*Amoris Laetitia*.'" Interview by Antonio Spadaro. *La Civiltà Cattolica*, March 1, 2017. https://www.laciviltacattolica.com/conversation-cardinal-schonborn-amoris-laetitia/.

Sharp, Larry. "The Doctrine of Grace in Calvin and Augustine." *The Evangelical Quarterly* (Apr-June 1980), 52.2, 84-96.

Skeel, David. "What Were Jesus and the Pharisees Talking About When They Talked About Law?" *Journal of Law and Religion*, 2007/2008, Vol. 23, No. 1, pp. 141-6.

Soba, Juan. "Ética y Teología Moral," *SCIO*, Nov. 2011, Vol. 7, pp. 77-115.

Sollier, Joseph. "Michel Baius." *The Catholic Encyclopedia*. Vol. 2. New York: Robert Appleton Company, 1907. http://www.newadvent.org/cathen/02209c.htm.

Squires, Stuart. "Jerome on Sinlessness: a *Via Media* between Augustine and Pelagius." *The Heythrop Journal*, July 2016, Vol. 57, No. 4, 697-709.

———. "Reassessing Pelagianism: Augustine, Cassian, and Jerome on the Possibility of a Sinless Life." Dissertation for the Degree of Doctor of Philosophy (Faculty of the School of Theology and Religious Studies of the Catholic University of America, 2013).

Staff, Toi. "Pope urged by Jews to take care over Pharisees talk." *The Times of Israel*, May 12, 2019. https://www.timesofisrael.com/pope-urged-by-jews-to-take-care-over-pharisees-talk/.

Serratelli, Arthur. "The faith confronting Neo-Pelagianism and Neo-Gnosticism." *Catholic News Agency*. May 17, 2018. https://www.catholicnewsagency.com/column/53883/the-faith-confronting-neo-pelagianism-and-neo-gnosticism.

Stravinskas, Peter. "Good Pharisees, bad Catholics, and the humble of heart." *Catholic World Report*, August 1, 2021. https://www.catholicworldreport.com/2021/08/01/good-pharisees-bad-catholics-and-the-humble-of-heart/.

Su, Kuen. "A Study on the Significance of Jesus' Pronouncement of the Seven Woes and Laments in Matthew 23." Doctor of Ministry Degree Thesis (Faculty of the Southern Baptist Theological Seminary, 2021).

Toke, Leslie. "Flagellants." *The Catholic Encyclopedia*. Vol. 6. New York: Robert Appleton Company, 1909. http://www.newadvent.org/cathen/06089c.htm.

Tranzillo, Jeffrey. "*Amoris Laetitia*, the Human Person, and the Meaning of Marital Indissolubility." *Homiletic & Pastoral Review*, August 1, 2016. https://www.hprweb.com/2016/08/amoris-laetitia-the-human-person-and-the-meaning-of-marital-indissolubility/.

"A Treatise Against Novatian by an Anonymous Bishop *Ad Novatianum*," as published by *EWTN*. https://www.ewtn.com/catholicism/library/treatise-against-novatian-by-an-anonymous-bishop-ad-novatianum-11427.

Trent. "6th Session," January 13, 1547. http://www.thecounciloftrent.com/.

———. "13th Session", October 11, 1551. http://www.thecounciloftrent.com/.

———. "22nd Session," Chapter VII, September 17, 1552. http://www.thecounciloftrent.com/.

van den Aardweg, Gerard, Claude Barthe, Philip Beattie, Jehan de Belleville, Robert Brucciani, Mario Caponnetto, Robert Cassidy, et al. "*Correctio Filialis de Haeresibus Propagatis*." July 16, 2017. https://www.correctiofilialis.org/.

Van Hove, Brian. "Brief Notices: Quantin, Jean-Louis. *Le Rigorisme chrétien*. [Histoire du Christianisme.] (Paris: Les Éditions du Cerf. 2001. Pp. 161. 95F paperback.)" *The Catholic Historical Review* (January 2002), Vol. 88, No. 1, 171-2.

Vatican II. *Gravissimum educationis*. October 28, 1965. Vatican.va.

Vatican Radio. "Pope Francis: if you want mercy, know that you are sinners" September 21, 2017. http://www.archivioradiovaticana.va/storico/2017/09/21/pope_francis_if_you_want_mercy,_know_that_you_are_sinners/en-1338134.

Vilijoen, Francois. "Jesus' Teaching on the 'Torah' in the Sermon on the Mount." *Neotestamentica* Vol. 40, No. 1 (2006): 135-55.

Vincent, Catherine. "Discipline du corps et de l'esprit chez les Flagellants au Moyen Âge." *Revue Historique*, Juillet / Septembre 2000, T. 302, Fasc. 3 (615), 593-614.

Viss, Simon. "Augustine and the Donatist controversy." Research Paper (Talbot School of Theology, 2018).

Weber, Nicholas. "Albigenses." *The Catholic Encyclopedia*. Vol. 1. New York: Robert Appleton Company, 1907. http://www.newadvent.org/cathen/01267e.htm.

———. "Cathari," *The Catholic Encyclopedia*. Vol. 3. New York: Robert Appleton Company, 1908. http://www.newadvent.org/cathen/03435a.htm.

Wedig, Mark. "Reception of the Eucharist Under Two Species." *Pastoral Liturgy*, November 27, 2010. http://www.pastoralliturgy.org/re-sources/0705ReceptionEucharistTwoSpecies.php.

Welborn, Amy. "You indietrist, you." *Charlotte was both* (blog), May 11, 2023. https://amywelborn.wordpress.com/2023/05/11/you-indiestrist-you/.

Williams, Brian. "The Tragedy of *Traditionis Custodes* in Two Pictures." Liturgy Guy (blog). October 18, 2022. https://liturgyguy.com/2022/10/18/the-tragedy-of-traditionis-custodes-intwo-pictures/.

Williamson, Zane. "Moral Rigorism and the Jansenist Monster under the Bed." *One Peter Five*, January 23, 2017. https://tinyurl.com/4u5u883y.

Wijngaards, John. *The Ordination of Women in the Catholic Church: Unmasking a Cuckoo's Egg Tradition*. London: Darton, Longman & Todd Ldt, 2001.

Wooden, Cindy. "Texts of Argentina homilies come with pope's notes on preaching." *Crux*, November 10, 2016. https://tinyurl.com/2p9dta4y.

www.ingramcontent.com/pod-product-compliance
Lightning Source LLC
Chambersburg PA
CBHW050852160426
43194CB00011B/2121